Power Sharing

New Challenges for Divided Societies

Edited by Ian O'Flynn and David Russell
Foreword by Donald L. Horowitz

Pluto Press

LONDON • ANN ARBOR, MI

First published 2005 by Pluto Press
345 Archway Road, London N6 5AA
and 839 Greene Street, Ann Arbor, MI 48106

www.plutobooks.com

This book has received financial support from the Northern Ireland
Community Relations Council which aims to promote a peaceful and
fair society based on reconciliation and mutual respect.

British Library Cataloguing in Publication Data
A catalogue record for this book is available from the British Library

ISBN   0 7453 2293 X hardback
ISBN   0 7453 2292 1 paperback

Library of Congress Cataloging in Publication Data applied for

10   9   8   7   6   5   4   3   2   1

Designed and produced for Pluto Press by
Chase Publishing Services Ltd, Fortescue, Sidmouth, EX10 9QG, England
Typeset from disk by Stanford DTP Services, Northampton, England
Printed and bound in the European Union by
Antony Rowe Ltd, Chippenham and Eastbourne, England

Contents

Part III   Deepening Democracy

Foreword

Donald L. Horowitz

In countries that are severely divided into contending ethnic groups, the consequences of such divisions can range from serious to catastrophic. In ordinary times, the struggle for relative advantage leads to a politics of inclusion and exclusion. The ascriptive character of group affiliations raises the spectre of exclusion that is permanent. In extraordinary times, especially when an ethnically biased state fails in its responsibility to protect its citizens, there are prospects for violence, up to and including civil war and genocide. The magnitude of the adverse consequences of ethnic conflict justifies the single-minded efforts of theorists of constitutional design, and of constitutional designers themselves, to devise institutions that can counter the politics of ethnic inclusion and exclusion.

There are differences among such theorists about the most effective constitutional designs for such societies. Some advocate the provision of consociational guarantees, while others favour incentives for politicians to behave moderately toward (and compromise with) members of groups other than their own. The latter is referred to in this volume as the 'integrative' approach. Both sets of theorists are rather single-minded in the pursuit of conflict-reducing institutions.

If the single-minded pursuit of institutions to counter destructive conflict is understandable, that does not mean that the discovery of apt institutions to cabin the conflict concludes the institutional business of severely divided societies. Ethnic conflict and violence may be dangerous, but they are not the only dangers facing such societies. Moreover, measures to reduce ethnic conflict to manageable levels may create their own externalities, adverse reactions or side-effects of necessary medicine.

This admirable and ambitious volume picks up where conflict-reduction theorists and practitioners leave off. Some of the distinguished contributors assess the shortcomings of the more common consociational prescriptions in Northern Ireland, Belgium, Macedonia, and Bosnia-Herzegovina. Growing polarisation in Northern Ireland, the near-demise of the Belgian state as a common enterprise, increasing segregation and local dominance of one community or another in Macedonia, the entrenchment of extremists and governmental immobilism in Bosnia and Herzegovina – all testify to the high costs of certain institutions put in place to end violence or the prospect of violence and state disintegration. These contributions, and another essay that questions the aptness of Lebanese institutions as vehicles to counter sectarianism, are all invaluably cautionary case studies that enjoin constitutional designers to proceed with an eye to adverse consequences of consociational schemes that are now visible from comparative experience. The essay on electoral systems then asks whether some combination of consociational and incentive-based institutions might produce more benign results.

Bringing together these experiences is by itself a most significant addition to the literature on approaches to conflict reduction in divided societies. The editors, however, go much further, because they do not aim merely to highlight some of the failings of common constitutional designs. They hope also to redress the omissions of constitutional designers obsessed with ethnic conflict alone.

A prominent source of omissions is the exclusive focus on ethnic groups as building blocks of the polity. If the logic of group-centred approaches to the construction of institutions is carried too far, there is no space for individuals who do not wish to identify, or identify exclusively, with a particular group. Liberalism is uncomfortable with certain forms of power sharing on a group basis. As constitution-makers concentrate on groups, group members may be at least equally concerned with alternative identities, as members of subgroups, or as women or as participants in networks that cross group lines.

And then there are the omissions that derive from the necessarily modest aspirations of those who design constitutions in order to reduce conflict. Those who worry about violence may be satisfied easily when there is a significant period of peace. Constitutional designers, with a few exceptions, have been notably silent about the need for reconciliation after protracted conflict. Some of the institutions they propose, premised on mechanisms of separate group assent to governmental action or on group separateness altogether, neglect the inevitable interactions among individuals and groups in any society. If the social order is seen as consisting solely of groups, there is an excellent chance that the resulting society will be stunted by the absence of a civic sphere and a civic culture. Instead of developing into a rich set of associations that stands apart from particular governmental configurations and sustains the democratic state, interactions among citizens who are merely members of groups

– or, more properly, of categories of people – will be thin and fragile. A group-centred state that impoverishes civil society will have a harder time preserving its own democratic foundation.

Within the covers of one volume, then, are contained multiple challenges to constitutional designers. There is a critique of consociational designs themselves, based on their performance in a number of settings. There is a critique of group-centred approaches in general for their neglect of identities apart from ethnic identities, both below the level of ethnic groups and at a comparable level. And there is a critique that challenges those satisfied with quiescence to repair the damage of the past and build a more secure social foundation based neither on groups nor on inter-group relations as such but upon a civic culture that may, at first, merely compete with group-based culture but ultimately render group antagonisms softer. In the long run, the efforts of constitutional designers really cannot survive unless their designs leave enough oxygen for a variety of identities to thrive and for new, wider identities to emerge. Given the range of human needs and aspirations, peace alone can only go so far.

Constitutional designs adopted at times of crisis are means to survival. If they save the society from protracted violence, that is well and good, but quiescence should develop into something more. If constitutional designs impede that evolution, perhaps they are the wrong designs. A good many constitutional committees and assemblies begin with preconceived and limited notions of the range of institutions worthy of consideration. This fine collection counsels constitutional designers to expand the menu from which they choose. For that reason alone, the collection should be widely read.

Introduction:
New Challenges for Power Sharing

Ian O'Flynn and David Russell[1]

POWER SHARING IN DIVIDED SOCIETIES

It is widely accepted by political analysts and policy makers alike
that power sharing is the most viable democratic means of managing
conflict in divided societies. In principle, power sharing enables
conflicting groups to remedy longstanding patterns of antagonism
and discrimination, and to build a more just and stable society for
all. Institutionally, there is an indeterminate number of ways in
which democratic power sharing can be realised. For example, the
choice of institutions and procedures may include provisions for
coalition government, guaranteed representation, legislative vetoes,
territorial devolution and federalism, functional autonomy, and
even trans-national structures agreed by treaty between sovereign
states. Yet despite this broad palate of institutional options, the
worry has long remained that power sharing may be uncritically
appropriated by those charged with designing and implementing
power-sharing institutions (see, for example, Barry 1975, p. 393).
Since no two divided societies are the same, what may work in one
context may flounder in another. But even where an initial choice
seems to work successfully, new and unforeseen problems may not
be all that far away.

In the heat of negotiations – such as those that led to the signings
of the Lebanese Ta'if Accord (1989), the Bosnian Dayton Accords
(1994), the Macedonian Ohrid Agreement (2001), and the Belfast
Agreement (1998), each of which is discussed in this collection
– political actors naturally tend to focus on the immediate issue
of ending violence. The institutional framework that emerges will
typically reflect this principal concern by enshrining mechanisms
that protect the vital interests of particular groups as a key means of
reducing tension and insecurity. Depending on the particular context,
it may also make special provision for human rights legislation and
equality standards, weapons decommissioning and demobilisation,
reform of internal security forces, the return of refugees and internally

1

displaced peoples, and so forth. Once the implementation process has begun, however, new and additional issues may arise that were not expressly addressed during the negotiation process but that nevertheless have crucial implications for the future success of a power-sharing agreement. These may include the need to promote reconciliation, address unforeseen tensions between individual and group rights, provide greater space for personal autonomy, as well as the need to promote and bolster a greater sense of overarching civic unity.

Those charged with the actual tasks of implementation have often been left with little direction with regard to how to deal with these latter issues. In one sense, this is hardly surprising. When negotiating peace agreements, politicians cannot reasonably be expected to anticipate all of the difficulties that a new political dispensation might bring. They may have to take vital decisions under the most pressurised of conditions, without ever having deliberated face to face with their political opponents – the same opponents with whom they will have to share power once negotiations have concluded. At a more general level, there is also the important point that, although the purpose of political institutions is to make political behaviour more predictable and stable, those institutions must be flexible enough to respond to and anticipate changing political imperatives (Goodin 1996, p. 22; Weale 1999, p. 34). In short, politicians cannot hope to determine every political issue in advance, for the reality is that once the new political institutions are established, day-to-day politics, the transitional domestic environment or, indeed, the international environment, will inevitably give rise to new and often unexpected challenges.

Of course, none of this lessens the responsibility that elected representatives and others charged with implementing power sharing have to address such difficulties once they have arisen. There is always the danger, however, that a negotiated agreement will be reduced to an event, an act played out on a certain day, usually crystallised around the moment of its formal signing. On such occasions, the key protagonists and sponsors typically declare the conflict over. But this declaration will rarely, if ever, reflect reality. Handshakes between former enemies, like those witnessed on the White House lawn between former Palestinian Chair Yasser Arafat and Israeli Prime Minister Yitzhak Rabin, do not mark the end of antagonism. Instead, experience suggests that such symbolic moments mark the beginning of the many difficulties that are yet to come. Although a way forward may have been agreed and documents may have been signed, the challenge of overcoming the actual, lived sources of division will typically remain. Consequently, there is always the potential that a given power-sharing initiative could stagnate or collapse under the weight of a complex implementation process.

The point, therefore, is that peace – or, more precisely, a meaningful and lasting peace – is not an event. Rather, it is something that is built over time – often in the face of severe adversity – between those who have experienced fractured relations that in some cases may extend back many generations. By the same token, democracy is not a single formula, but a complex set of political institutions and underlying principles that must be continually shaped and renegotiated by the members of a divided society as their relationships with each other grow and necessarily transform. This is not to say that divided societies cannot learn from one another. On the contrary, there is a long tradition within the comparative politics literature of borrowing and lending between societies struggling to cope with their divisions (see, for example, Darby 2003). This tradition has provided many crucial insights, drawn from cases as different as South Africa, Northern Ireland, Israel/Palestine, the Basque country, Colombia, Fiji, Sri Lanka and beyond. Yet, despite its undoubted successes, the primary focus of this comparative paradigm continues to be on the creation of power-sharing instruments, rather than on the considerable unintended consequences that often result.

UNINTENDED CONSEQUENCES

This collection grew out of the need to fill a perceived vacuum both in the literature and in practice. More specifically, it aims to take seriously the unintended consequences of power sharing and, correspondingly, to suggest ways in which those consequences might be appropriately addressed. As such, this collection is not concerned with how violent conflict might be ended, or with how the transition to democracy might initially be made. Rather, its concern is with how peace and democracy might be bolstered and sustained in societies that have already made the transition to power-sharing government and that are struggling to deal with the challenges that transition brings. More specifically, the book aims to thematise and question whether the way in which power sharing has been institutionalised in different societies:

- perpetuates inter-communal conflict by institutionalising difference at the political level;
- inhibits the transition from conflict management to conflict resolution by encouraging extremism;
- stifles internal diversity and recognition in the name of communal identity and group concerns;
- fails to recognise cross-cutting identities and leaves insufficient space for individual autonomy.

As already mentioned, internal power sharing is necessary to prevent dominant groups or communities from subjugating others. And yet, depending on the particular way in which it is institutionalised, power sharing can be bought at much too high a cost for the communities themselves, their individual members, and those in society who do not wish to (or who cannot) participate in political life along communal lines. The four themes just listed are intended to highlight ways in which this may occur.

Although conceptually distinct, the four themes give expression to different dimensions of the same underlying concern: namely, whether the choice of power-sharing institution is likely to have a negative, rather than positive, impact on a divided society's ability to build a sustainable democracy for everyone in that society. This concern is enormously complex and admits of no easy answers – so much so that it continues to drive, for example, the longstanding debate between advocates of consociational versus integrative power-sharing. Consociational power-sharing is most closely associated with the work of Arend Lijphart (1969, 1977, 2004) and more recently with that of John McGarry and Brendan O'Leary (1993, 2004). It is based on the assumption that the best way to deal with division is, at least in the first instance, by taking division seriously. As Lijphart explains:

> It is in the nature of consociational democracy, at least initially, to make plural societies more thoroughly plural. Its approach is not to abolish or weaken segmental cleavages but to recognise them explicitly and to turn the segments into constructive elements of stable democracy. (1977, p. 42)

Thus, consociational approaches aim to treat conflicting communities as the basic building blocks of political engagement by institutionalising them as distinctive or separate entities within the power-sharing framework. As the case of the Netherlands demonstrates, this approach can succeed over time in dealing successfully with division and in building a just and peaceful democracy for all. Indeed, it can even help create conditions that – given appropriate circumstances and prudent public policies – might mitigate tensions to such a point that the significance of perceived differences and the corresponding need for power sharing wither away. Against this view, however, advocates of integrative forms of power sharing – most prominently associated with the work of Donald Horowitz (1985, 2001, 2004) and Benjamin Reilly (2001) – argue that there are a great many other cases in which consociationalism has had the opposite effect. They argue that by institutionalising groups as if they were separate and distinctive entities, consociationalism not only tends to treat each group as if it were a monolithic whole, but consequently runs a serious risk of deepening the very divisions it was meant to address.

By way of alternative proposal, Horowitz and Reilly have instead stressed the need for greater political integration between the members of conflicting communities as well as across society as a whole. To this end, they argue that rather than designing rigid power-sharing institutions in which elected representatives have to work together after elections have taken place, sustainable democracy is more likely to be achieved through the provision of electoral incentives that reward political parties and leaders who are willing to compromise with one another across the political divide and, by compromising, fend off the uncompromising extremes within their own communities (Horowitz 2001, pp. 92–3; see also Reilly 2001, p. 11 and *passim*).

Now, in the light of the four themes outlined above, it might be concluded that integration is always the preferred option. Up to a point, the chapters in the collection lend support to this conclusion, given their tendency to argue against the rigid institutionalisation of group identity and the concomitant need to find greater space for those in society who cannot be so neatly classified. From the outset, however, we want to insist that this collection is not hostile to consociationalism or other forms of power sharing (regional devolution, federal structures and the like) that advocate separation. The collection's overall thrust does suggest that integration is, in the ideal case, preferable to separation. However, we recognise that in certain contexts, power-sharing models like consociationalism that advocate separation may actually be the more feasible option. After all, it makes little sense to insist, for example, that integration should be the guiding principle of political engagement in contexts like Kosovo, the Congo basin, Kashmir or Sudan, where divisions are so deep and the memories of recent violence are so real. In such contexts, separation may indeed be the only viable institutional option, at least in the first instance (where secession and partition are not viable).

That said, the chapters in this collection clearly show that there are real problems with consociational democracy in particular and with the broader notion of separation in general. Accordingly, where integrative power-sharing is realistically possible, we maintain that it should be the default position of political engagement. Even where it is not possible to opt for integration in the first instance, it should nevertheless remain a fundamental objective, actively pursued by policy makers in a determined fashion, and properly resourced from the beginning of any post-agreement implementation process.

WHAT THIS COLLECTION ARGUES

In discussing these and other related issues, the collection adopts a broad, multidisciplinary approach, drawing as it does on the expertise of contributors from the fields of political science, sociology, legal and political theory, psychology and the non-governmental sector. Given the sheer complexity of the new challenges for power sharing – not to mention their obvious urgency in the face of so many recent political events – we believe that such an approach is both necessary and warranted.

The collection itself is divided into three parts: 'Conceptual Issues', 'Case Studies' and 'Deepening Democracy'. As its title indicates, the first of these sections considers a number of key conceptual issues underlying the choice of power-sharing institution in the light of their implications for the four themes outlined above. Very often, theoretical thinking about practical issues is either neglected or altogether rejected on the grounds that it offers very little in the way of concrete guidance. However, as the four chapters in the opening section of this collection clearly demonstrate, such scepticism is misplaced. Institutional choice must be (in practice, will be) constrained by empirical possibilities. But empirical possibilities themselves depend on conceptual constructions (see Taylor 1985) that are never value-neutral. As Robert Goodin argues:

> The case for some sort of empirical theory informing policy choices is intuitively obvious. We choose policies hoping to produce certain kinds of results, and we must know how the system is wired in order to know which

lever to pull. ... But to understand must be theoretical, not just the product of accumulated practical experience or random hunches, if we are to be able to anticipate all the side effects of the policy and say how the system will respond under altered conditions or in the long term, of which we have no experience. (1982, pp. 4–5)

Against this background, Ian O'Flynn (chapter 1) considers what democratic values imply for the choice of power-sharing institution. In particular, he shows how the values of equality, autonomy and inclusion can enable institutional designers to strike an appropriate balance between the need to protect groups and the need to protect their individual members. This line of thinking is consistent with a number of recent developments within international law, as demonstrated by Tom Hadden (chapter 2). However, Hadden also shows that international law has not followed a single, linear trajectory, but has instead vacillated between a concern for separation and a concern for integration.

Naturally, political leaders have a crucial role to play in determining the character of political engagement in divided societies. As Duncan Morrow (chapter 3) argues, although leaders are constrained by both external and internal factors, they can exert considerable influence nonetheless. If appropriately incentivised, they can, Morrow argues, help move the political process from antagonism to mutual accommodation, and from mutual accommodation to eventual civic unity. Naturally, for this to occur, much will depend on the particular kind of institutional incentives that leaders and their constituents face. While the precise nature of those incentives has been central to the debate over consociational versus integrative power sharing, Stefan Wolff (chapter 4) argues that as far as the choice of electoral system is concerned, these two schools of thought need not be considered mutually exclusive. On the contrary, Wolff argues that there are sound theoretical reasons that count against the tendency to draw rigid divisions between these two approaches to power sharing.

The conceptual considerations presented in this collection's first part form the backdrop against which five test cases are examined and evaluated in its second part. These cases are: Northern Ireland, Belgium, Macedonia, Bosnia and Herzegovina, and Lebanon. The perennial problem, of course, for collections such as this is how to justify the particular choice of test case. There are a great many divided societies in the world today, and so it is necessary to avoid arbitrary selection while at the same time realising that there are limits to the number of investigations that can possibly be undertaken.

Accordingly, a number of related considerations have driven the particular selection presented here. The five test cases selected should be familiar to comparative scholars. As such, the collection seeks to add to an existing body of literature and paradigm of social scientific research. Crucially, however, this very familiarity makes them all the more suitable for addressing the unintended consequences of power sharing. These five test cases are often 'first ports of call' for scholars and practitioners wishing to discover how they might set about redressing inter-communal discord. It makes sense, therefore, that we should use them as starting points in our efforts at drawing attention to the kinds of issues that this collection seeks to explore. Since there is already an established practice of borrowing and lending between these five cases, the hope is that this collection will provide a baseline analysis from which a more expansive empirical investigation can be conducted in the future.

Each of our test cases is therefore analysed in terms of one or more of the four central themes outlined above. Anthony Oberschall and Ken Palmer (chapter 5) examine the power-sharing arrangements established in Northern Ireland under the terms of the 1998 Belfast Agreement. They argue that although a great many people in Northern Ireland are favourably disposed to greater cross-community cooperation and integration, the choice of consociational arrangements means that sectarianism will most likely prevail in both institutionalised politics and community relations for the foreseeable future. Kris Deschouwer (chapter 6), too, is critical of Belgium's consociational arrangements. Although he recognises that those arrangements have their good points, the rigid institutionalising of communal identities has done little to lessen divisions between the two main communities. Instead, the logic of ongoing devolution that characterises contemporary Belgian politics effectively means that there is no real political centre within the state and, correspondingly, no real sense of Belgian national identity.

In his analysis of the case of Macedonia, Florian Bieber (chapter 7) draws attention to the challenge of recognising diversity and encouraging moderation. In particular, he argues that the 2001 Ohrid Agreement neglects certain minority groups for the sake of political expediency while simultaneously failing to take sufficient consideration of conflicts *within* communities. In the second of our Balkan test cases, Marie-Joëlle Zahar (chapter 8) argues that two factors are central to understanding the difficulties attaching to sharing power in Bosnia and Herzegovina: leader intransigence and foreign intervention. Although the relation between these two factors is complex, Zahar argues that Bosnia's power-sharing institutions are inherently flawed and succeed, such as they do, only because of foreign intervention in favour of the status quo. Finally, David Russell and Nadim Shehadi (chapter 9) examine the 1989 Lebanese Ta'if Accord in order to explore the difficulties of promoting a concept of national reconciliation in a society where communal differences are the foundation for political life. They argue that the particular institutions chosen do not lead to the creation of public policies that might encourage citizens to look beyond their differences.

Traditionally, the study of power sharing has tended to focus, for the most part, on questions of institutional design. In this collection, however, we take the view that democratic power sharing is a much broader concern, one that should also be understood to involve the wider public sphere in general, and the institutions of civil society in particular (Habermas 1996, pp. 359ff). In essence, democracy is not just about institutions, leaders and political parties, but is about everyone in society. Correspondingly, the responsibility to make democracy work does not rest simply with elected representatives and other government officials, but ultimately falls to all of us. This is, of course, the ideal. In practice, power sharing can be institutionalised in such a way that it effectively precludes certain forms of political engagement while rewarding others. It can, as the themes above suggest, stifle within-group diversity in the name of communal identity and group concerns, while failing to create sufficient space for cross-cutting identities and personal autonomy. The third and final part of this collection, 'Deepening Democracy', addresses these concerns.

Although the public sphere is an enormously complex political phenomenon, we maintain that no account of the new challenges for power sharing could plausibly ignore the (often subjugated) position of women within this sphere. Rachel Rebouché and Kate Fearon (chapter 10) examine how the institutionalisation of group identities can impact negatively on women by creating a false choice between women's identity and group coherence. In response, they stress the need to think about power sharing in ways that better recognise and accommodate the complexity of women's interests and experiences both within and across groups. The need to better accommodate women's experiences in such ways connects up with a more general need to create space for cross-cutting identities and shared interests that might potentially unite the members of otherwise conflicting communities. Manlio Cinalli (chapter 11) argues that although social networks are central to building the integrationist outcomes that this collection favours, to date little attention has been paid to how such networks operate within the context of divided societies. Cinalli advances a four-part typology that, when applied to specific cases, shows why the prescription of institutional solutions cannot be separated from the empirical assessment of relationships and exchanges across the broader public sphere.

Cross-cutting networks not only encourage people to look beyond the things that divide them but, in so doing, often provide a platform for future reconciliation. Since reconciliation is a primary goal of any peace process, it needs to be adequately provided for within the terms of a power-sharing agreement. But, as Brandon Hamber and Gráinne Kelly (chapter 12) argue, because the idea of reconciliation is often badly understood, it typically remains insufficiently addressed. In response, they offer a new, systematic definition and analysis of the concept of reconciliation as well as offering a series of positive suggestions as to how this goal could be advanced in divided societies seeking to build a more secure democracy. Finally, Robin Wilson (chapter 13) draws the various strands of this collection together in order to show how power sharing might be rendered consistent with the aim of creating an overarching sense of civic unity. In particular, he highlights dangers attaching to the rigid conceptualisation of group identities and interrogates the conceptual contradictions attaching to such approaches.

The challenges that divided societies face can vary tremendously, both in form and intensity. Consequently, our thinking about the best way to deal with those challenges must take seriously the fact that no one institutional solution will be right for every type of situation. And yet, the dominant tendency, both in the literature and in practice, has been to opt for separation over integration. Separation can be an appropriate guiding principle for those charged with the task of designing power-sharing institutions, as supporters of consociationalism have long defended. But to think that it is applicable in every case can inhibit our ability to deal with the new challenges that power sharing brings and, correspondingly, our ability to build a more sustainable democracy. The chapters in this collection provide a sample of the many challenges that attach to sharing power. Those challenges are among the most pressing that we face today, not just because of their implications for the members of divided societies, but also because of their implications for peace and democracy globally.

NOTE

1. We wish to thank our publishers, Pluto Press, for their help and patience throughout the course of this project. Our thanks also goes to three anonymous referees, as well as to Roger MacGinty and Albert Weale, for their constructive comments.

REFERENCES

Barry, B. (1975) 'The Consociational Model and Its Dangers', *European Journal of Political Research*, 3, 393–412.

Darby, J. (2003) 'Borrowing and Lending in Peace Processes', in J. Darby and R. MacGinty (eds), *Contemporary Peace Making: Conflict, Violence and Peace Progresses*. Basingstoke: Palgrave Macmillan, pp. 245–55.

Goodin, R. (1982) *Political Theory and Public Policy*. Chicago, IL: The University of Chicago Press.

—— (1996) 'Institutions and Their Design', in R. Goodin (ed.), *The Theory of Institutional Design*. Cambridge: Cambridge University Press, pp. 1–53.

Habermas, J. (1996) *Between Facts and Norms: Contributions to a Discourse Theory of Law and Democracy*, trans. W. Rehg. Cambridge: Polity Press.

Horowitz, D. L. (1985) *Ethnic Groups in Conflict*. Berkeley, CA: University of California Press.

—— (2001) 'The Northern Ireland Agreement: Clear, Consociational, and Risky', in J. McGarry (ed.), *Northern Ireland and the Divided World: Post-Agreement Northern Ireland in Comparative Perspective*. Oxford: Oxford University Press, pp. 89–108.

—— (2002) 'Constitutional Design: Proposals versus Processes', in A. Reynolds (ed.), *The Architecture of Democracy: Constitutional Design, Conflict Management and Democracy*. Oxford: Oxford University Press, pp. 15–36.

Lijphart, A. (1969) 'Consociational Democracy', *World Politics*, 21 (2), 207–25.

—— (1977) *Democracy in Plural Societies*. New Haven, CT: Yale University Press.

—— (2004) 'Constitutional Design for Divided Societies', *Journal of Democracy*, 15 (2), 96–109.

McGarry, J. and O'Leary, B. (1993) *The Politics of Ethnic Conflict Regulation*. London: Routledge.

—— (2004) 'Stabilising Northern Ireland's Agreement', *Political Quarterly*, 75 (3), 213–25.

Reilly, B. (2001) *Democracy in Divided Societies: Electoral Engineering for Conflict Management*. Cambridge: Cambridge University Press.

Taylor, C. (1985) 'Interpretation and the Sciences of Man', in *Philosophy and the Human Sciences: Philosophical Papers 2*. Cambridge: Cambridge University Press, pp. 15–57.

Weale, A. (1999) *Democracy*. Basingstoke: Palgrave Macmillan.

Part I
Conceptual Issues

1

Democratic Values and Power Sharing

Ian O'Flynn[1]

THE CHOICE OF DEMOCRATIC VALUES

At one point or another, many of us may have wondered why democratic power-sharing proves so difficult in some divided societies. It is true that there is no such thing as a perfect democracy, at least not in the real world. But since there are numerous countries around the globe where power sharing, in one form or another, has been relatively successful, we must wonder what it is that makes the difference. Why is it that groups and communities in countries like Switzerland and the Netherlands have managed to prosper – not in spite of power sharing, but precisely because of it – while those in countries like Sri Lanka and Macedonia have struggled to move beyond a mere tentative commitment to sharing power? Why is it that Great Britain can move with some success towards greater devolution, while Belgium seemingly moves ever closer to partition?

No one chapter can possibly hope to offer anything more than a partial perspective on these enormously complex and contested issues. However, even partial perspectives can add to our understanding of the challenges that democratic power sharing brings, and help build new solutions to old problems. In this spirit, I want to offer a philosophical perspective on what might best be described as a matter of measurement. We know that when people are engaged in violent conflict, they can measure progress in terms of territory gained or lost. But in countries that have already made the transition to democracy, and are striving to build sustainable power-sharing institutions, progress can be much more difficult to measure. It can be more difficult to measure because the values and standards by which we might assess that progress – values like equality, freedom, inclusion and so forth – are often vaguely defined and badly understood.

There are doubtless many reasons why democratic values sometimes prove so problematic. Perhaps the most basic reason, however, is how to choose from the many different values to which we might conceivably appeal and, correspondingly, how to decide what that choice implies for the course that power sharing ought to follow. The ongoing debate between advocates of consociational versus integrative power sharing provides a clear illustration of what is at issue here: while both recognise the importance of the values of inclusion and moderation to conflict management and resolution, the different weight that each accords to those values results in what are seemingly conflicting institutional prescriptions. Thus, if democratic values really are to provide clear and unambiguous standards by which we might assess the progress of a power-sharing democracy, we need to be explicit about the priority that we give to some values and not to others, as well as about the institutional implications of that choice (see Weale 1999, pp. 40–2). In order to explore what is at issue here, this chapter will consider the account of democratic values advanced by Robert Dahl in his *Democracy and Its Critics* (1989). While I maintain that this prominent account is plausible in its own right, I will suggest a number of ways in which it needs to be developed with respect to the challenges of sharing power in divided societies.

DAHL ON DEMOCRATIC VALUES

Dahl's account of democratic values – or what he variously refers to as democratic ideas, principles or assumptions – is situated within a much broader project that aims to show that democracy is a better form of government than any of its rivals (Dahl 1989, p. 84 and *passim*). Here, I will simply assume that, although far from easy to establish and maintain, democracy represents the best hope for divided societies as their members struggle to build a just and stable political society (Sisk 1996, p. 29). Following Dahl, I will also assume that in a democracy citizens should be regarded as equally well qualified, taken all around, to participate in the political process (Dahl 1989, pp. 97–8), an assumption which he elaborates in terms of two key democratic values: intrinsic equality and personal autonomy. To these two values, I will add a third: the value of inclusion. Like Dahl, I take it that the value of inclusion is implicit in the values of intrinsic equality and personal autonomy. However, the value of inclusion is worth considering in its own right since it draws our attention to a number of further questions that are of crucial importance with respect to how democracy should proceed in divided societies.

Intrinsic equality

According to Dahl, virtually all arguments for democracy ultimately fall back, even if only by implication, on the value of intrinsic equality. This value, associated with Kant but defended by philosophers of different schools, holds that each individual has independent moral standing and hence is valuable in his or her own right. It holds, furthermore, that because our moral standing cannot be reduced to that of any other, all individuals are intrinsically equal (Dahl 1989, pp. 84–5; see also Dworkin 1970, p. 11; Weale 1999, p. 58). Although the value of intrinsic equality has proved immensely powerful as an abstract ideal, it has, however, proved notoriously vague in practice. Philosophers disagree about the precise respects in which intrinsic equality should be ascribed to individuals, and about the requirements, if any, that this value places upon democratic practices and institutions. Like Dahl, I agree that the interpretation that seems 'most relevant to the democratic process is expressed in the principle of equal consideration of interests' (Dahl 1989, p. 86). But even here there is scope for disagreement. It is not clear, for instance, whether equal consideration of interests can be secured by affording individuals no more than a standard range of civil and political rights, or whether in some circumstances further institutional measures are also required.

While Dahl's discussion turns on the intrinsic equality of individuals, a key claim in many divided societies is that this value can also be ascribed to groups or communities. As Peter Jones explains, the suggestion here is that because groups can be attributed with a moral standing that is separate from the moral standing attributed to their individual members, they can be treated as if they were valuable in and of themselves (Jones 1999, *passim*). In Northern Ireland, for example, the term 'parity of esteem' is often used to express the idea that the two conflicting communities, British unionists and Irish nationalists, should be afforded just such a status (see Pollak 1993). Parity of esteem features in the 1998 Agreement as a guiding political principle and, as such, has played an important role in ensuring that 'the identity, ethos and aspirations of both communities' have equal standing (Agreement 1998, Constitutional Issues, article 1 (v)). In a similar vein, Quebec governments take it as axiomatic that French culture in Quebec is valuable in its own right and hence should be preserved for the future. To this end, they have introduced a series of stringent language and employment laws that 'actively seek to create future members of the community' (Taylor 1994, p. 58).

From one perspective, institutional guarantees of status can help reduce insecurities and tensions between groups, and hence help lessen the difficulties that they can face in sharing power. But from another perspective, it is difficult to see how the thought that intrinsic equality can be ascribed to groups can be rendered compatible with ascribing intrinsic equality to their individual members (Habermas 1994, pp. 110–11; Barry 2001a, p. 50). Institutionalising groups as if they were valuable in their own right seemingly assumes that groups are static, or that groups mean the same thing to each and every member. This, however, can hardly be the case. The term 'Serb', for example, does not refer to a single entity but to a range of associations and institutions – including the Orthodox Church, political parties and so forth – that offer a range of definitions of what being 'Serbian' means and that act in a range of ways to pursue those definitions, often in competition with one another. How this competition plays itself out will depend on institutional and other contexts: Kosovo Serbs, for example, are not the same as Serbs in the remainder of Serbia. But whatever the context, the point is that group identity is not a property, a set of essential attributes that all members must inevitably possess, but a relationship that members establish and re-establish among themselves (Parekh 1999, p. 68). To think otherwise is to run the risk of trapping people within rigidly defined categories that may be untrue to the ways in which they view themselves and the world about them. In other words, by prioritising one interpretation of a group's identity over others, we may well end up failing to treat some of its individual members as valuable in and of themselves.

Although these considerations might lead us to conclude that groups cannot be valuable in their own right (see, for example, Jones 1998, p. 36), the trouble is that they are often *perceived* to be intrinsically valuable by their individual members. Like it or not, perceptions matter greatly in divided societies, as does the corresponding ability to act as a collective entity (Rothchild 1986, pp. 87–93; Sisk 1996, pp. 13–14). This is not to suggest that we should never try to change those perceptions – or to 'diminish their pretensions', to use Neil MacCormick's phrase (1996, p. 566) – especially when they work against the maintenance of a just and stable power-sharing democracy. But what we cannot do is discount those perceptions, simply because we think they are misguided. The simple fact of the matter is that Christians and Muslims in Lebanon, Serbs, Bosniaks and Croats in Bosnia and Herzegovina and Walloons and Flemings in Belgium do not simply participate in political life as individual citizens, but also as distinct groups with vital communal interests to protect.

On the face of it, then, the trouble would appear to be this. As Dahl contends, any convincing account of democracy must appeal to the value of intrinsic equality as ascribed to individuals. But since we must also take seriously the fact that groups, too, are often viewed as intrinsically valuable, the danger is that these two imperatives may conflict. The question, therefore, is what to do. Do we simply have to live with this potential tension and muddle through as best we can when conflicts arise? Or perhaps the sensible thing to do is to avoid getting caught up in philosophical debates about the nature and scope of democratic values, favouring instead an incremental, piecemeal approach that allows values to emerge under their own steam (but see Goodin 1982, pp. 3–4 and chapter 2)? In what follows, I want to show that such conclusions are too hasty. Taken on its own, intrinsic equality does appear to come up short as a standard by which to measure the progress of a power-sharing democracy. However, following Dahl, I will argue that when intrinsic equality is combined with a second fundamental democratic value – the value of personal autonomy – the case for appealing to democratic standards becomes much more powerful.

Personal autonomy

According to Dahl, the value of intrinsic equality may be a necessary condition of democracy, but it is not a sufficient condition. It is not sufficient because, although intrinsic equality means that a just democratic system must aspire to treat each citizen's interests with equal consideration (and, empirically speaking, may well be unstable unless it does so), it is simply too weak to justify the basic democratic idea that citizens should, all things considered, have an equal say in the democratic process. As Dahl explains, it would not offend this value if I were to claim that since I know what is best for you, and since I can be trusted to advance your interests as if they were my own, then I ought to speak for both of us (1989, pp. 87–8). In other words, it would not be offensive because although the value of intrinsic equality implies that each person's interest must be treated with equal consideration, it leaves two further questions unanswered:

(a) who best judges that interest? and (b) who best safeguards and promotes it?

In response, Dahl argues that a more robust justification for democracy can be constructed by joining the value of intrinsic equality to a second fundamental democratic value. He terms this value the 'assumption of personal autonomy' which straightforwardly says that 'no person is, in general, more likely than yourself to be a better judge of your own good or interest or to act to bring it about' (1989, p. 99). Admittedly, the value of personal autonomy has been the source of some dispute among political philosophers (see, for example, Barry 2001b, pp. 118–23). Yet for present purposes, what is significant is not so much the particular stance that Dahl takes on this value, but that he appears to draw no great distinction between a number of important dimensions of it.

For example, Dahl sometimes seems to suggest that people should be treated *as if* they are the best judges of their own interest, whereas at other times he seems to suggest that people actually *are* the best judges of that interest. The former is a normative claim that might rightly play its part in the justification of democracy, whereas the latter is simply an empirical claim that may or may not be true in particular cases. In the present context, what is perhaps more important is that Dahl does not always distinguish clearly between who best judges an interest and who best safeguards and promotes it. Although both feature in his analysis, I contend that the second of these two dimensions is often the more decisive consideration, especially since the realities of modern political life are such that representative democracy is by and large unavoidable (Mill 1991 [1861]).

Interestingly, Dahl's own examples (slavery and the subjugation of women) seem to support this contention (1989, p. 104). While countless other examples could easily have been cited, the important point to note here is that the failure by some to safeguard and promote the interests of others, particularly when those others have (or are perceived to have) a different group identity, has been a principal justification for establishing political systems based on power sharing. Moreover, this failure also helps to explain why the dominant tendency, both in the literature and in practice, has been to call for the institutionalisation of group identities as a key means of protecting members' interests – through, for example, the provision of reserved seats and mutual vetoes within a legislature (see, for example, Lijphart 1977).

Now, it is perhaps easy to forget that this dimension of the value of personal autonomy is not just a matter that affects relations *between* groups, but also has crucial consequences for relations *within* groups. Institutionalising group identities may help protect groups from one another and hence afford them a more effective voice within the democratic process. But it may also turn a group's identity into a commodity over which its leaders must compete in order to gain or retain political power. For example, the tendency of so-called 'ethnic entrepreneurs' to mobilise politically for personal gain has been well documented. So, too, has their proclivity for playing upon existing fears and prejudices when more moderate members of their group attempt to make conciliatory gestures towards members of competing groups (see, for example, Horowitz 2001, 2002; Sisk 1996, p. 83). Since this means that moderates must always be aware of losing support to extremists who typically portray themselves as holding true to the group's 'authentic' identity and aspirations, moderates can also be led to treat the group as if it were a monolithic whole.

The danger, therefore, with institutionalising group identities is that it may make it difficult for political leaders to remain responsive to, and hence effectively promote, the full diversity of members' interests. Otherwise put, it may make it difficult for those who do not necessarily conceive of their identity along group lines to have their interests effectively represented. In saying this I do not mean to deny that, in some instances, the only option is to institutionalise competing group identities, especially in contexts where the memories of violent conflict are still fresh and where insecurity is wholly rife. Nor do I mean to deny the rather obvious fact that, for instance, Israeli Arabs, Russian Estonians, Kashmiri Muslims or Chinese Malaysians do not simply seek to engage in political life as individual citizens but also as distinctive groups that have vital collective interests to protect (see Parekh 1999, p. 72). However, I contend that insofar as a commitment to the value of personal autonomy entails a commitment to democracy, those charged with designing power-sharing institutions should ultimately aim towards a very different vision of what power sharing should involve, even if that vision is not obtainable in the shorter term.

I maintain that it is possible to design power-sharing institutions in a way that is compatible with both the value of personal autonomy and the peremptory need in divided societies to protect groups from one another. The approach that I have in mind calls for a form of power sharing containing mechanisms to ensure that those who see themselves as belonging to distinctive groups can participate effectively as such within the democratic process, but that does not bind members' capacity for effective participation exclusively to those mechanisms. Special language provisions provide a good illustration of what is at issue here. On the one hand, they are often included in power-sharing arrangements as a key means of creating equality between competing groups; but on the other, they can be institutionalised in such a way that group members need not be required to speak the language (but see Taylor 1994, p. 58). Either way, the value of personal autonomy implies that this choice should be left open. But this is not all. In so doing, it also leaves it to people to decide for themselves whether groups can be intrinsically valuable, or whether the value of intrinsic equality should only be ascribed to individuals.

Far from being unrealistic, this more fluid approach to power sharing is, as Tom Hadden's chapter in this volume enables us to see, consistent with a number of recent developments in international law. In particular, it is consistent with the basic thinking that underpins both the United Nations Declaration on the Rights of Persons Belonging to National or Ethnic, Religious and Linguistic Minorities (1992) and the European Framework Convention on the Protection of National Minorities (1995). Once again, I want to stress that this approach may not be appropriate in every context. In some divided societies, especially those that have recently emerged from periods of intense, internecine violence, more rigidly institutionalised forms of power sharing and identity may well be necessary to counteract deep feelings of insecurity and mistrust between groups. However, to the extent that we accept that democratic institutions can and should be informed by the values of intrinsic equality and personal autonomy, divided societies should aim to achieve those standards in the longer run.

Inclusion

With Dahl, I accept that the value of inclusion follows from, or is implicit in, the values of intrinsic equality and personal autonomy (Dahl 1989, pp. 99, 129). After all, the point of those two values is to justify the view that each citizen who is bound by a collective decision should be equally included in its making. It has long been argued, of course, that there is no way in which democracy or its values can determine who should be citizens; democracy can begin to function only once the citizen-body has been defined (see, for example, Dahl 1989, chapter 14; but see Saward 1998, chapter 7). However, it is not true to say that intrinsic equality and personal autonomy are entirely silent on this issue. They suggest that however we think about the value of inclusion, that value should be defined as broadly as possible – or as Dahl puts it, intrinsic equality and personal autonomy 'provide reasonable grounds for adopting a criterion that approaches universality among adults' (Dahl 1989, p. 129). That said, the issue remains enormously difficult, not least of all with respect to divided societies.

It might be argued that, by aiming at a standard of inclusion that approaches near universality among adults, we may be tempted to overlook a basic fact about divided societies: divided societies are societies divided among groups. Consequently, while the aim of including adults in general is indeed laudable, the first concern should be that of making space for groups (see McGarry and O'Leary 1995). There is reason to think, however, that this argument is somewhat overstated. Divided societies can, and often do, contain a great many people who do not identify with the main contending groups.

> These include recent immigrants, those who seek to break away from their communities of origin, those of a mixed religious heritage and those for whom political struggles related to class, gender, or sexual orientation are of far greater concern than ethnic, national or religious differences. (O'Neill 2003, p. 386)

But whereas we might be tempted to think that the aim of including all such people within the democratic process has to take its place behind the task of finding a workable means of including the main contending groups, I believe this thought to be mistaken. Broadening the scope of inclusion does not merely enhance the quality of life of those who stand to gain directly, but has implications for society as a whole. For just like groups, individuals who are at liberty to choose the terms in which to express themselves politically are more likely to participate in the kind of debate, and contribute towards the sorts of democratic decisions, that could build a better future for everyone in society (O'Flynn 2004, pp. 556–7).

In my view, this last point is all too often overlooked by those charged with designing power-sharing institutions. On the face of it, one obvious exception is the 'integrative approach' advocated principally by Donald Horowitz (1985) and Benjamin Reilly (2001). This approach argues for the adoption of an electoral system (especially the 'alternative vote' or 'instant run-off') that rewards moderate politicians who are willing to compromise with politicians from the other side and, by compromising, enables them to fend off the uncompromising extremes within their own communities. In so doing, it also encourages them to take seriously the interests of citizens more generally, and hence adds greater weight to the votes of those who do not wish participate in political life along group lines (O'Flynn 2003, pp. 142ff). The trouble is, however, that by advocating electoral systems that reward moderates, integrative approaches run the risk of doing damage to the value of inclusion: while fostering moderation is obviously a good thing, opting for an electoral system that 'aims for moderation rather than broad representation in the legislature and executive' (Lijphart 2004, p. 98) may result in a 'spoiler momentum' that ultimately makes democratic politics unworkable (Zahar 2003).

Against this kind of background, it is perhaps easy to see why, for example, Larry Diamond should conclude that, 'Where cleavage groups are sharply defined and group identities (and intergroup insecurities and suspicions) deeply felt, the overriding imperative is to avoid broad and indefinite exclusion from power of any significant group' (1999, p. 104; quoted in Lijphart 2004, p. 100). The obvious question, though, is what to do with extremists once they are returned to power.

For those like Arend Lijphart (1977) who advocate consociational forms of power sharing, democracy is, in the first instance, about inclusion. Accordingly, the initial task is to devise a proportional electoral system that returns a legislature that is highly representative of society as a whole; in short, moderates, extremists and others in society should be included in the democratic process. Once politicians have been returned to power, consociational guarantees like the mutual veto and group (or 'segmental') autonomy are then meant to encourage politicians to moderate their claims so that political compromises might emerge. But as we know from cases like Northern Ireland and Lebanon, consociational institutions do not always have this effect. On the contrary, to the extent that consociational institutions operate on the assumption that 'high fences make good neighbours' (Wilson and Wilford 2003, p. 6), they not only tend to treat competing group identities as if they were rigid or fixed, but, for reasons already explained, often end up encouraging within-group competition and extremism.

Insofar as the value of inclusion follows from the values of intrinsic equality and personal autonomy, our ability to respond to the kind of difficulty at which we have arrived stands as a good test of the capacity of democratic values to provide clear and unambiguous standards by which we might assess the progress of a power-sharing democracy. In order to show that democratic values really do provide viable standards, I suggest the following. With Lijphart, Diamond and others, I agree that electoral systems must be as inclusive as possible; they must, in other words, provide for the greatest possible range of electoral choice and society-wide representation. I therefore agree that proportional electoral systems are more appropriate than systems like the alternative vote that may not be sufficiently inclusive. At the same time, I also share Horowitz's and Reilly's worry that consociational devices like the mutual veto and group autonomy tend to reify group identities, play into the hands of extremists, and consequently undermine the values of intrinsic equality and personal autonomy. Yet rather than accept that we have therefore reached an impasse – both philosophically and institutionally – we should instead explore the possibility of combining proportional electoral systems with power-sharing institutions that allow for greater fluidity of identity.

For example, PRSTV has served Northern Ireland well in terms of creating a relatively accurate fit between each party's share of the vote and its share of the seats in the Northern Ireland Assembly (CAIN 2004). In practice, this electoral system has ensured that extremists and moderates from both communities have been included in the legislature, while executive formation rules have further ensured that moderates and extremists have been included in the cabinet (see O'Leary 1999). Arguably, however, the presence of moderates and extremists within the one cabinet has not only led to an increased risk of cabinet inertia with respect to tackling particularly divisive issues, but has contributed in no small measure to ongoing political instability in Northern Ireland (see Horowitz 2001, 2002). The question, therefore, is whether there are principled reasons to think that executive formation rules should be reformed – for example, by insisting that cabinets as a whole, along with individual nominees, must be ratified by a weighted majority in the legislature – so as to make it more difficult for those holding extremist views to gain cabinet positions. Put another way, the question is whether there are sound reasons to think that although a legislature should reflect the diversity of opinion found in society, the make-up of a government cabinet need not directly do so. I suggest the following.

First, a power-sharing system that makes it harder for extremists to gain cabinet positions need not necessarily curtail their ability to engage freely in political debate or their efforts to persuade others to see things from their point of view. In fact, it might even be argued that there is nothing unusual in this arrangement since, in any democratic system, the right to hold seats in a legislature does not automatically translate into the right to hold executive office. Moreover, the existence of a vibrant opposition can even been seen as crucial for the health of the democratic process itself, preventing political inertia and ensuring that government really does act on behalf of everyone in society. Secondly, and perhaps more significantly, it is crucial to see that democratic inclusion is not simply about the inclusion of moderate and extremist political parties. As in the 'Serb' example highlighted earlier, those charged with designing power-sharing institutions should pay greater attention to the range of diverse interests and opinions that might be found within any particular group, as well as across society as a whole. Inclusion should go beyond mere party politics. It should also provide the opportunity for those in the wider public sphere – the media, churches, the voluntary sector and the like – to engage in a meaningful way in political life. In this sense, one of the greatest challenges for power sharing is how to ensure that everyone in society can have their say, however they wish to express that say. The value of inclusion should cast its net so that the full range of interests in society can be voiced. Nowhere is this more important than in a divided society that is endeavouring to build a sustainable democracy.

CONCLUSION

The values by which we might measure the progress of a power-sharing democracy can be hard to define and can be even harder to apply in practice. Nevertheless, by drawing on the work of Robert Dahl, I have tried to show just why it is that the values of intrinsic equality, personal autonomy and inclusion have such important implications for thinking about the form that power-sharing institutions ought to take. More specifically, I have argued that power sharing should, as far as practicably possible, make it as easy as possible for people to choose between participating in the democratic process as individual citizens or as members of distinct groups. In other words, it should avoid the rigid institutionalisation of group identities in favour of an approach that is more sensitive to the diversity of people's interests. Admittedly, these prescriptions may not be feasible in every context, at least not in the short run. But, as I have argued, there are good reasons why divided societies should strive to achieve them in the longer run.

NOTE

1. I wish to thank Donald Horowitz, Peter Jones, Graham Long, David Russell and Robin Wilson for writing enormously helpful comments on an earlier draft of this chapter. They may not, of course, agree with everything in this printed version.

REFERENCES

Agreement Reached in the Multiparty Negotiations (1998). Belfast: The Stationery Office.

Barry, B. (2001a) 'The Muddles of Multiculturalism', New Left Review, 8, 49–71.

—— (2001b) Culture and Equality: An Egalitarian Critique of Multiculturalism. Cambridge: Polity Press.

CAIN (2004) Northern Ireland Conflict, Politics and Society. Available at http://cain.ulst.ac.uk/.

Dahl, R. (1989) Democracy and its Critics. New Haven, CT: Yale University Press.

Diamond, L. (1999) Developing Democracy: Toward Consolidation. Baltimore, MD: Johns Hopkins University Press.

Dworkin, R. (1970) 'A Special Supplement: Taking Rights Seriously', New York Review of Books, 15 (11). Available at http://www.nybooks.com/articles/10713.

European Framework Convention on the Protection of National Minorities (1995). Available at http://conventions.coe.int/Treaty/en/Treaties/Html/157.htm.

Goodin, R. (1982) Political Theory and Public Policy. Chicago, IL: University of Chicago Press.

Habermas, J. (1994) 'Struggles for Recognition in the Democratic Constitutional State', in A. Gutmann (ed.), Multiculturalism: Examining the Politics of Recognition. Princeton, NJ: Princeton University Press, pp. 107–48.

Horowitz, D. (1985) Ethnic Groups in Conflict. Berkeley, CA: University of California Press.

—— (2001) 'The Northern Ireland Agreement: Clear, Consociational, and Risky', in J. McGarry (ed.), Northern Ireland and the Divided World: Post-Agreement Northern Ireland in Comparative Perspective. Oxford: Oxford University Press, pp. 89–108.

—— (2002) 'Explaining the Northern Ireland Agreement: The Sources of an Unlikely Constitutional Consensus', *British Journal of Political Science*, 32 (2), 193–220.

Jones, P. (1998) 'Political Theory and Cultural Diversity', *Critical Review of International Social and Political Philosophy*, 1 (1), 28–62.

—— (1999) 'Group Rights and Group Oppression', *The Journal of Political Philosophy*, 7 (4), 353–77.

Lijphart, A. (1977) *Democracy in Plural Societies*. New Haven, CT: Yale University Press.

—— (2004) 'Constitutional Design for Divided Societies', *Journal of Democracy*, 15 (2), 96–109.

MacCormick, N. (1996) 'Liberalism, Nationalism and the Post-Sovereign State', *Political Studies*, 44 (3), 553–67.

McGarry, J. and O'Leary, B. (1995) 'Five Fallacies: Northern Ireland and the Liabilities of Liberalism', *Ethnic and Racial Studies*, 18 (4), 837–61.

Mill, J.S. (1991 [1861]) 'Considerations on Representative Government', in J. Gray (ed.), *Mill: On Liberty and Other Essays*. Oxford: Oxford University Press, pp. 203–467.

O'Flynn, I. (2003) 'The Problem of Recognising Individual and National Identities: A Critique of the Belfast Agreement', *Critical Review of International Social and Political Philosophy*, 6 (3), 129–53.

—— (2004) 'Why Justice Can't Have it All: In Reply to O'Neill', *Ethnicities*, 4 (4), 545–61.

O'Leary, B. (1999) 'The Nature of the Agreement', *New Left Review*, 233, 66–96.

O'Neill, S. (2003) 'Justice in Ethnically Diverse Societies: A Critique of Political Alienation', *Ethnicities*, 3 (3), 369–92.

Parekh, B. (1999) 'Defining National Identity in a Multicultural Society', in E. Mortimer (ed.), *People, Nation and State: The Meaning of Ethnicity and Nationalism*. London: I. B. Tauris, pp. 66–74.

Pollak, A. (ed.) (1993), *A Citizens' Enquiry: The Opsahl Report on Northern Ireland*. Dublin: Lilliput Press.

Reilly, B. (2001) *Democracy in Divided Societies: Electoral Engineering for Conflict Management*. Cambridge: Cambridge University Press.

Rothchild, D. (1986) 'Hegemonial Exchange: An Alternative Model for Managing Conflict in Middle Africa', in D. Thompson and D. Ronen (eds), *Ethnicity, Politics and Development*. Boulder, CO: Lynne Rienner, pp. 65–104.

Saward, M. (1998) *The Terms of Democracy*. Cambridge: Polity Press.

Sisk, T. (1996) *Power Sharing and International Mediation in Ethnic Conflict*. Washington, DC: United States Institute of Peace.

Taylor, C. (1994) 'The Politics of Recognition', in A. Gutmann (ed.), *Multiculturalism: Examining the Politics of Recognition*. Princeton, NJ: Princeton University Press, pp. 25–73.

United Nations Declaration on the Rights of Persons Belonging to National or Ethnic, Religious and Linguistic Minorities (1992). Available at http://www.unhchr.ch/thml/menu3/b/d_minori.htm.

Weale, A. (1999) *Democracy*. Basingstoke: Palgrave Macmillan.

Wilson, R. and Wilford, R. (2003) 'Northern Ireland: A Route to Stability?', Birmingham: The Devolution Papers.

Zahar, M.-J. (2003) 'Reframing the Spoiler Debate in Peace Processes', in J. Darby and R. MacGinty (eds), *Contemporary Peacemaking: Conflict, Violence and Peace Processes*. Basingstoke: Palgrave MacMillan, pp. 114–24.

2
Integration and Autonomy: Minority Rights and Political Accommodation

Tom Hadden[1]

DIFFERING PERSPECTIVES

Choosing structures to resolve conflict and build a sustainable democracy in multiethnic states and societies is difficult. The issues typically look somewhat different from legal and political perspectives. Human rights lawyers tend towards the development of general principles which are to be applied on a universal basis. National politicians and political scientists tend towards more pragmatic policies aimed at managing current problems and, if they aspire to statesmanship, achieving longer term peace, stability and prosperity.

There are also significant regional variations in the approach to these issues. Europeans often focus their attention only on long established 'national' minorities and have less interest in making equivalent provision for more recent immigrant communities. Asians often have to deal with even more diverse religious and ethnic communities, not least the different strands of Islam, Hinduism and Buddhism and the widespread Chinese diaspora. Africans often face a huge number of different ethnic and linguistic communities thrown together into composite states by colonial rivalries. Latin Americans often face the problem of dealing with an ex-colonial ruling class, indigenous communities and the descendants of the slave trade.

Members of different ethnic communities themselves also tend to adopt differing approaches to their situations. Some are passionately committed to the maintenance of their distinctive identities and cultures. Others seem more interested in integrating with the rest of the population, finding satisfying lifestyles and jobs for themselves or their families and maintaining only those aspects of their traditional cultures which fit with those objectives.

The underlying objective for all those involved must be to find a way of accommodating these differing perspectives within a human rights framework.

UNDERLYING HUMAN RIGHTS PRINCIPLES

The prevailing focus from a human rights perspective has typically been on the rights of individual members of minorities rather than on their relationship with majorities. But there has been a progressive shift in recent years in the approach of the human rights community from almost exclusive focus on the prevention of discrimination towards the recognition and accommodation of minorities and the adoption of positive measures to protect their existence and facilitate the expression of their distinctive cultures. The Universal Declaration on Human Rights of 1948 under article 2 prohibited discrimination on the ground of 'national or social origin'. The European Convention on Human Rights of 1950 under article 14 added discrimination on the ground of 'association with a national minority'. Both were otherwise silent on the rights of minorities or their members. The development of a more positive approach began with article 27 of the International Covenant on Civil and Political Rights of 1966 which granted a right to members of minorities to 'enjoy their culture, practise their religion and use their language'. The most recent formulations in the United Nations Declaration on the Rights of Persons Belonging to National or Ethnic, Religious and Linguistic Minorities of 1992 (referred to hereinafter as the United Nations Declaration) and the European Framework Convention for the Protection of National Minorities of 1994 (referred to hereinafter as the European Framework Convention) have again shifted the focus from the rights of individual members of minorities to the imposition of duties on states to protect the existence of minorities and take action to facilitate their development (Thornberry 1991).

These developments have tended to overshadow, if not entirely replace, the longstanding debate on the practicality of the right of peoples to self-determination. Though this right was given pride of place in article 1 of both the International Covenant on Civil and Political Rights and the International Covenant on Economic, Social and Cultural Rights, the human rights community has found it difficult to give it much practical effect. The United Nations Human Rights Committee which deals with individual complaints under the International Covenant on Civil and Political Rights has ruled that it cannot deal with complaints over the denial of self-determination since it has no way of deciding who should represent a people.[2] The International Court of Justice has found it equally difficult to decide on who is to be regarded as a people in contested territories.[3] And national governments have consistently insisted that the principle of the territorial integrity of states must take precedence over any claim to self-determination that would involve secession, except in the most extreme circumstances (Musgrave 1997).[4] There is consequently increasing interest in the concept that minorities may have a right to various forms of autonomy, based on a combination of the terms of these new instruments and a more flexible interpretation of the right of peoples to self-determination (Hannum 1996; Gilbert 2001). This too clearly has a separatist thrust in the sense that it envisages a form of society in which members of minorities may not only maintain their distinctive identities and cultures but also establish separate institutions and structures to govern their own affairs on an indeterminate range of issues.

This new focus, however, has not displaced the more general human rights principles of mutual tolerance, non-discrimination and individual equality before the law, which are reflected in the inclusion in the new minority instruments of the right of individual members of distinctive communities not to be treated as such against their will. These principles point towards a somewhat different form of society in which the objective is the inclusion of members of all religious or ethnic communities in a pluralist and multicultural environment through integrated institutions and structures in which all can participate on an equal basis. There is a continuing and probably unavoidable tension in these various principles between the assertion of primacy for individual rights and the demands of minorities for group or communal rights, a tension that cannot always be resolved by the standard response that minority rights are granted only to their individual members (see Raz 1986, pp. 107–9).

CHANGING PATTERNS

The development of general principles of universal application is also made more difficult by the fact that there is usually constant and cumulative change in the balance between majority and minority communities. This may be due to demographic changes, to patterns of population movement and immigration, to the extent of intermarriage, and to the degree to which members of those communities wish to maintain their distinctive communal affiliation. There is also concern that undue focus on the membership of one or other majority or minority community may conceal the extent to which many individuals have or feel themselves to have multiple identities (see, for example, Gutmann 1994). These features of majority and minority communities are of particular concern to political scientists, who are interested in the processes of social change. Hence the focus by political scientists and politicians on the need to maintain flexibility in their response to changing conditions. Human rights lawyers typically find it easier to make provision for more static conditions. The problem posed by these constantly changing patterns is reflected in the difficulty which the human rights community has had in reaching any consensus on the definition of a minority for the purposes of international instruments or in linking human rights principles to different forms of democracy.

THE CHOICE OF STRATEGIES

The underlying issue for both lawyers and politicians is how far they should go in encouraging greater integration between different communal groups, even at the cost of diminishing their distinctive traditions and cultures, or in permitting or promoting those distinctive traditions and cultures. It is certainly not obvious from a political perspective that measures to promote communal differences are always to be preferred to those designed to achieve greater integration. Nor is it obvious that members of different communities should be left entirely to their own devices – or those of their communal leaders – in choosing between integration and separation or autonomy. There are genuine choices to be made about the long-term objectives of national policy in this area. There are numerous examples of local and national conflicts arising from the assertion of communal identities and demands, just as there are examples of the harmonious accommodation of distinctive communal cultures whether in an integrated multicultural environment or with different forms of territorial or functional autonomy.

Definitions and terminology

To clarify the nature of this choice it is important to distinguish at least three broad approaches to dealing with minority issues at a national level: assimilation, integration and autonomy:

- *assimilation* is generally understood to involve the merging of the separate identity and culture of distinctive communities with the dominant national identity and culture;
- *integration* may be understood as involving the recognition of the identity and culture of those who wish to maintain a distinctive community and the implementation of measures to ensure their effective participation as such in all aspects of the political, economic, social and cultural structures of the country in which they live;
- *autonomy* may be understood to involve the creation of separate structures through which members of a distinctive community may exercise effective control over their own political, economic, social or cultural affairs on a regional, local or functional basis.

Each of these approaches is acceptable at an international level, subject to the explicit provision in article 5(2) of the European Framework Convention that policies of assimilation are not to be imposed against the will of those affected by them.

There is an additional problem of terminology in this context which stems from the variable and confusing use within the human rights community of the concepts of multicultural, intercultural and related policies. The distinction drawn within the United Nations Working Group on Minorities between multicultural education (education in separate schools for distinctive communal groups) and intercultural education (education in separate or integrated schools about other communities and cultures), for example, is not widely understood and runs counter to the more general usage of the terms.[5] It may therefore be desirable to relate these terms more directly to the distinctions between assimilation, integration and autonomy:

- societies and policies based on an assimilative approach could be described as *mono-cultural*;
- societies and policies based on the recognition and accommodation of various distinctive communities and cultures within a broader integrated and socially inclusive framework could be described as *multi-cultural*;
- societies and policies based on the provision of separate or autonomous institutions or structures for each main community or culture could then perhaps be described as *auto-cultural* or *solo-cultural*.

As in some other areas of human rights activity, the selection of appropriate and meaningful terminology may be as important to securing public support as the formulation of detailed policy and practice.

Flexible guidelines

The fact that each of these general approaches is regarded as legitimate suggests that the most appropriate role for the international human rights community in setting standards may be to provide flexible guidelines and examples of good – and bad – practice rather than to prescribe specific rights and obligations applicable in all circumstances (Hadden 2003). It may then be possible to distinguish spheres and conditions in which policies of integration may be desirable and other spheres and conditions in which the provision of separate structures and facilities may be desirable. A distinction has already been drawn by Eide between the need for individual equality in the common political domain and for special measures of recognition and accommodation in the communal domain (Eide 1994). But it must also be recognised that in both cases positive measures by national governments and international agencies may be required. Strict individual equality in national elections is unlikely to achieve effective participation by representatives of minorities in the structures of national government (Kymlicka 1995). Nor is general freedom for all communities to organise their educational and cultural affairs likely to result in effective freedom for members of those communities to choose between integration and separation. There are real choices of political direction to be made in this context which should in principle be recognised by the international human rights community rather than concealed in general formulations.

Areas for integration

The objective or aspiration of policies of integration, as has been indicated, is to create an inclusive society in which members of different ethnic, religious and linguistic communities may mingle and share in the full range of social, economic and political activity without having to abandon their distinctive characteristics or cultures. In an era of increasing diversity in many countries, as a result of population movement and various forms of globalisation, this is an entirely appropriate policy objective. It complies fully with the human rights principles of individual and communal equality, social inclusion, and mutual tolerance. There is also some evidence that it may help to avoid the dangers of communal conflict arising from physical separation and economic competition and the resulting growth of divisive stereotypes based on lack of contact and knowledge (Horowitz 1985).

The most obvious sphere for an integrative approach is that of national government. The Vienna Declaration and Programme of Action and other international human rights instruments make it clear that all states should have a system of national government 'representing the whole people belonging to the territory without distinction of any kind'.[6] The United Nations Declaration likewise provides under article 2(3) that minorities should be able to participate effectively in national or regional government decisions concerning them. Since by their very nature minority communities are unlikely to win substantial numbers of legislative seats in ordinary democratic elections, special measures may be required to ensure reasonable levels of representation in national parliaments, in national political parties and in government, as indicated in the Lund Recommendations on the Effective Participation of National Minorities in Public Life.[7] In cases where minorities are widely dispersed, provision for a separate electoral roll and reserved seats or for positive action by national political parties in the selection of candidates may be needed to secure any representation in the national parliament, as in New Zealand and Pakistan. Concern over the separatist impact of maintaining separate voting rolls, however, has led to the abandonment of separate voting rolls in Pakistan.

In cases where a society is deeply divided into two or three major communities, each with its own ethnic or communal political parties, as in Northern Ireland, Lebanon or Sri Lanka, provision for some form of proportional allocation of ministerial posts may be needed to avoid the risk that permanent exclusion of one or other community from government may lead to serious conflict. The dangers of 'ethnic entrepreneurs' establishing political power on this basis and of entrenching ethnic divisions and conflict on a permanent basis, however, are well recognised. Hence the importance of the provision in the most recent human rights documents of a right for individuals to choose not to be treated as a member of a specific minority.[8]

A second sphere in which integration is likely to be appropriate is in the membership of appointed public bodies and the agencies of law enforcement at a national level. The Montreal Declaration on the independence of the judiciary, for example, calls for the membership of the judiciary to be reflective of the community, and the United

Nations Code of Conduct for Law Enforcement Officials calls for the police to be representative of the community as a whole.[9] The Commonwealth guide to Best Practice for National Human Rights Institutions calls for their membership collectively to 'reflect gender balance, the ethnic diversity of society and the range of vulnerable groups'.[10] It is relatively straightforward to make constitutional or legislative provision for appointment to such bodies to be made on a representative basis, as for example in South Africa in relation to appointments to the judiciary and other state bodies, and in Northern Ireland in relation to recruitment to the police and appointments to the Northern Ireland Human Rights Commission.[11]

A third sphere in which integration is generally favoured is in public-sector employment. Though there are no prescriptive international standards in this context a number of states in which there are substantial linguistic or ethnic minorities, such as Canada, South Tyrol and Northern Ireland, have adopted measures designed to secure a fair balance in public-sector employment (Hadden and Craig 2000).

It should be noted that measures adopted for all these purposes tend to give priority to the claims of the group to reasonable or fair participation or representation rather than to the claims of individuals to absolute equality of treatment in terms of their qualifications or experience. Most relevant international instruments contain provisions exempting such measures from the prohibition against discrimination. Article 8(3) of the United Nations Declaration, for example, provides that measures taken to implement the Declaration shall not be considered contrary to the principle of equality; article 4(3) of the European Framework Convention provides that measures adopted to promote full and effective equality for members of national minorities shall not be considered to be an act of discrimination.

Areas for autonomy

The underlying purpose of the grant of autonomy to a minority community, whether on a territorial, local or functional basis, is to offset the feeling of more or less permanent exclusion from political power which affects most minorities. This is closely related to the underlying rationale of the right to self-determination, that any qualifying people should be able freely to determine their political status, to pursue their economic, social and cultural development and dispose of their natural wealth and resources. Since the criteria for the definition or identification of a minority are broadly similar to those for a people, it can be argued that, insofar as it is practical within an established state, the right of a qualifying minority to effective participation in decisions which concern it should include the right to pursue its own economic, social and cultural development and to be granted effective political autonomy to that end.

The most obvious sphere for the grant of autonomy is in respect of regional or local government in areas where a particular minority or community is concentrated. This too may call for positive measures, notably in the drawing of administrative or electoral boundaries in such a way as to ensure the inclusion of as many members of the relevant minority or communal group as is practicable or in creating special administrative structures or powers different from those which apply in other more homogeneous regions. There are numerous examples of this approach as a means of avoiding or attempting to resolve communal conflicts. As has been demonstrated in recent presentations to the United Nations Working Group on Minorities, special autonomous status and powers have been granted on a territorial basis in parts of Finland, Hungary, Romania and Russia.[12] A similar approach has been adopted or proposed with a view to ending persistent conflicts in Bosnia, Kosovo and Sri Lanka.

There may also be scope for the granting of functional as opposed to territorial autonomy to members of distinctive minorities or communities which are more widely scattered and which do not form a clear majority in any major locality. Agencies or institutions may be created on this basis for the promotion of minority languages or cultures throughout the national territory. Separate courts or tribunals may likewise be established for the administration on an autonomous basis of distinctive religious or social laws or customs for members of the relevant community. A prominent example is the granting of functional autonomy on linguistic and educational affairs to the two main communities in Belgium (Hadden and Craig 2000).

The adoption of measures of this kind involves a somewhat different form of inequality from those which may be required to promote integration. Instead of ignoring differences in individual qualifications or experience which might otherwise be relevant, different forms of administration or treatment may be established for individuals on the basis of their national or ethnic, religious or linguistic characteristics. The underlying justification for what might otherwise be regarded as racial or religious or linguistic discrimination is the preservation of communal values or customs and ultimately of the community itself.

There are also some corresponding difficulties and dangers. As the number and diversity of established and immigrant communities increases in many countries, there is an obvious problem in identifying which communities are entitled to autonomy for particular purposes and which are not. The stronger the formulation of any emerging right to autonomy, the greater the difficulty in avoiding allegations of discrimination between different communities. There is also a risk of increasing fragmentation and separatism. And almost any form of territorial autonomy – and some forms of functional autonomy – brings with it the difficulty of protecting the rights of new minorities within the autonomous area or function. The more complex and diverse the society, the greater may be the advantages of pursuing policies of integration.

Areas for policy choice

Even if it is accepted that there are some circumstances in which human rights principles point clearly in the direction of either integration or autonomy, there will remain many areas in which it is not possible to say which should be adopted without making a policy choice.

The major sphere in which a choice between policies of integration and autonomy is almost always required is education. It is widely recognised that one of the most effective means of promoting or achieving national unity and/or a plural and tolerant multicultural society is by providing common state schools which recognise the distinctive culture of each community and which are attended by the vast majority of children. It is also recognised that the maintenance or development of a minority culture and communal solidarity is greatly facilitated if separate schools are attended by most or all the children of each main community. There have also been claims that in some areas of communal disadvantage, notably educational achievement, the provision of separate rather than integrated schools produces better results for the disadvantaged group (Brooks 1996). The main international instruments are somewhat equivocal on this issue. Most provide that members of minority communities are entitled to establish and maintain separate communal schools at their own expense, but that state authorities are entitled to restrict state funding to common schools. Article 13(2) of the European Framework Convention, for example, provides that the exercise of the right for members of national minorities to establish their own schools shall not entail any financial obligations for the state.

The continuing debate within the human rights community on the distinction between multicultural, intercultural and integrated education reflects but does not always explain or resolve this fundamental policy choice. There is, accordingly, scope for greater clarity in the relevant international standards on the permissible alternatives, notably the choice between providing multicultural education in integrated schools and giving state support to separate community or faith schools. There is also a need for further consideration of the application of anti-discrimination principles in cases where some but not all minority communities are given state support for the maintenance of their own schools, notably on the extent to which national policies on the recognition of particular communities, such as those involved in the Belgian Linguistics case,[13] should be permitted to prevail over the principles of equality in state funding. This is an area in which detailed guidelines on the potential impact of various policies and on examples of good practice would be particularly valuable.

There are similar issues of national policy objectives with respect to some other areas of economic and social life. Formal legislative requirements (by setting targets or quotas) or financial incentives (by contract compliance provisions) can be introduced to encourage communal balance in private-sector employment with a view to avoiding the kind of communal segregation which often develops in an unregulated economy. This approach has been developed as a means of promoting both economic equality and multicultural values by prescriptive national legislation in a number of countries, notably the United States, Canada, Northern Ireland and South Africa. Alternatively incentives may be provided for autonomous economic development within minority communities with a view to eliminating or reducing the patterns of economic disadvantage which often become established. This may be particularly important in promoting appropriate economic development in indigenous communities in rural areas (Salomon and Sengupta 2003). Here, too, there is obvious scope for the development of guidelines on good practice in respect of differing situations.

More difficult issues may arise in respect of residential segregation. There are understandable reasons for members of distinctive minority communities to want to live in the same parts of towns and cities, if only to facilitate the enjoyment of their culture and to increase their sense of security. But the development of mono-ethnic ghettos and the associated communal separation in education and economic activity is often regarded as a primary cause of communal tension and conflict. This is a matter of current concern in respect of immigrant communities in many developed countries, as for example in response to recent disturbances in some English towns. There are fewer examples of effective legislative or financial intervention in this area. But it is clear that positive action may be required to create the conditions for greater integration in both public- and private-sector housing.

National and regional variations

It cannot be assumed that the same general approach on all these matters can be applied on a universal basis. A large number of factors must be taken into account in deciding on the most appropriate balance or combination of measures to promote integration or autonomy. The nature, size, location and distribution of each minority community are obviously relevant. So too is the number of actual or potential claims for special treatment. It is likely to be more practical to grant a measure of autonomy to a well established indigenous or rural minority than to several different ethnic communities in a large city, even if the number of people involved is much larger. The history and nature of the state in which the communities live must also be taken into account. Different policies may be appropriate in well-established states in which there is a dominant community with a coherent national identity from those in which there is a greater degree of ethnic diversity and a greater danger of fragmentation. And in divided societies in which two or more large communities are competing for political or economic domination, entirely different strategies may be called for.

All these factors may contribute to the development of different norms and guidelines for the major world regions. As already indicated, practice in Europe has been to encourage the grant of various forms of autonomy to well-established 'national' minorities, but to adopt integrationist strategies for more recent immigrant communities. In countries in sub-Saharan Africa in which there are much larger numbers of indigenous communities and a concern to develop or create a new post-colonial national identity, the arguments for a more general integrationist approach may be stronger. In Asia and Latin America there are stronger pressures to grant various forms of territorial autonomy to indigenous minorities and in some cases to develop systems of functional autonomy on some social and legal matters for different religious communities.

THE LIMITATIONS OF A RIGHTS-BASED APPROACH
TO CONFLICT RESOLUTION

All these issues require further work and discussion within the human rights community at both regional and international levels. The United Nations Working Group on Minorities has already played a valuable role in providing an international forum for the claims of a wide range of minority communities. It has also encouraged the development of clearer thinking in the human rights community on issues of multiculturalism and autonomy within the framework of the United Nations Declaration. Given the wide variation in the range of legitimate approaches which have been outlined above, there may not be much scope for the formulation of more detailed and prescriptive international rights or standards. But there is clearly scope for the development of guidelines and examples of good practice for the wide range of different circumstances in which the claims of minorities must be considered at a national level. This is an area in which the United Nations and other regional human rights bodies may perhaps be able to develop a constructive role in the provision of technical assistance rather than an exclusive focus on assessment or adjudication of current state practice. An important element in this is likely to be a more coherent focus on the different circumstances and pressures which are relevant in the major world regions and sub-regions.

But human rights lawyers must also recognise the limitations of a rights-based approach in this area. Talk of inalienable individual and communal rights is fine in the courts and in the classroom. On the streets and in the ghettoes it may have a very different impact. Lawyers have a lot to learn from politicians and political scientists on the arts of negotiation and compromise in dealing with conflicting rights and interests. There is no legal answer to questions such as who has a right to autonomy or when there is a right to power sharing. Nor should there be.

NOTES

1. An earlier version of this contribution was presented at an international seminar on 'An Emerging Right to Autonomy' at the Danish Centre for Human Rights in April 2002.
2. *Lubicon Lake Band v Canada*, Communication No.167/1984.
3. *Western Sahara Advisory Opinion*, (1975) International Court of Justice Reports, 4.

4. See the Vienna Declaration and Programme of Action, 1994, which specifies cases in which the state does not have a government representing the whole people of the territory without any distinctions.
5. See the *Report of the Montreal International Seminar on Intercultural and Multicultural Education*, UN Doc. E/CN.4/Sub.2/AC.5/2000/WP.4, para 6.
6. The wording is derived from the General Assembly Declaration on Friendly Relations and Cooperation among States, Resolution 2625(XXV) 24 October 1970.
7. Foundation for Inter-Ethnic Relations, 1999; the preparation of the Recommendations was sponsored by the High Commissioner for National Minorities of the Organisation for Security and Cooperation in Europe.
8. The strongest formulation is in article 3(1) of the European Framework Convention; see also article 3(2) of the United Nations Declaration.
9. Adopted by General Assembly Resolution 34/169 of 17 December 1979.
10. Commonwealth Secretariat, *National Human Rights Institutions: Best Practice*, London 2001.
11. Constitution of the Republic of South Africa, art. 174(2); Northern Ireland Act 1998, s. 68(3).
12. For a general summary of the work of the Working Group in this area see Hadden, *International and National Action for the Protection of Minorities: the Role of the Working Group on Minorities*, UN Doc. E/CN.4/Sub.2/AC.5/2004/WP.3.
13. European Court of Human Rights (1968) Series A No.6; the court upheld the right of the Belgian government to divide the country into linguistic regions in which only French and Flemish schools respectively would receive state funding.

REFERENCES

Brooks, R. L. (1996) *Integration and Separation: A Strategy for Racial Equality.* Cambridge, MA: Harvard University Press.
Eide, A. (1994) *Possible Ways and Means of Facilitating the Peaceful and Constructive Solution of Problems Involving Minorities.* UN Doc. E/CN.4/Sub.2/1993/34.
Gilbert, G. (2001) *Autonomy and Minority Groups: A Legal Right in International Law?* UN Doc. E/CN.4/AC.5/2001/CRP.5.
Gutmann, A. (ed.) (1994) *Multiculturalism: Examining the Politics of Recognition.* Princeton, NJ: Princeton University Press.
Hadden, T. (2003) *Towards a Set of Regional Guidelines or Codes of Practice on the Implementation of the Declaration.* UN Doc. E/CN.4/Sub.2/AC.5/2003/WP.1.
Hadden, T. and Craig, E. (2000) *Integration and Separation: Rights in Divided Societies.* Belfast: Centre for International and Comparative Human Rights Law.

Hannum, H. (1996) *Autonomy, Sovereignty and Self-Determination: The Accommodation of Conflicting Rights*. Philadelphia, PA: University of Pennsylvania Press.

Horowitz, D. (1985) *Ethnic Groups in Conflict*. Berkeley, CA: University of California Press.

Kymlicka, W. (1995): *Multicultural Citizenship: A Liberal Theory of Minority Rights*. Oxford: Oxford University Press.

Musgrave, T. (1997) *Self-Determination and National Minorities*. Oxford: Oxford University Press.

Raz, J. (1986) *The Morality of Freedom*. Oxford: Clarendon Press.

Salomon, M. and Sengupta, A. (2003) *The Right to Development: Obligations of States and the Rights of Minorities and Indigenous Peoples*. London: Minority Rights Group International.

Thornberry, P. (1991) *International Law and the Rights of Minorities*. Oxford: Oxford University Press.

3
Breaking Antagonism?
Political Leadership in Divided Societies

Duncan Morrow

All societies contain conflict. Divided societies, however, often struggle to find and implement democratic institutions that can manage conflict in ways that can be generally accepted as legitimate. In this sense, divided societies can be defined as societies in which there is no transcendent democratic principle that enables legitimate, collective decisions to be taken on anything like a consistent basis (Wright 1987, pp. 1–25). Instead, they are typically marked by more than one claim to legitimacy, as competing ethno-national groups or communities vie to impose their internal transcendence on the will of others. Instead of a unified *demos* – a fundamental, intrinsic requirement of democracy (Dahl 1989, p. 207) – there are two or more 'peoples', and hence two or more sources of democratic legitimacy. Under such conditions, a decision-making mechanism that enables one group to prevail over the other is, by definition, hierarchical and oppressive, and hence undemocratic.

The implications for politics in such a context are profound, for it is simply impossible to 'do' democratic politics in divided societies when division itself appears to infect every aspect of political life. There are numerous ways in which such divisions can, and have been, approached and analysed. This chapter, however, focuses on only one aspect of politics in divided societies, namely, the role of political leaders and leadership. To this end, it traces a logic of political engagement that moves from antagonism to mutual accommodation and finally to the ideal of a shared future for all. Political leadership has a crucial role to play in propelling this logic forward. However, not only is there an indeterminate range of variables that may upset and even undermine that development, but, as this chapter tentatively concludes, much may depend on the role that international instruments might conceivably have to play.

POLITICAL LEADERSHIP IN DEEPLY DIVIDED SOCIETIES

According to the dictionary definition, a leader is 'a person who causes another to go with them, by guiding or showing the way or who directs the actions and opinions of others by example, persuasion or action'. This definition carries with it the general sense of going first, of direction-setting. But it also suggests that what leaders do, either by act or omission, and how those actions or omissions impact upon their supporters, matters enormously for the success of a given power-sharing system within a given territory.

In divided societies, leaders typically aim to speak for and advance the interests of their own ethno-national group or community rather than the interests of the electorate as a whole. Insofar as this is the case, leadership in a divided society connotes a form of political behaviour that is quantitatively, if not altogether qualitatively, different to that which typically occurs in societies where an overarching sense of common citizenship or civic bond prevails. Trust in the democratic process is usually premised upon the assumption that the rule of law obtains, and that the civic bond will enable citizens to accept the legitimacy of decisions with which they disagree. Yet, under conditions of group or communal antagonism, trust in the political system is often weak or even largely absent. Ultimately, the promotion of particular communal interests can predominate over the promotion of any common interest or conception of the public good. Indeed, where conflict is deeply embedded, and where the political incentives structure does little to create or encourage a stronger sense of the public good, there is little chance power-sharing democracy will succeed in the longer run.

For present purposes, then, the point to stress is that although power sharing is often viewed as the most feasible – indeed, perhaps the only feasible – means of ensuring a just and stable democratic system, much turns on how leaders relate to one another within those institutions. Again, this is not to deny that the behaviour of political leaders in a divided society is not, to some degree or another, structured and constrained by the choice of power-sharing institutions (see, generally, Peters 1999), or by external and systemic factors such as the precise balance of power both within the territory and beyond, the degree of ongoing inter-group violence and the financial, human and military resources available to the group. Nevertheless, experience suggests that, far from being entirely bound by those constraints, leaders often have considerable room for manoeuvre.

More specifically, they are typically challenged with guiding their followers in one of three broad directions: *antagonism*, with a view to asserting the primacy of ethno-national group identity; *management and mitigation*, with a view to cooperation between competing ethno-national groups; and *negotiated arrangements* for the balance of power and transformation, in which antagonism is replaced by a common allegiance to institutions and procedures which promote legitimacy and solidarity beyond the group. I will now consider each of these approaches in turn.

Leadership as antagonism

The primary task of a state and its institutions is the protection of its citizens from external or internal threat. To speak of ethnic or inter-communal antagonism, therefore, is simply another way of describing an endemic internal threat. Under conditions of widespread fear or resentment – which can persist despite (and sometimes precisely because of) the creation of power-sharing institutions – leadership is often reduced to articulating resistance and opposition to the perceived threat. Similarly, heroism is equated with a willingness to resist the enemy to the last, or to rally the people to their source of common allegiance in the face of a common opponent, even if this means making power sharing unworkable. Ethnic antagonism, embedded in an historic conflictual relationship, is a fertile ground for the establishment of this kind of isolationist and exclusionary leadership.

A good illustrative example of antagonistic, ethno-political leadership and its effects on power sharing is the case of the former Yugoslavia during the 1990s. Much of the commentary on this particular case is at pains to underline the complex economic and international factors which ultimately defined the crisis. However, it is clear that the willingness of the various national leaderships to promote and direct ethnic chauvinism – as the case of Bosnia and Herzegovina examined in this volume clearly illustrates – contributed both to their own popularity within their respective groups and to the collapse of inter-ethnic power sharing (Glenny 1992).

Tito's Communist Yugoslavia had survived on the myth of 'Brotherhood and Unity', forged in the final years of the Second World War and dependent on the relative stability which Yugoslav 'non-alignment' generated in the Balkans during the Cold War. While it is true that Tito's Communist partisans had recruited a multinational army by 1945, the leadership of the army (with the exception of Tito himself) was overwhelmingly Serb and their bitter opponents were the overwhelmingly Croat Ustashe. Furthermore the Serb Chetniks, although also defeated in the war, shared the partisan history of resistance to Fascism. The ethnically contested zone of Bosnia saw numerous appalling massacres of civilians, leaving a locally complex residue of bitterness and resentment (Malcolm 1997). Communism's answer to this was an authoritarian single-party regime with a strong cult of personality which firstly took ruthless revenge on the Ustashe and then, following Tito's break with Stalin, promoted the myth that ethnic nationalism and communal differences had been superseded by the common bond of Communist ideology. Following the 'Croat Spring' in 1971, the Communist Party was forced into a new accommodation with nationalist pressure and established a system of single-party federalism. In the subsequent decades, however, the collapse of communism across Europe and Russia precipitated the descent into militant ethnic nationalism.

Slobodan Milošević's seizure of control of the Serbian Communist Party in 1987 is a case study in ethnic populist leadership. On a visit to the restless province of Kosovo, heartland of Serb national myth, Milošević announced to a beleaguered Serb crowd that 'No one shall ever beat you again'. Most observers believe that the remark arose in the heat of the moment, but it catapulted Milošević from Party bureaucrat to popular Serb hero overnight. Within months he had taken over the Party and had clear designs on a newly centralised Yugoslavia. In 1988, Milošević orchestrated a massive re-enactment of the last battle of the medieval Serbs at Kosovo Polje, bussing in thousands of Serbs to Kosovo for the event. For non-Serbs, the implications were unmistakable. The relatively wealthy Slovenes, safe in their alpine hideaway, made haste to prepare for independence, especially when Milošević became President of Yugoslavia in 1989. And in the first free elections in Croatia, the revisionist nationalist historian, Franjo Tudjman, was elected to oppose the Serbian leader. Throughout Yugoslavia, the scene was therefore set for ethnic confrontation, promoted by unashamedly chauvinistic politicians. Leadership was equated with ethnic self-assertion, and success defined in terms of military defeat or victory. Furthermore, the elimination and expulsion of ethnic enemies became the pattern of inter-group activity in Eastern Slavonia (Croatia) in 1991, in Bosnia from 1992 until 1994, in Knin from 1994, in Kosovo since 1999 and in parts of Macedonia in 2001 (Silber and Little 1996).

In Croatia, the supposedly supra-national *Jugoslovenska Narodna Armija* (JNA) was ruthlessly deployed by Milošević to defend the Serb enclaves from Croatian control. Second World War memories of Ustashe brutality against the Croat Serbs and resentment at the suppression of Partisan revenge on the Croat Ustashe became the basic currency of political exchange, as Milošević made it clear that Serbs outside Serbia would be protected by the JNA. The Croat government, too, revelled in re-enactments of Croatia's medieval past, and repudiated the Communist notion that Serbs and Croats shared a common language. When Bosnian Muslims and Croats voted for full independence in a referendum in 1992 in the face of a nearly universal boycott by Bosnian Serbs, the Serbs with access to support from Milošević and the JNA began the process of partitioning Bosnia along ethnic lines. The goal was to ensure that all Serbs within Bosnia were integrated within a Greater Serbia. Their methods were mass murder and expulsion, now known across the world through the euphemism of 'ethnic cleansing', as the Serbs took control of 70 per cent of the territory. Milošević took the policy to a new scale when up to 500,000 Kosovar Albanians were evicted or fled their homes for Montenegro or Macedonia.

The crisis of Yugoslavia cannot be laid at the door of any one political leader. What is true, however, is that the storm of ethnic antagonism which Milošević used to secure and maintain power in Serbia came to dominate political engagement in the Balkans. Tudjman in Croatia, aided and abetted by the Kosovo Liberation Army (KLA), adopted similarly ruthless strategies, albeit in more restricted circumstances, while Izetbegović in Bosnia and Rugova in Kosovo were not immune from using chauvinistic demagoguery for political ends. (Lest it be imagined that the tendency to ethnic leadership was confined to collapsing ex-communist states, Greece continues to insist that Macedonia cannot be recognised under its preferred name for fear of establishing border claims on Greek territory.) Whether the causes were ethnic, the narrative of the Balkans after 1990 was therefore one of inter-ethnic incompatibility fuelled by mutually self-asserting groups further fuelled by antagonistic leadership.

What the case of the former Yugoslavia suggests, then, is that where antagonism exists, political leadership will tend to emerge to try to exploit it. Having built a constituency around ethnic solidarity, politicians have a perverse but clear incentive to maintain it. Having acted on it, ethnic antagonism is almost certainly deepened, recreating the (vicious) circle of antagonism and aggressive political leadership for a further generation. The tragedy of such leadership, however, is that it is simultaneously attractive to beleaguered peoples and only capable of delivering results through massive violence. In the Balkans, the decision to exploit ethnic antagonism was superficially successful for a rising political class, but it created such chaos that the Western world ultimately felt obliged to step in four times (in Croatia in 1992, in Bosnia in 1995, in Kosovo in 1999 and in Macedonia in 2001) to generate short-term stability. While these interventions put a stop to the worst excesses of ethnic cleansing, the processes of reintegration and resettlement have proved slow, and the deployment of foreign troops in Bosnia is now into its tenth year. Most significantly, putting a stop to violence is not the same as establishing a new common transcendence that might support the successful functioning of sustainable power sharing. Election results in Bosnia and ongoing tension in both Macedonia and Kosovo show a continuing, local preference for ethnically separatist leadership (Job 2002). The very fact that troops continue to be deployed in both contexts is evidence of the fragility of any power-sharing experiment under such conditions. Without a decisive shift from ethno-nationalism, antagonistic leadership continues to provide fuel for tomorrow's difficulties.

Leadership to manage conflict

Violence, or even the threat of violence, is its own worst advertisement. Especially after periods of serious trauma, political leaders are often drawn into, or encouraged by their followers into, the search for a sustainable democratic alternative. Yet, paradoxically, the experience of violence simultaneously makes meaningful trust difficult, if not subject to terminal suspicion. Even in a period of relative calm, the argument for maintaining vigilance remains.

This, then, is the dilemma of leadership in a power-sharing society: on the one hand, the delegitimisation of active inter-communal violence sows the seeds of mutual recognition, the acceptance of diversity and a tentative commitment to a sense of solidarity that transcends the ethnic group; but on the other hand, in the absence of a mutual willingness to set aside often fundamental disputes on the nature and legitimacy of the state, politics often becomes limited to a question of mitigating conflict, minimising violence and creating mechanisms for direct negotiation and decision making, rather than for resolution, reconciliation or transformation.

Framed against the background of this dilemma, the stability of a power-sharing political system partly lies in the development of clear understandings between leaders concerning their behaviour towards each other and on their capacity to 'deliver' a permanent end to destabilising violence from within their own community. In this context, 'partnership' itself becomes the principle of successful democratic political leadership. Successful political leaders are power brokers and dispensers, as well as enforcers of internal discipline. Inevitably, however, mechanisms which seek to 'contain' antagonism are vulnerable to shifts in the balance of power, either externally or internally. Such systems continue to 'contain' violence in both senses of the word: the volcano is not extinct but instead is merely dormant. In the long run, the question confronting systemic partnerships is whether they will decay in the direction of a return to antagonism or whether they are the forerunners of a more stable, deeper democratic compromise.

Hence, what is often overlooked is the fact that partnership does not resolve the dilemma of leadership in a power-sharing society but establishes a new culture of stability from which to take further decisions about how to move the political process forward in the hope of creating a better transcendent society for all. One of the difficulties of theories of accommodation, however, is that they often tend to present accommodation as an alternative model of democracy rather than as a precursor to something better.

For example, foremost among accommodation and theories of power sharing is Arend Lijphart's theory of consociation (Lijphart 1969, 1977, 2004), which initially drew on the experience of four internally divided but basically democratic societies in Western Europe. Lijphart's acceptance of collective rights for distinct groups and political mechanisms such as proportionality in the allocation of government posts, and of the security offered by the mutual veto and the promotion of autonomous cultural development, has attracted leaders of ethnic groups seeking some sort of accommodation but requiring minimal change within groups. Problematically, however, consociationalism now seems to have grown into a theory of accommodation with application to all divided societies rather than a less grandiose description of the pragmatic arrangements reached in a variety of states as each seeks ways to accommodate inter-group conflict. The result is that too much attention is paid to the similarity of institutional, power-sharing structures, while not enough attention is paid to the health and long-run viability of underlying relationships between communities and their leaders. In divided societies, the negotiation of power-sharing structures will never suffice in the long run unless they are underpinned by common understandings and expectations between leaders, and the implications of those expectations for future, society-wide reconciliation.

Consociational power sharing (and power sharing more generally) provides a framework for accommodating the competing aspirations of different ethno-national groups. As such, that framework recognises the existence and legitimacy of competing aspirations; but it also institutionalises leaders' willingness to submit those aspirations to exclusively democratic means. In other words, power sharing means that political leaderships have foregone the option of supporting violence as a viable means of achieving their community's political ends, and instead have submitted to the logic of collective deliberation and decision making. Whereas in the Netherlands consociation has proved to be the precursor of a stable society based on equal citizenship, Belgian consociation – as Kris Deschouwer's chapter in this volume demonstrates – has become a euphemism for the slow decay, and possible future break-up, of the state. Since the first major constitutional reform of 1970, Belgium has undergone a series of institutional and procedural changes, all of which have pointed to the ultimate separation of Flanders and Wallonia. Previously integrated political parties are now split along ethno-linguistic lines. Powers continue to be systematically transferred from the central government to the segregated political and cultural authorities. Only Brussels, a largely French-speaking city within Dutch-speaking Flanders, and the institutions of the royal family and Belgian football have acted to keep consociation from transforming into full separation. Even aspects of trade and foreign policy are now conducted directly by the separate communities (Fitzmaurice 1996).

The point, therefore, is that while there is enormous value in political partnership between leaders as a mechanism to manage potentially violent conflict in the direction of non-violence and mutual accommodation, there must be clarity on the long-term direction and purpose of cooperation. Northern Ireland provides a classic case of the dilemma underlying power sharing where structures *precede* political relationships that transcend purely sectional interests. Following 30 years of ongoing inter-communal trauma, the majority of Northern Irish politicians accepted an Agreement drawn up on largely consociational lines in 1998, although they had little experience of working with one another except as antagonists (but see

Horowitz 2001, 2002). Unlike Belgium, there was no easy mechanism in Northern Ireland to establish communal segregation since the two communities, British unionist and Irish nationalist, are intermingled; and unlike the Netherlands, the history of violent antagonism continued to act as a brake on leaders seeking accommodation. Failure to agree on core institutions of law and order (the reform of criminal justice, policing, demilitarisation and army retrenchment) in 1998 meant that leaders were unable to deliver a definitive end to violence and partnership proved unstable at best.

In general terms, under conditions of uncertainty, politicians in Northern Ireland have continued to prefer antagonism to accommodation, and both to reconciliation and transcendence, with nationalist and unionist leaders unable to reach anything like a workable, stable partnership. Fortunately, the prior history of (failed) inter-communal violence and strong international pressure (largely applied by Bill Clinton's US government) to agree on new partnership arrangements ensured that there would be no full-scale return to violent conflict. Successful power sharing has paradoxically emerged between the wider British and Irish states, both of which have placed a strong emphasis on the rule of law and non-violence as understood across the European Union. Moreover, after 11 September 2001, Western tolerance for active insurgency disintegrated, further pressurising Northern Irish politicians to subordinate their respective national claims to liberal democratic forms of legitimacy. The challenge for the Northern Irish political leadership emerging from violence and conflict was to acknowledge that no local government was possible without sharing, even though this meant promoting partnership and a new shared transcendent legitimacy over antagonism. And up to a point, this challenge has been met. However, what remains to be seen is whether the particular institutions now in place can provide sufficient opportunities for leaders to move beyond antagonism, or whether antagonism is so deeply institutionalised that no such transcendence is in practice possible (cf. Wilford and Wilson 2003, p. 116).

Leadership to end antagonism?

Although consociational power sharing does not, of itself, resolve conflict, it does submit antagonism to wider rules and regulations about partnership and non-violence. To that degree, it represents an opportunity to develop new political relationships over time that stress the importance of shared (or what I have been referring to as 'transcendent') democratic values. Many democrats, however, continue to object that consociationalism's compromise with antagonism simply allows antagonism to be turned into a principle of democratic legitimacy with many negative consequences for liberty and equality, cross-cutting identities, the development of an overarching civic bond, and so on. In other words, they object that consociationalism allows antagonism to become the default position of political engagement, rather than creating space in which a new, more transcendent logic might begin to emerge.

That said, it must be admitted that the ultimate outcome of consociational experiments cannot be decided in advance. There are examples where consociational structures have morphed into the more normal type of democratic system – the Netherlands is often cited as the classic example – and others where consociational structures have failed finally to move beyond antagonism and have instead collapsed – such as Cyprus and Lebanon in the 1970s. Much ultimately depends on the nature and quality of the partnership that emerges between political leaders – or, put more directly, on how leaders decide to operate the institutions of state – which either embodies recognition of a wider solidarity or uses the cover of partnership to continue war by other means.

A decision to seek an end to antagonism involves a profound recognition that no single community can prevail by violence or that ending a relationship of antagonism is more important than victory. The trouble is, of course, that where there is a history of trauma, reneging on the sacred claims of the ethnic nation, or a decision not to pursue a wider claim for justice, leaves leaders vulnerable to the accusation of betrayal, even of endangering their own people. In Northern Ireland in the 1970s, the political leaders of Ulster unionism, such as Brian Faulkner, were ultimately destroyed from within their own camp by radicals who disapproved of any deal to share power with Irish nationalists. Thirty years later, the chief among his opponents, Ian Paisley, was poised to take the same steps he had so despised earlier. In the case of Mahatma Gandhi, his support for an inter-cultural secular state for India led to his assassination by a radical Hindu nationalist. Transformational leadership in divided societies often comes with a direct personal cost.

There is, and can be, no single model of leadership to end conflict in deeply divided societies, not least of all because 'élite behaviour seems to be more elusive and less susceptible to empirical generalisations than mass phenomena' (Lijphart 1977, p. 54). As our discussion thus far suggests, however, whatever form a model takes, it must inevitably involve a decision against violence, taking steps into the unknown and a willingness to shoulder extreme political risk. In a society that has been characterised by ethnic antagonism, the decision to end antagonism always involves a step outside the ritualised known. In practice, promoting a stable relationship requires new forms of political engagement that run contrary to the antagonism which shapes the prevailing mode of antagonistic relationship. Transformational leadership goes beyond the detail of negotiation not only to promote an end to the past, but moreover to provide a vision of a shared future. The key role of leadership in seeking to move beyond inter-communal conflict is not just that of negotiating a power-sharing agreement, but of demonstrating to one's electorate that the new world of cooperation is indeed safe.

In South Africa, for example, the release from jail of Nelson Mandela in 1989 represented a turning point. Mandela had resisted release on a number of previous occasions, preferring to wait for an appropriate political moment and a change in the white leadership. Although F.W. de Klerk had been identified with the right of the ruling National Party, the ending of the Cold War offered a new context. In the course of the negotiations which followed, de Klerk appears to have come to the conclusion that a final deal with a Mandela-led ANC represented the best hope for avoiding a conflagration in South Africa. De Klerk's key role was to recognise this and to secure formal white approval at key points in the negotiations. Mandela's historic role was to be the black African whom it became safe for white South Africans to lose to. Instead of a deal, talks in South Africa became strictly about the transfer of power and the safety of the losers. Instead of an angry black insurgency, South Africa emerged as the rainbow nation. Of course, the strategic context and the detailed negotiations of the National Party and ANC were critical. Having suffered through lengthy imprisonment under apartheid, Mandela had the iconic authority under the transcendence of the old struggle to influence the terms of the new world. What Mandela, and to a degree de Klerk, established was a new transcendence beyond majority rule within which all of the citizens of South Africa could believe they were safe. In the absence of this leadership, it is difficult to imagine how a transition could have been negotiated so smoothly. In a context of antagonism, where fear and anger are rational and trust absurd, it was the achievement of the leadership in South Africa to imagine a new common citizenship (Deluca 2000).

A similar role was played in 1960s America by Martin Luther King and the Southern Christian Leadership Conference, whose dedication to non-violence convinced whites outside the South that the federal government should intervene to support civil rights. King's dream became the new American dream, and 'Civil Rights' became an American necessity, not simply a campaign by Southern blacks. The possibility that even the legacy of slavery and failed reconstruction could be eased by political leadership demonstrated that antagonism is not necessarily impermeable. Admittedly, the political, social, economic and cultural difficulties that have since emerged confirm that single acts of leadership create opportunities for transformation but do not eliminate the difficulties in a single act. What they can do, however, is create new understandings of legitimacy which at least open the possibility of a shared future. Transformational leadership requires that the possibility of a new transcendence which encompasses everyone is made visible in the actions and words of political leaders. Such charismatic leadership cannot be manufactured or dictated. But its effects are critical.

CONCLUSION

As Thomas Hobbes knew, the problem of internal violence threatens all societies. Unless violence is contained, it ultimately threatens to destroy all human life. In divided societies, the problem of antagonism is the starting point of political life, not its conclusion. After the Second World War, the United Nations promoted universal values of human rights as the transcendent rules governing the legitimate use of power. Today, the international system, formally at least, recognises that not all things are equal. The difficulties of translating 'universal values' into meaningful politics are most acute for political leaders precisely where they are most necessary: where political relationships are shaped not by trust but by antagonism. The logic of hostility – of political power unmitigated by legitimate democratic authority – is that power must be kept from others, not shared on an equal basis.

The actions of political leaders in such settings are often critical to the outcome. There is a strong dynamic towards inter-group antagonism which makes ethnically divided societies dangerous weak points in the international system. The emergence of political leadership to exploit these cleavages is probably inevitable. Consequently, if there is to be a broad movement towards acceptable international standards, issues of conflict resolution must not simply be left to the emergence of 'good leaders', but must also be recognised as a wider international responsibility. Internally, a broad consensus on non-violence has enabled Canada to go further than other Western states in trying to articulate a new balance between unity and diversity within clearly democratic values, largely because the Quebec question has been free to challenge both the presumptions of equal citizenship and the simplicities of doctrines of national self-assertion within a peaceful democratic framework. In the American South, the decisive issue was not individual leadership but the capacity of leadership to trigger the intervention of the Supreme Court and the federal authorities. In Northern Ireland, agreement has only been possible because of international insistence on sharing. Even in Bosnia, Dayton has enforced its minimum order through international insistence. Leadership in ethnically divided societies is critical, but it is seldom sufficient.

REFERENCES

Dahl, R. (1989) *Democracy and its Critics*. New Haven, CT: Yale University Press.

Deluca, A. R. (2000) *Gandhi, Mao, Mandela and Gorbachev: Studies in Personality Power and Politics*. Westport, CT: Praeger.

Fitzmaurice, J. (1996) *The Politics of Belgium: A Unique Federalism*. Boulder, CO: Westview Press.

Glenny, M. (1992) *The Fall of Yugoslavia*. London and New York: Penguin.

Horowitz, D. (2001) 'The Northern Ireland Agreement: Clear, Consociational, and Risky', in J. McGarry (ed.), *Northern Ireland and the Divided World: Post-Agreement Northern Ireland in Comparative Perspective*. Oxford: Oxford University Press, pp. 89–108.

—— (2002) 'Explaining the Northern Ireland Agreement: The Sources of an Unlikely Constitutional Consensus', *British Journal of Political Science*, 32 (2), 193–220.

Job, C. (2002) *Yugoslavia's Ruin*. Lanham, MD: Rowman and Littlefield.

Lijphart, A. (1969) 'Consociational Democracy', *World Politics*, 21 (2), 207–25.

—— (1977) *Democracy in Plural Societies*. New Haven, CT: Yale University Press.

—— (2004) 'Constitutional Design for Divided Societies', *Journal of Democracy*, 15 (2), 96–109.

Malcolm, N. (1997) *Bosnia: A Short History*. New York, NY: New York University Press.

Peters, B. G. (1999) *Institutional Theory in Political Science: The 'New Institutionalism'*. London and New York: Pinter.

Silber, L. and Little A. (1996) *The Death of Yugoslavia*. London and New York: Penguin.

Wilford, R. and Wilson, R. (2003) 'Northern Ireland: Valedictory', in R. Hazell (ed.), *The State of the Nations 2003*. Exeter and Charlottesville: Imprint Academic.

Wright, F. (1987) *Northern Ireland: A Comparative Perspective*. Dublin and London: Gill and McMillan.

4

Electoral-Systems Design and Power-Sharing Regimes

Stefan Wolff[1]

Electoral-systems design is a key mechanism in the broader institutional design approach to the resolution of conflict in multiethnic societies. As such, it is closely connected with a longstanding debate on what design of political institutions is best suited to channel inter-communal conflict into peaceful democratic competition. The two predominant schools in conflict resolution today – integrative and consociational power sharing – take very distinct views on which electoral systems stand the best chance of contributing to the successful management of conflict. These two interlocked debates on institutional and electoral-system design are the focus of this chapter. In exploring the arguments put forward by integrationists and consociationalists and by advocates of different electoral systems, this chapter examines their theoretical merits and empirical manifestations and argues against rigid divisions between the two approaches to power sharing.

POWER SHARING IN MULTIETHNIC SOCIETIES AND THE SIGNIFICANCE OF THE ELECTORAL SYSTEM

Power sharing in multiethnic societies means that institutional arrangements exist that constrain purely majoritarian democracy, a constraint that the majority of political agents in a given society accept in the hope that it will enable the institutions of government to discharge their duties effectively and efficiently and at the same time be recognised as legitimate. The debate on power sharing – the various institutional forms it may take and its general suitability for the settlement of ethnic conflicts – has proceeded for many years. At a basic level, two predominant types of power-sharing institutions – integrative and consociational – can be distinguished. Consociational power sharing is most closely associated with the work of Arend Lijphart, who identified four structural features shared by consociational systems – a grand coalition government, segmental autonomy, proportionality in the voting system and in public sector employment, and minority veto (1977, pp. 25–52). Lijphart argued that these characteristics, more or less prominently, were exhibited by all the classic examples of consociationalism: Lebanon, Cyprus, Switzerland, Austria, the Netherlands, Belgium, Fiji and Malaysia.

Integrative power sharing, in contrast, emphasises that rather than designing rigid institutions in which elected representatives have to work together *after* elections, political stability is more likely to be achieved if electoral formulas are devised that reward candidates for moderation and cross-communal appeals *before* elections, thus effectively excluding extremists who appeal to a narrow sectarian constituency. This school of thought is most prominently associated with the work of Donald Horowitz (1985), and more lately with that of Timothy Sisk (1996) and Benjamin Reilly (2001). Reilly, in particular, has contributed much to a more systematic development and understanding of the theory of centripetalism:

> a normative theory of institutional design designed to encourage three related but distinct phenomena in divided societies: (i) *electoral incentives* for campaigning politicians to reach out to and attract votes from a range of ethnic groups other than their own ... (ii) *arenas of bargaining*, under which political actors from different groups have an incentive to come together to negotiate and bargain in the search for cross-partisan and cross-ethnic vote-pooling deals ... and (iii) *centrist, aggregative political parties* or coalitions which seek multi-ethnic support... (Reilly 2001, p. 11; emphasis in original)

From the perspective of consociational power sharing, post-election institutional design is the more important component, while integrative power sharing stresses that, almost regardless of the design of government institutions, post-election cooperation among the leaders of different ethnic groups is more likely if such cooperation begins before elections actually take place. This does not mean, however, that consociationalists reject the importance of electoral-systems choice. On the contrary, Lijphart, for example, has been a longstanding advocate of list-proportional representation (PR) as it ensures representation of a wide range of political parties with different interests and opinions. Integrationists like Horowitz, Sisk and Reilly also advocate PR electoral systems, but tend to favour preferential systems,[2] and especially the Alternative Vote (AV) and the Single Transferable Vote (STV). This means that in both schools a link is made, correctly, between electoral-system design and election result on the one hand, and the feasibility of election results for the stability of post-election power-sharing institutions on the other.

Thus, according to both the consociational and integrative approaches, what is particularly important in societies underpinned by power sharing is that electoral-systems and institutional designs actually 'match', in the sense that electoral systems generate outcomes that enable democratic institutions to function. This means that electoral processes are crucial factors in determining the degree to which political processes in multiethnic societies will be characterised by moderation and inclusiveness as the two key factors of political stability. To explain why this is the case, the electoral process can itself be analysed in terms of four constituent dimensions: election systems, election campaigns, the conduct of elections and election results.

Election systems

An election system includes a number of different aspects, such as:

- an electoral formula (majority systems, PR systems, mixed systems, etc.);
- regulations on assembly size (number of seats available in the legislature);
- regulations on district magnitude (the number of seats contested per constituency);
- regulations on voting and ballots (blocked versus non-blocked lists; open versus closed lists);
- threshold criteria (minimum share in votes cast to qualify for representation under PR systems; also known as 'quorum').

While the choice of an electoral formula must not be overestimated in its capacity to determine election outcomes, it does have clear and measurable consequences, also known as an electoral system's 'technical effect' (see Lijphart 1994; Reilly 2001). The debate in the academic literature is split between advocates of moderation and advocates of inclusiveness. Accordingly, the choice is allegedly either to follow Horowitz and other advocates of the integrative approach to power sharing and opt for an electoral system that encourages and rewards moderation, even at the cost of giving up on the equally important democratic value of inclusion; or to follow Lijphart and adopt the consociational approach and opt for an electoral system that produces highly inclusive outcomes, but does not necessarily encourage moderation.[3] The crucial difficulty attaching to this choice, however, is that stability in multiethnic societies is often as much a function of moderation as of inclusion. Power sharing can only run smoothly if there is a significant degree of moderation among those who are participating in the political process. Yet, it is also generally accepted that stability may be increased if all relevant groups are represented (both moderates and extremists).

Unlike majority/plurality systems, PR systems tend not to provide clear majorities in legislative assemblies and therefore often result in coalition governments. However, unlike PR systems, majority/ plurality systems have the disadvantage that significant segments of the voting population in each constituency will not regard themselves as represented because 'their' party's candidate did not win the available seat. Such crucial differences notwithstanding, a PR list system (in large multi-member constituencies), does have one crucial element in common with majority/plurality systems: they both fall into the category of non-preferential electoral systems that do not allow voters to rank parties or candidates according a specific preference – that is, voters cannot indicate another choice (or choices) should their preferred candidate fail to obtain enough votes to win a seat or rank candidates within party lists (under a PR list system).

Among non-preferential electoral formulas, PR systems are clearly preferable insofar as they offer a much greater likelihood of elections delivering results that make the formation of grand coalitions more likely because they virtually guarantee the representation of different ethnic groups. By contrast, for majority/plurality systems to perform the same function, very specific circumstances need to be present, such as a high degree of compactness of ethnic-group settlements coinciding with electoral district boundaries. However, some of the disadvantages of majority/plurality systems are then simply transposed to the level of intra-group political competition. In situations in which different political parties compete with one another within one ethnic group, majority/plurality systems may be able to guarantee the political representation of the *ethnic* group but not necessarily of all significant *visions* within it. Thus, stable power sharing would potentially be much more difficult to achieve as the legislature may not include all key players or at least not in proportion to the support they receive within a given community.

From the point of view of integrative power sharing, neither non-preferential PR nor majority/plurality systems offer any significant opportunities for the formation of durable pre-election coalitions.

Advocates of this type of power sharing have therefore focused on the virtues of preferential voting systems, especially the Alternative Vote (AV), the Supplementary Vote (SV), and the Single Transferable Vote (STV) (cf. Fraenkel and Grofman 2002; Horowitz 1991; Reilly 2001). Admittedly, the strength of empirical evidence in support of the usefulness of any of these preferential voting systems in the context of integrative power sharing in multiethnic societies is very thin (Reilly 2001). Significantly, however, what can be shown empirically is that post-election coalition-building among parties representing different ethnic communities is possible (if admittedly rare or unusual) without both consociational institutional designs and preferential voting systems: Bulgaria, Macedonia, Romania and Slovakia all use PR systems of one type or another and are governed by multiethnic coalitions. By the same token, the application of a preferential and proportional voting system (STV) can be combined with a more rigid consociational structure of the institutions of government. Even though, at present, Northern Ireland is not a shining example of success, there is at least a compelling theoretical argument that favours such an approach.

For consociational institutions to function and perform well, a (widely representative and therefore necessarily broadly inclusive) grand coalition is required. STV in this context can contribute to achieving both of these aims: its proportional character ensures an inclusive composition of the assembly elected, while its preferential character is at the same time likely to favour the election of moderate politicians and the formation of pre-election coalitions (but see below for specific conditions). By the same token, the application of open-list PR systems, as in South Tyrol, can have similar effects: list PR guarantees a high degree of inclusiveness while the openness of the lists allows voters to cast preferences for specific politicians thus making it possible that candidates on the lower end of a party list still can be elected if, for example, their personal appeal or that of their agenda attracts a sufficient number of preference votes.

Having said this, one needs to bear in mind that the preferential character of STV and open-list PR carries dangers to the extent that it does not guarantee that more moderate politicians will be chosen. From this perspective, Lijphart's insistence that the PR list system is preferable to STV and that closed lists are better than open lists because this asserts the dominance of (party) elites continues to be a credible observation (Lijphart 2002, p. 53). Yet Lijphart (2002, p. 44) appears to miss the point when he claims that strong incentives – namely, the chance to exercise executive power – exist for political leaders after elections to compromise even if there have been no pre-election pacts. While this may well be the case in many instances, political leaders who gain power on a confrontational election platform in order to maximise votes from within their own ethnic community not only contribute to the polarisation of society, but also create expectations and a climate of adversarial, 'no-compromise' post-electoral politics. Once elected to office, they may opportunistically change their mind, but their electorates are less likely to do so, thus potentially leading to a situation in which inclusive institutions lack moderation and, what is worse, legitimacy (cf. Norris 2002). In other words, a closed-list PR system may ensure that party leaderships obtain a larger degree of autonomy from their party and their constituents, but such a system does not necessarily encourage, let alone guarantee, elite moderation.

Returning to the issue of the effect that electoral formulas have, apart from the so-called 'technical effect' and its implications, consideration also needs to be given to their psychological effects on voters, which in turn shape the prospects of success for particular parties. As electoral formulas reward certain voting behaviours while constraining others, voters may opt to vote tactically; they may, that is, try to use the technical effects of the electoral system to effect one outcome and/or prevent another (cf., e.g., Hartmann 2000; Venice Commission 2000). For example, if an electoral formula disadvantages smaller parties, voters who may be ideologically closest to such parties may decide not to 'waste' their vote and instead vote for a larger party. Such decisions are more easy to make in majoritarian/plurality systems, while they may not be necessary in PR systems.[4] The technical effects of wasted votes in preferential systems, especially STV, is more difficult to estimate for the voter, and thus 'strategic voting' is, to some extent, constrained. As Reilly points out:

> In enabling all voters to express their preferences, elimination-based systems like AV and STV inadvertently make some preference orderings count more than others [because] the *order* of this transfer of preferences from eliminated candidates to those still in the running is essentially arbitrary: the secondary preferences of those who chose a relatively unpopular candidate are counted before the preferences of those who chose a more popular candidate. (2001, p. 163; emphasis in original)

As for assembly size and district magnitude, the rule of thumb is that the larger the assembly size and the higher the district magnitude, the more inclusive, from a party representation perspective, the assembly where non-preferential electoral rules are adopted. The high district magnitude requirement favours PR systems applied in a single state-wide constituency or in several large, multi-member constituencies, or integrated mixed-member systems that have the same effect.[5]

The choice between blocked/non-blocked lists and open/closed lists determines the ability of voters to 'personalise' their vote. Closed and blocked lists only offer the choice of voting for a predetermined party list (that is, the voter chooses a party list on which the ranking of candidates is predetermined by the party itself – the standard system used in Bulgaria, Macedonia, Romania and Slovakia). Closed, non-blocked lists allow the voter to rank individual candidates from one party (that is, they have one vote for a party, but can register a preference as to who they would like to see represent this party in the assembly, as is, for example, the case in elections in South Tyrol). Open and non-blocked lists allow voters to cast their votes across party lines and to express their preference for individual candidates on such lists (the so-called panachage model, used for example in local elections in Poland). In relation to non-blocked lists, it is important to bear in mind that, while these limit the ability of party executives to determine who represents the party in the assembly, they also increase intra-party competition and can encourage factionalisation. By the same token, such lists introduce an element of accountability into the PR system and improve the relationship between voter and representative (cf. Hartmann 2000; Venice Commission 2000). Thus, even within PR list systems, a degree of preferentialism can be introduced which can, theoretically at least, encourage pre-election coalitions and functioning post-election power sharing, and thus have a favourable impact on political stability as it promotes moderation and inclusiveness in post-election political processes in multiethnic societies.

Two other issues in relation to election systems are the degree of their complexity and the extent to which voters are familiar with them. Very often in multiethnic societies, election systems reflect the complexity of issues that they are intended to address, namely, to contribute to delivering moderate and inclusive government. Unsurprisingly, this can imply complex rules and regulations, the practical consequences of which cannot always be accurately predicted by either their designers or the voters (see Farrell 2001, pp.

193ff; Fraenkel and Grofman 2002). The introduction of new electoral systems or reform of existing systems therefore requires public information and education campaigns to ensure voters properly understand the mechanics of the election and the consequences of their vote. Familiarity with a given electoral system can, however, be a double-edged sword: on the one hand, familiarity enables voters to make better informed decisions about how to use their vote, while on the other, it can also mean that sections of the electorate are more likely to distrust results, especially if they have experienced discrimination and disadvantage in the past.

Election campaigns

In many ways, election campaigns reflect the nature of inter-ethnic relations while often foreshadowing the nature of post-election politics. This is particularly the case where the higher the stakes the more likely it becomes that the campaign will have a polarising and radicalising effect on different groups. As Horowitz has shown, predictability is particularly linked to three patterns of ethnic violence in electoral contests: pre-emptive strikes, break-outs and lock-ins (2001, pp. 295–308). Pre-emptive strikes are aimed at enhancing a particular community's chances of electoral success, for example by driving out, intimidating or otherwise influencing voters whose vote may go to a different political party. Pre-emptive strikes therefore accept ascriptive elements of party affiliation, which is in contrast to break-outs where an effort is made to reduce this ascriptive element in order to overcome a particular electoral disadvantage.

Break-outs often appear as attempts on the part of an existing political party to expand beyond its traditional core ethnic constituency; if this is perceived as threatening by other parties and their followers relying on ascriptive elements, violence is a likely result (Horowitz 2001, pp. 295–308). Pre-emptive strikes and break-outs are both types of pre-election violence, while lock-ins trigger post-election violence, and are thus more relevant in the context of election results, which I discuss below. Campaign-related violence may be locally contained or more widespread, depending on the stakes and the demographic distribution of groups. Its likelihood will also depend on the general nature of inter-ethnic relations and the legacy of past campaign conduct. Pre-emptive strikes and break-outs both reflect strategic choices made in relation to inclusiveness and/or moderation of political processes. Pre-emptive strikes signal a move by extremists to limit the inclusiveness of post-election institutions, while break-outs are a reflection of attempts to achieve a greater degree of inclusiveness.

Another factor of election campaigns which has a bearing on the degree of inclusiveness and moderation in any post-election political process is that of campaign promises and, more generally speaking, election manifestos. Ruling out certain coalitions or polarising communities and politicians does not bode well for a post-election process in which a moderate and inclusive government needs to be formed. Either politicians stick to their campaign pledges and the government that emerges in the aftermath of an election is exclusive and/or extremist, or politicians falter on their promises and potentially lose the support of their constituencies, which may then be exploited in turn by hardliners within or outside parliament and/or the governing party. On the other hand, campaigns fought on substantive rather than on ethnic issues offer greater promise of post-election political processes that are inclusive and characterised by moderation as they allow for the formation of government coalitions based on policy overlap, rather than convenience or necessity.

Electoral systems that induce pre-election cooperation and moderation do not necessarily exclude confrontational and even violent election campaigns. Even though Reilly (2001) shows with the example of Papua-New Guinea that a preferential voting system (in this case, AV) does have a positive effect on the conduct of election campaigns, Horowitz's (2001) findings on electoral riots strongly suggest that political parties and their supporters who feel threatened by preferential voting systems – because they are unlikely to be able to gain sufficient cross-communal support to guarantee them a number of seats equal to those they may have achieved under non-preferential systems – may choose violence to 'compensate' for this and, for example, intimidate voters to cast preferences in their favour. Consequently, while preferential voting systems may be beneficial for the longer-term stability of power-sharing institutions of both the integrative and consociational type, their influence on the conduct of election campaigns and (as I will show below) on the conduct of elections themselves is more limited, and, in the short term, not necessarily conducive to conflict management and democracy-building.

These last observations underscore the close relationship that exists between intra-community and inter-community dynamics in the context of election-based political systems. The more vulnerable (moderate) politicians feel in relation to out-bidding by extremists, the more likely they are to adopt tough stances at election times, and the more they do so, the more vulnerable they will be after elections. Even if they win, moderates may easily lose the support of their voters if extremists can point out that essential campaign promises have been broken. Put another way, where party systems are divided along communal lines, elections can increase intra-community political competition, and make this intra-community political arena more important than the inter-community one. As a consequence, politicians compete for a clearly defined pool of votes in their own community, and in order to win a major share in it they must prove that they are the best representatives of their community's interests. It is easy to see how such a situation plays into the hands of extremists and disadvantages moderates.

The conduct of elections

Similar to campaigns, the conduct of elections often reflects the general state of inter-ethnic relations and can foreshadow the nature of the post-election political process and the feasibility of power sharing. Taagepera and Shugart (1989) identify a number of 'pathologies': fraud, malapportionment, gerrymandering and turnout. While fraud and turnout are pathologies that are not specific to power-sharing contexts, malapportionment and gerrymandering have particular significance, both from an institutional design perspective and from the perspective of practical experiences.

Malapportionment occurs, for example, when voters living in significantly larger constituencies are represented by the same or even fewer numbers in parliament than those of significantly smaller constituencies. The first implication of this is that malapportionment is only possible in electoral systems that have at least two constituencies. Malapportionment can be a consequence of population movement (for example, voluntary segregation or ethnic cleansing) which diminishes or increases the number of voters in existing, territorially-defined constituencies, or of unequal population growth (for example, due to higher birth rates, emigration or immigration) which diminishes or increases the number of voters in existing communally defined constituencies. It can also be a deliberate strategy to increase or decrease the representation of a particular segment of a given population. Thus, the 1960 constitution of Cyprus predetermined the number of members of parliament to be elected within each of the two major communities – Greek and Turkish Cypriots – but gave Turkish Cypriots a higher share of seats in parliament than they would have been entitled to under an exactly proportional system. In this instance, malapportionment was a factor that contributed to the breakdown of consociational power sharing. While malapportionment is not specific to consociational systems, but can, in principle, also occur in integrative power-sharing regimes, its use is more likely in the former, given its stronger emphasis on inclusive representation, even at the cost of over-representation.

Gerrymandering, in contrast, does not primarily concern equality or proportionality within and across constituencies, but constituency boundaries themselves. While malapportionment can be a consequence (or aim) of gerrymandering, the latter is more concerned with the voter composition of particular constituencies. Gerrymandering seeks to create as many majorities for a particular party or community as possible by drawing constituency boundaries in such a way that in each constituency a small majority is feasible and/or by concentrating as many voters of opposing parties in one constituency in order to eliminate them from the electorate in others which would then fall to the party that re-drew boundaries. In Northern Ireland, for example, the Unionist Party government in the 1950s and 1960s drew electoral boundaries for local councils in such as way that unionist candidates in electoral areas with nationalist majorities could still obtain a majority of seats. To ensure the 'sustainability' of this system, the allocation of public housing followed the same prerogative of guaranteeing unionist control of electoral wards.

Proportional-representation systems and electoral formulae based on multi-member districts are generally less prone to gerrymandering than majority/plurality systems where there is normally only one 'winner' per constituency. Hence, gerrymandering can be used, and may in fact be required, for the operation of an integrative power-sharing regime: the AV system, favoured by Horowitz, requires ethnically heterogeneous constituencies, which may have to be created through changing constituency boundaries. This is not a problem in itself, but in the context of deeply divided societies it once again raises the issue of the extent to which electoral engineering undermines its own intentions by encouraging perceptions of unfairness and manipulation at the expense of particular parties whose opportunities for having their candidates elected will be significantly reduced. While it may be possible to achieve moderation among those elected to office by reducing inclusiveness, such techniques are more likely to increase polarisation and extremism among those excluded from the process of government. STV also requires multiethnic constituencies but, as a proportional electoral system, the effects of gerrymandering are less likely to be perceived as unfair as it is less likely that specific parties will be completely excluded.

Integrative and consociational power-sharing regimes both rely on so-called 'pathologies' of electoral systems to increase the chances of election results that fit the underlying assumptions of both models – moderation and inclusiveness (albeit differently weighted). Yet, clearly, the more they depend on this kind of manipulation – that is, the more serious these pathologies – the more they will send a signal to (some) voters and politicians that elections are unfair. On the other hand, if electoral engineering goes hand-in-hand with broad public consultation and information exercises, it remains a valuable and legitimate tool for conflict resolution and institutional design. In addition, proper judicial and administrative processes can go a long way not only to ensure that pathologies are minimised, but also that election outcomes are accepted, even if they do not reflect each community's, or each party's, aspirations (Lyons 2002; Venice Commission 1991). Thus, while the proper use of gerrymandering and malapportionment cannot guarantee fully inclusive and moderate post-election governments, they can, nevertheless, contribute to a more stable post-election political process.

Election results

Election results, especially the composition of an elected assembly and the subsequent stability of power-sharing regimes, are particularly important in two ways. First, they determine the extent to which political institutions obtain or retain sufficient levels of authority and legitimacy. Secondly, they decide on the composition of a legislature and an executive, and as such can often determine whether compromise and coalescent government will prevail, or whether the political process will stagnate and, in the worst case scenario, collapse into violence.

On the surface, both of these points seem to be related primarily to the stability of any post-election political process, but especially in multiethnic societies they inevitably also raise issues of inclusiveness. Election results that do not broadly reflect the level of diversity within a given society *and* within its constituent communities are unlikely to be acceptable to those who do not feel that they are adequately represented. This brings me back to the third pattern of violence in electoral contests identified by Horowitz (2001), namely, the lock-in situation. Horowitz distinguishes pure lock-in, which occurs when elections confirm the continuation of dominant, demographic majorities, from an artificial lock-in, in which elections result in a victory of the minority (as caused by a party-political split of the majority or an election system that translates a majority of votes into a minority of seats). Consequently, violence has different points of origin: the minority in case of a pure lock-in (such as in Northern Ireland in the 1960s), while the violent backlash is likely to come from the majority in cases of artificial lock-in (such as in Fiji after the 1999 elections).

However, the acceptability of election results also depends on the conduct of election campaigns and the elections themselves, on the stakes in elections and, more generally speaking, on the state of inter-ethnic relations in a given society. In 'normal' democracies, the right to vote must not be confused with the right to representation (Grofman et al. 1992, pp. 129f.), and especially not to have one's interests represented by the party one has voted for and/or in that party's anticipated strength. Power-sharing institutional designs seek to address this point by providing mechanisms in which all significant groups in a multiethnic society see their interests represented and aspirations reflected in post-election political processes. As already explored, different approaches to power sharing seek to achieve this in different ways – through specific electoral systems that strengthen a moderate middle ground in a given society which can ideally lay claim to representing the views of larger sections of different ethnic communities or by designing institutions in which representatives of these groups have to cooperate after elections. Hybrid versions that combine elements of both approaches have significant theoretical appeal, even though the empirical ground on which this assertion rests remains thin. In other words, election results that produce broadly acceptable moderate politicians in the institutions of government, as well as institutions that regulate their participation and include safeguards against the exploitation of minorities, combine the most appealing elements of both approaches to power sharing without compromising the integrity of an overall institutional design aimed at non-violent, democratic conflict management in multiethnic societies.

SOME CONCLUSIONS

Channelling conflict in multiethnic societies into non-violent, democratic processes is a difficult endeavour at best. Apart from the immensely complex environments of conflicting claims and political strategies of internal and external actors, divisions among scholars on how best to address often protracted and symbolically-charged conflicts in multiethnic societies have not helped the practical business of conflict management either. The two predominant approaches of integrative and consociational power sharing, for example, are themselves deeply divided over how best to achieve political processes that can command authority, pass and implement legislation, maintain public order and security, and respond to changes in public opinion. I have argued that the often-posited choice between inclusiveness and moderation – as exemplified in the two basic models of integrative and consociational power sharing – is misguided because stability in deeply divided societies is as much a function of inclusiveness as it is of moderation. Therefore, hybrid systems combining elements of both consociational and integrative power sharing may be best equipped to achieve sustainable democratic power sharing. Despite some reservations, especially because of the shaky empirical basis for such a 'mixed' approach, I have tried to show that there is significant theoretical appeal in an approach that combines preferential voting with elements of consociational institutional structures.

The most important direct consequences of elections are obviously their results. While it is true that the choice of electoral systems and the fine-tuning of specific rules can shape election outcomes, it is ultimately the will of the voter that determines the overall composition of assemblies and governments. However, in the same way that polarisation and extremism are courses of action that can be chosen or avoided, so are post-electoral political processes not foregone conclusions. Parliaments and governments have, and make, choices as to how to conduct politics. Clear, absolute majorities do not have to lead to the neglect of minority interests; multi-party coalition governments do not have to be unstable or to collapse at the first difficult decision.

Apart from the role of politicians, another qualification of the direct impact of elections on moderation and inclusiveness in political processes in multiethnic societies is the broader design of political institutions. Recent scholarship and political practice have developed a wide range of power-sharing mechanisms that can be usefully employed in the process of state construction and democratic consolidation in multiethnic societies: consociations, ethno-federalism, territorial autonomy, and the like, are all designs that can mitigate electoral outcomes that would otherwise have 'complicated' inter-ethnic relations. Careful institutional design is, therefore, a necessary (although admittedly not a sufficient) component in all efforts to achieve moderate and inclusive political processes in multiethnic societies, and as such a useful complement to the design of electoral systems. The key to success is to make sure that electoral systems fit in the more general institutional design of a given polity and that 'mismatches' between the two, which might easily exacerbate existing inter-ethnic tensions, are avoided through careful institutional design. To take these precautions may complicate electoral processes, but it is necessary in order to ensure that elections in multiethnic societies lead to moderate and inclusive government that allows for stable, non-violent and democratic political processes in which conflicts can be managed peacefully.

NOTES

1. An earlier version of this chapter was presented as a paper entitled 'The Ethnopolitical Dynamics of Elections' at the Annual World Convention of the Association of Nationality Studies in April 2003 in New York and subsequently published as ECMI Working Paper No. 17 (Wolff 2003).
2. Preferential systems allow voters to rank candidates according to preference, thus enabling them to express further choices if the preferred candidate does not obtain enough votes to be elected. This is meant to encourage candidates to broaden their appeal (i.e., moderate their policies) beyond their own ethnic constituency.
3. I am grateful to the editors of this volume for bringing this point to my attention.
4. Vote wastage in PR systems does, however, become relevant where thresholds apply.
5. High thresholds, however, can cancel out the benefits of PR systems, making election results sometimes even less inclusive than if the same election had been conducted under a majority/plurality system (e.g., Turkey's 10% threshold completely distorts election results, allowing parties with about 30% of the vote to obtain more than 50% of the seats).

REFERENCES

European Commission for Democracy through Law (Venice Commission) (1991) *General Report to the CSCE Seminar of Experts on Democratic Institutions.* Strasbourg: Council of Europe [CDL (1991) 031e-restr].
—— (2000) *Electoral Law and National Minorities.* Strasbourg: Council of Europe [CDL-INF (2000) 4].
Farrell, D. M. (2001) *Electoral Systems: A Comparative Introduction.* Basingstoke: Palgrave Macmillan.

Fraenkel, J. and Grofman, B. (2002) 'Evaluating the Impact of Electoral Reform on Interethnic Accommodation: The Alternative Vote in Fiji'. (Unpublished paper. Manuscript in author's possession.)

Grofman, B., Handley L., and Niemi, R. G. (1992) *Minority Representation and the Quest for Voting Equality*. Cambridge: Cambridge University Press.

Hartmann, C. (2000) 'The Strengths and Weaknesses of Existing Electoral Models as Instruments for Managing Ethnic Conflict'. (Unpublished paper. Manuscript in author's possession.)

Horowitz, D. L. (1985) *Ethnic Groups in Conflict*. Berkeley, CA: University of California Press.

—— (1991) *A Democratic South Africa? Constitutional Engineering in a Divided Society*. Berkeley, CA: University of California Press.

—— (2001) *The Deadly Ethnic Riot*. Berkeley, CA: University of California Press.

Lijphart, A. (1977) *Democracy in Plural Societies*. New Haven, CT: Yale University Press.

—— (1994) *Electoral Systems and Party Systems: A Study of Twenty-seven Democracies, 1945–1990*. Oxford: Oxford University Press.

—— (2002) 'The Wave of Power Sharing Democracy', in A. Reynolds (ed.), *The Architecture of Democracy: Constitutional Design, Conflict Management and Democracy*. Oxford: Oxford University Press, pp. 37–54.

Lyons, T. (2002) 'Postconflict Elections: War Termination, Democratisation and Demilitarising Politics'. Fairfax, VA: Institute for Conflict Analysis and Resolution, George Mason University. Working paper No. 20.

Norris, P. (2002) 'Ballots Not Bullets: Testing Consociational Theories of Ethnic Conflict, Electoral Systems and Democratisation', in A. Reynolds (ed.), *The Architecture of Democracy: Constitutional Design, Conflict Management and Democracy*. Oxford: Oxford University Press, pp. 206–47.

Reilly, B. (2001) *Democracy in Divided Societies: Electoral Engineering for Conflict Management*. Cambridge: Cambridge University Press.

Sisk, T. D. (1996) *Power Sharing and International Mediation in Ethnic Conflict*. Washington, D.C.: United States Institute of Peace Press.

Taagepera, R. and Shugart, M. S. (1989) *Seats and Votes: The Effects and Determinants of Electoral Systems*. New Haven, CT and London: Yale University Press.

Wolff. S. (2003) 'The Ethnopolitical Dynamics of Elections'. *ECMI Working Paper No. 17*. Flensburg: European Centre for Minority Issues, available online at http://www.ecmi.de/doc/download/working_paper_17.pdf.

Part II
Case Studies

5

The Failure of Moderate Politics: The Case of Northern Ireland

Anthony Oberschall and L. Kendall Palmer

Hopes were high in 1998 that the Belfast Agreement would mark the beginning of a peaceful resolution of the violent conflict between Irish nationalists and British unionists[1] in Northern Ireland. Although the worst instances of sectarian violence between these two communities have now receded, sectarian politics nevertheless persists and blocks the full implementation of the Agreement. In this chapter, we argue that there is a contradiction at the heart of the Belfast Agreement that obstructs the emergence of a non-sectarian, centrist governing coalition. In turn, this contradiction works against the goals of peaceful coexistence and inter-communal reconciliation. In our view, the power-sharing legislative assembly, executive committee and electoral system established under the Agreement are flawed in that they serve to entrench, and have even encouraged, sectarian division. In contrast, the Agreement's approach to questions of human rights, justice, policing and equality appears to be designed to foster greater integration between the two communities. We believe that people in Northern Ireland are favourably disposed to greater cross-community cooperation and integrative power sharing but that there is no governing force to legitimate and support such grassroots preferences and dispositions. In the absence of such a force, it is our contention that sectarianism is likely to dominate both in politics and in community relations more generally in Northern Ireland.[2]

NATIONAL IDENTITY AND STATE

When violent conflict broke out in Northern Ireland in the late 1960s, 76 per cent of Catholics considered themselves Irish while 71 per cent of Protestants considered themselves British. Since then, little has changed. Social-attitude surveys show that in 2002, 75 per cent of Protestants considered themselves British while 62 per cent of Catholics considered themselves Irish. On the central constitutional question, a similar pattern emerges. In 1968, 84 per cent of Protestants were opposed to a united Ireland, while in 2002, 83 per cent wanted Northern Ireland to remain in the United Kingdom. While this might suggest a picture of social and political stagnation, there has, however, been a crucial change since the outbreak of the conflict. In 1968, 82 per cent of Protestants approved 'the right for people in the North to take up arms ... and fight to keep Northern Ireland British'. However, in 2002, 68 per cent said that they would accept a united Ireland if a majority ever voted for it. Among Catholics in 2002, although 68 per cent wanted to become part of a united Ireland, 93 per cent said they would accept a continuance of Northern Ireland's current constitutional status even if a majority never voted for it. In short, survey data suggest that Catholics want equality within Northern Ireland more than they want a united Ireland, and they believe they are on the way to achieving it (NILT 2002; Rose 1971).

Looking at the salience of the symbolic dimensions of nationality in Northern Ireland, one can see a cup that is either half full or half empty. Once again, 2002 survey data suggest that people do not feel as intimidated as they once did by paramilitary murals, flags and kerb paintings, and that the most common reaction to the Union Jack and the Irish Tricolour is neither pride nor hostility, but indifference. Many Catholics and Protestants agree that their respective cultural traditions are by and large protected in present day Northern Ireland (cf. Hughes and Donnelly 2003). Of course, it is not our intention here to present an unrealistic, or even utopian, picture of how people in Northern Ireland think about national identity. Evidence clearly shows that when national and sectarian symbols intersect with security and justice issues, they remain contentious – as they do, for example, with respect to issues such as the name and uniform of the police force on the Protestant side, Orange Order parades on the Catholic side, and weapons decommissioning for both (Irwin 2003; NILT 2002).

The point, therefore, is that while the picture is a complex one, it would seem that there is much to be positive about. There is at least some willingness among people in Northern Ireland to take a softer approach to questions of national identity and to the question of the constitutional status of Northern Ireland. And yet despite these positive social developments, there is a marked and paradoxical growth in political division and polarisation, as 'the people of Northern Ireland appear to be moving away from the voices of moderation and accommodation and back to their separate political camps' (Irwin 2003, p. 71). Division is especially pronounced among unionists on just about every important aspect of the Belfast Agreement and its implementation, be it power sharing with Sinn Féin, security and police reform, North–South institutions and relations, and so on. It manifests itself in the battles between the Democratic Unionist Party (DUP) and the Ulster Unionist Party (UUP), as well as within the UUP itself, on the scope for political compromise, rooted in deep-seated, historical cleavages within Protestantism (Alcock 2002). The anti-Agreement rejectionists, who are mainly DUP supporters, have consistently refused to share power with Sinn Féin as long as the paramilitary Irish Republican Army (IRA) – with whom Sinn Féin is inextricably linked – holds on to its weapons; they view the policies and reforms embodied in the Agreement as steps in a covert design for abandoning Northern Ireland by the United Kingdom, and charge Prime Minister Tony Blair with betrayal. This paradoxical divergence between people's positive aspirations and the negative realities requires further analysis and explanation.

As we will argue, this divergence is best understood within the context of a wider discussion about the contradictory nature of the actual power-sharing arrangements established under the terms of the Belfast Agreement. In a divided society like Northern Ireland, efforts at peace-building, grassroots conciliation, public policy and cooperation among political leaders are equally important and should be viewed as mutually reinforcing. Yet flaws contained in the power-sharing structures established under the Belfast Agreement appear to institutionalise the politics of sectarianism and lead to the creation of contradictory public policy that stymies grassroots reconciliation initiatives. In our view, the Belfast Agreement could be revised in ways that provide stronger incentives and mechanisms for a winning coalition of the middle drawn from conciliatory unionist, nationalist, and centrist groups (such as the Alliance Party and Women's Coalition) that favour cross-community cooperation and inter-communal reconciliation. In short, we contend that self-sustaining peace in Northern Ireland demands stable democratic institutions of the kind that will promote a common commitment to a shared future, and correspondingly, a non-sectarian civic culture.

CONTRADICTIONS AND AMBIGUITIES OF THE BELFAST AGREEMENT

During the multi-party negotiations that lead to the signing of the Belfast Agreement, the key parties to the process were principally concerned with ensuring the long-term cessation of violence, with reaching an agreement on how to deal with the constitutional question, with finding an appropriate form of power sharing, and with legislating for an extensive equality agenda. This was no small task, and the parties had to deal with many vexed issues in haste to ensure that the deadline set for Good Friday 1998 would be met.

More specifically, the negotiations took the form of a three-stranded approach: Strand One dealt with relationships internal to, or within, Northern Ireland; Strand Two concerned North–South relationships between Northern Ireland and the Republic of Ireland; while Strand Three dealt with East–West relationships between the Irish government, the British government, and the devolved legislative bodies in Scotland, Wales and Northern Ireland. In Strand One, the Agreement provides for a local legislative assembly that is built on the four basic principles of consociational power sharing: it establishes a 'grand coalition' government, communal or 'segmental' autonomy in many institutions, proportionality in representation and resource allocation, and a mutual veto on pivotal political decisions (Lijphart 1977; O'Leary 1999). Advocates of consociationalism typically start from the premise that communal identities are relatively fixed or immutable and, for this reason, they maintain that it is naive to think that communal loyalties can easily be overcome or supplanted by the creation of a more conciliatory, integrated identity (Sisk 1996, pp. 35–6). However, this not only suggests that consociational power sharing is more comfortable with sectarian divisions than it ideally ought to be – especially if inter-communal reconciliation is a valued goal – but it has led some of its critics to argue that this particular form of power sharing is an inherently 'unstable option that lies somewhere between partition and inter-ethnic integration' (Wilson 2002, p. 10).

Much has already been written on the more specific shortcomings of consociational power sharing (see, for example, Barry 1975a and 1975b). Rather than rehearsing these shortcomings here, the point that we want to stress with respect to the Belfast Agreement is the unsatisfactory balance that it strikes between power sharing and social policy. To secure agreement on key political mechanisms for government, the Agreement's negotiators agreed to sidetrack some responsibility for certain issues to newly created commissions and public bodies for later implementation. These issues included weapons decommissioning, police reform, criminal justice, contentious parades, human rights, and equality. Broad principles of integration favoured by the British and Irish governments were expressed in the terms of reference of these commissions and public bodies, but such principles clearly contrast with the idea of communal or segmental autonomy promoted by consociational politics. Crucially, recent experience in Northern Ireland clearly suggests that as commissions confront justice, equality, fairness and other principles of social justice with the realities of sectarian particularism in legislative bodies, the casualty becomes the former, integrative dimensions of the Belfast Agreement. This contradiction has come to plague and derail the implementation of the Agreement as a whole such that, at the time of writing, political life in Northern Ireland is characterised by growing political extremism and diminishing prospects for better community relations.

A further ambiguity stems from the (in our view) unsatisfactory way in which the Agreement addresses the crucial constitutional question that lies at the heart of the conflict. The Agreement was sold to unionists as a means of ensuring Northern Ireland's place within the United Kingdom while, at one and the same time, it was sold to nationalists as an opportunity to bring about a united Ireland (O'Leary 1999, pp. 91–2). This ambiguity has likewise returned to haunt the implementation of the Agreement. Many unionists view every step in the implementation process as a 'falling domino' on the road to a united Ireland, while the same steps are perceived by many nationalists as 'way stations' to the further assimilation of Northern Ireland within the United Kingdom. Constitutionally, the Agreement recognises Northern Ireland as part of the United Kingdom; but it also allows that sovereignty could be ceded to the Republic of Ireland by a majority vote at some future point. Yet by granting that an issue of such political magnitude can be decided by a mixture of changing demographics and simple majoritarianism, insecurity and suspicion have been institutionalised at the core of an agreement that was meant to ensure stability for all sides to the conflict. Thus, although consociational power sharing depends on cooperation between political leaders, this cooperation remains unlikely in Northern Ireland as long as the constitutional question remains the subtext for all contentious issues (see also Wilson 2002).

CRITICS OF THE BELFAST AGREEMENT

Non-cooperative, indirect bargaining during the negotiations of the Belfast Agreement has left a bitter legacy. The Northern Ireland political parties bargained little with one another face to face, and therefore the vast majority of the deal was struck through indirect negotiations with the British and Irish governments acting as intermediaries. The parties were not long in discovering that whoever made the most credible threats to the peace process would get the most concessions from the two governments. But each concession, expressed in ambiguous language, upset some previous concession promised to another party, thus creating uncertainty and a lack of finality. Mistrust and obstructionism, rather than trust and cooperation among Northern Ireland's political leaders, is the legacy of the Belfast Agreement and its stumbling implementation (Mallie and McKittrick 2001; Mitchell 1999). The following examples are intended to illustrate what is at issue here.

One key problem that critics have identified is that there is no true cabinet government or executive. Ministries are allocated to the parties in proportion to their numbers in the Assembly according to a mechanical algorithm known as the d'Hondt rule (O'Leary 1999, pp. 95–6). As such, ministers are not chosen by – nor are they responsible to – a cabinet team under a Prime Minister and hence they can obstruct a coherent government policy and pursue a narrow interest agenda. To be sure, the Assembly can veto a specific budget item to influence a maverick minister. However, in practice such checks on a minister's actions are not feasible because they threaten to unravel complex budgetary compromises. This is why we maintain that, as far as the cabinet formed under the terms of the Agreement is concerned, power without accountability has to change if Northern Ireland is to move more successfully towards the creation of a political system that is responsive to the diverse interests in society (Horowitz 2001, p. 104; Horowitz 2002, p. 210; Wilson and Wilford 2003, p. 9).

Critics also believe that structures for governing are generally top heavy, over staffed, too expensive, inefficient and invite gridlock. Northern Ireland currently has 108 Assembly Members elected in 18 parliamentary constituencies (also 18 Westminster MPs and three members of the European Parliament), as well as 26 District Councils. Critics further argue that there is an excessive number of executive departments, partly as a consequence of consociational principles in the executive branch, and the corresponding need to satisfy the demands of communal autonomy. The Agreement has also mandated the creation of new commissions – in particular, the new Human Rights and Equality Commissions – with their own budgets and staffs, complicated decision-making rules, and overlapping responsibilities.

While much expenditure goes on salaries, money is also spent on reaching agreement in endless rounds of meetings and workshops, as well as on hundreds of pamphlets explaining various schemes for tolerance, cooperation and reconciliation.

According to our research findings, many unionists believe that these commissions are not accountable to public opinion or to elected Assembly members and hence are undemocratic; that they fund programmes to meet ethnic quotas (arguably, though not intentionally, in keeping with consociational norms) rather than to meet need; and that they have even been prepared to direct money to some local programmes controlled by paramilitaries as a means of 'bribing' them to accept a programme in their 'territory'. By contrast, some nationalists reported that these commissions are actually designed to divert, or even subvert, the equality, social justice, community development and human rights goals of the Belfast Agreement into harmless byways; they also argue that their members are unrepresentative of the citizenry. The British government agreed to these commissions because it hoped to foster greater inter-communal conciliation. Yet given the ways in which they are now perceived by members of both communities, nationalist and unionist, it must be obvious that this convoluted apparatus as a whole now needs streamlining. In the next section, we underpin this case by considering the way in which the outworkings of the Agreement have exacerbated inter-communal perceptions.

CLASHING PERCEPTIONS

The Agreement was meant to foster reciprocity and trust, with each side delivering on its share of the bargain. There is, however, disillusionment with asymmetry of achievement. According to interviews which we conducted with members of both the nationalist SDLP and unionist UUP, with members of the Assembly, as well as with several academics, the common perception is that nationalists got all they wanted, namely, power sharing, police reform, reform of the criminal justice system, rapid demilitarisation (British army retrenchment), prisoner release, and North–South institutions (joint institutions for cooperation between the Republic and Northern Ireland), all of which were painful concessions made by the unionist parties. By contrast, the general perception is that the one concession unionists truly wanted in return, namely, weapons decommissioning by the IRA, has not happened in full or with transparency, despite numerous assurances and promises from the British and Irish governments. As a result, unionists tend to feel betrayed: it is important to understand that for them, weapons decommissioning is a trust issue, a public test of Sinn Féin's commitment to abandoning violence and to the acceptance of non-violent and democratic means of political change. Decommissioning is symbolic of that commitment, a commitment which has not so far been made unconditionally.

It is our contention, then, that far from being confidence-building, implementation of the Belfast Agreement – such as it is – has amplified mistrust among key political actors and agents on both sides. For example, North–South institutions are, at present, weak and underdeveloped. The North–South Ministerial Council, whose actions are subject to the approval of both the Irish Dáil (or national parliament) and the Northern Ireland Assembly, was established to supervise implementation bodies (on such matters as food safety, trade and tourism, water pollution, and language) which affected people on both sides of the border. Although one might wonder how pollution in the Foyle and other shared waterways can be controlled unless there is cooperation on environmental measures by the two governments, the general air of mistrust surrounding the Agreement has led to a situation in which one rejectionist unionist interviewee feared that North–South institutions are nothing more than 'a wedge in the door' towards an eventual united Ireland.

Another example of divergent interpretations of the Agreement's outworking is 'demilitarisation' – the retrenchment of the British army and removal of border fortifications, as well as the disbanding of the (predominantly Protestant) police reserves. Some unionist interviewees feel exposed and vulnerable to renewed terrorism and see demilitarisation as further evidence of the British government's wish to disengage from Northern Ireland. One interviewee claimed that the border with the Republic is wide open to weapons, explosives and terrorist traffic. In point of fact, however, according to top security officials that we interviewed, security against terrorists now rests on good cooperation and intelligence sharing between security bodies on both sides of the border, which has led to the successful interception of illegal explosives shipments by the Real Irish Republican Army (RIRA). An army presence in fortified barracks and military border patrols is not now necessary for the security of Northern Ireland. Surveillance of known IRA activists is continuing as a matter of prudence, not as a matter of imminent threat.

Police reform is another contentious issue. Sinn Féin wants an entirely new police force and, until that comes about, refuses to encourage Catholics to become police officers or to participate in the District Policing Partnerships, a lynchpin for police accountability and citizen input into policing. In contrast, unionist political parties perceive police reform as yet another step in the ongoing process of surrender by the state to paramilitary rule. The head of the Northern Ireland Policing Board thinks the professionalisation of the police force is on a successful track. Meanwhile, local community leaders and mediators on a sectarian interface in London/Derry deal with sectarian youth violence by keeping the police at arm's length (see below). With such cognitive distortions derived from lack of trust and selective perception, cooperation on reforms and public policy is problematic.

The upshot of this analysis is that public disillusionment and disappointed expectations have eroded support for the Agreement – though not for achieving peace. According to Colin Irwin, for example, 'trust, quite simply, is in "free fall" for all the pro-Agreement parties, and for the Irish and British governments, in both the Protestant and Catholic communities' (2003, p. 75). The Belfast Agreement is complex, if not complicated: beyond the written text there are verbal understandings, promises, commitments, practices and deliberate ambiguities that have diluted responsibility and muddied the goals and steps in peacemaking. These uncertainties reward irresponsibility, recriminations, charges and counter-charges, and obstruction.

COMMUNITY RELATIONS

The sectarian legacy of violent conflict – which impacts on both communities but especially on their respective working-class neighbourhoods – has not, in our opinion, been sufficiently addressed by elite negotiations and agreements on government. The top-down political process of the Northern Ireland Assembly at Stormont and the activities of commissions and committees established under the Agreement influence and interact with grassroots, bottom-up practices, accommodations, and local institutions that shape separation and integration, cooperation and continued conflicts, between Protestants and Catholics. There is no lack of laws, agencies and programmes intended to improve community relations, advance social justice, and achieve a lasting peace in Northern Ireland.

There is the Community Relations Council and the District Council Community Relations Programme; the Community Relations Unit of the Office of the First Minister and Deputy First Minister; 'equality and equity' policies backed with fair employment legislation, an Equality Commission, the Human Rights Act of 1998, the Education Reform Order of 1989 and its Education for Mutual Understanding and Cultural Heritage mandates, a Targeting Social Need initiative, and the statutory duty placed on public authorities to promote good relations between persons of different religious persuasion, political opinion or racial group in accordance with Section 75 of the Northern Ireland Act 1998. Most directly, the commissions and various programmes finance many local activities, including the work of non-governmental organisations (NGOs). Crucially, however, the top-down sectarian politics institutionalised by the consociational power-sharing formula and bottom-up peacemaking and normalisation efforts are often on separate tracks, to the detriment of cross-community reconciliation.

Evidence suggests that social attitudes are more cooperative towards, and tolerant of, greater integration than sectarian politics and election outcomes would lead one to believe. A major survey in 1996 concluded that 'most people in Northern Ireland want to live together rather than apart, and ... even on those matters on which there is most disagreement there are some possible compromises' (Hadden et al. 1996, p. 3). These findings indicate that a lot has changed since 1968 when a majority in both communities agreed that 'people with the same religion ought to stick together' (Rose 1971, p. 495). Three recent surveys tracking community relations from 1989 to 1999, analysed by Hughes and Donnelly (2003), show that a substantial majority of Catholics and Protestants in 1999 expressed a preference for living in mixed neighbourhoods, working in a mixed environment, and schooling their children in a mixed school. Ninety-one per cent agree that government should give top priority to equal treatment, and 64 per cent believe that government already does. This contrasts with the 69 per cent of Protestants in 1968 who opposed anti-discrimination legislation in employment and housing (Rose 1971, p. 481). Added to this, the latest Northern Ireland Life and Times Survey (NILT 2003) found that large majorities among Catholics, and a majority among Protestants, would prefer mixed neighbourhoods, mixed schooling for their children, and an integrated workplace. Indeed, three out of four respondents said that they would not mind if a close relative were to marry outside of their religion. Moreover, almost no one reported having been abused verbally on account of their religion or having been unfairly treated in a shop or business. Yet despite these indicators, no political party, movement, group or policy initiative has so far managed to mobilise this huge pool of citizens willing to cooperate and share institutions across the sectarian divide.

Of course, individual preferences and dispositions favourable to greater inter-communal mixing in Northern Ireland do not translate automatically into integrated neighbourhoods and schools (Schelling 1984). Add fear, mistrust, and social pressures, as Shirlow (2003) found in the Ardoyne district of North Belfast, and the result is robust sectarian separation. These findings lead us to conclude that only a public policy supportive of shared neighbourhoods is likely to translate individual preferences and dispositions into real choices and living patterns. This integrative approach has not, however, been typical in the post-Agreement years. Politically led initiatives aimed at a promoting reconciliation have not dominated peace-building efforts at the community level.

When social relations are burdened with a legacy of discrimination and intimidation, public policy has to even the playing field between and across communities. Consider education. Parents want not only quality education; they want their children treated equally and fairly by professional teachers and administrators. They want their children protected from peer harassment. They want the curriculum, both statutory and 'hidden', not to be biased against their group. As long as their concerns are not addressed, some parents will prefer separate schooling even though they are favourably disposed to shared education. Our research indicates that what people desire above all is to live in a 'normal' society, by which they mean an end to insecurity, fear, threats, intimidation and violence. They want security, controls on anti-social behaviour, acceptable standards of public services, clean air, proximate primary schools, local empowerment through neighbourhood associations, and the like, some of which a public programme can and ought to provide.

In the absence of an institutional underpinning at the political level, greater social integration is not likely to occur. Instead, people view separation (in the physical sense of peace walls and territory, and the psycho-social sense of avoidance and sectarian encapsulation) as the guarantor of security in daily life, and they view cross-community transacting as burdened with uncertainty and trouble one should avoid. As one interviewee put it, 'mothers find it safer to have two playgrounds for their children on both sides of a peace wall than to share the same playground'. Local authorities have come to accept (even when opposing) avoidance and separation because it is preferable for mothers to have playgrounds they will send their children to, rather than build and locate playgrounds where they will not be used. Much the same applies to housing, schools, and other activities and facilities that might be shared, but are not. Even the middle class is 'comfortable in separation' (author interview).

One consequence of institutional failure is that sectarian conflict and tensions at interfaces are increasingly dealt with through local mediators and institutions rather than through state agencies and commissions created by the Belfast Agreement for conflict management. In Derry, a leading businessman mediated between the Loyalist Orange Order and the Nationalist Bogside Residents' Association for a peaceful Apprentice Boys' parade in 2003 instead of turning to the Parades Commission. According to a Derry community mediator, when youths at interfaces engage (or threaten to engage) in sectarian name calling, stone throwing and flag waving, mediators and community leaders communicating over mobile phones call meetings to defuse and cool tempers. The police act only as a last resort. In short, local residents and institutions have to cope with the culture of violence in their midst and cannot afford to wait for that time when the police will become accepted as impartial arbiters.

Many community groups and NGOs conduct workshops, programmes and activities with youths, parents, drug addicts, and ex-paramilitaries to teach tolerance and non-violence in communal relations. However, these gains should not be overestimated since the culture of violence has proved resilient. Sectarian mobilisation has not ceased just because there has been a peace process. Dominic Bryan's (2001) research on Orange Order parades, for example, has found that the 'blood and thunder' marching bands of Protestant working-class youth, some with links to Loyalist paramilitaries, enact a provocative symbolic sectarian repertoire with flags, banners, songs and music. Such mobilisation is closely tied to the political culture of contention, territorial control, and sectarian domination, and occasions clashes between those youths and Catholic residents along contested parade routes, or between those youths and the police when parades are banned or rerouted.

IS NORTHERN IRELAND A 'NORMAL' SOCIETY?
SHOULD IT BECOME ONE?

One may well ask what Northern Ireland would look like if it were a 'normal' society characterised not by sectarianism but by the positive expression of cultural diversity. Today, but for two minor exceptions in the shape of the Alliance Party and the Women's Coalition, the political parties in Northern Ireland are sectarian. Only 5 per cent of school children attend mixed schools. In working-class residential areas at sectarian interfaces, contentious flags, opposing national colours painted along pavements and physical barriers in the guise of peace walls sharply separate almost entirely homogeneous sectarian neighbourhoods. Many potentially shared activities (including sports) remain separate. Workplaces are, however, mixed, and so are higher education institutions. The civil service, the largest employer in Northern Ireland, has made huge strides on integration. The police have made a start, with 50/50 entry-level recruitment for new officers, while many border fortifications have been dismantled.

Why, then, are these positive developments not enough? Under ideal conditions, a 'normal' society would have a multi-party governing coalition, as in many European democracies, with a joint-policy against sectarian divisions. More people from both the Catholic and Protestant communities would share institutions such as schools and neighbourhoods because their dispositions and preferences would be unconstrained by intimidation, adverse public opinion or lack of opportunity. Couples in mixed marriages would be more easily accepted by both families and in both communities. Police and their families would be able to live anywhere they wished, and would not have to inspect their vehicles for hidden bombs. Separation and division would be based on in-group preferences and not on security concerns and the legacy of sectarian intolerance. An ideal, 'normal' society would have some sectarian politics but would not be at risk of sectarian violence.

Although an ideal is, of course, just that, the point of our chapter has been to argue that the top-down peace process ought to deliver more for ordinary people and should be in keeping with, and complement, the integrationist strategy favoured in the social reform agenda. More specifically, we contend that the consociational-style power-sharing institutions established under the terms of the Belfast Agreement have fortified sectarianism and hence have not served people in Northern Ireland well. Consequently, no cross-community, centrist party coalition has taken root; in fact, recent election results dramatically demonstrate the extent to which the more extreme parties, the DUP and Sinn Féin, have gained at the expense of all of the more moderate parties. For these reasons, we maintain that the institutional structures for governing Northern Ireland established under the Belfast Agreement should be revised in ways that could enable centrist, cross-community mobilisation and public discourse to compete successfully with political sectarianism. The hope is that such revisions could better articulate citizen preferences and dispositions for greater sharing, and could align the integrative goals and policies of the commissions and committees with those of the Assembly, instead of the current mismatch.

NOTES

1. Although relations are complex, most Irish nationalists are Catholic, whereas most British unionists are Protestant. Accordingly, the terms 'Catholic' and 'Protestant' are often used as ethnic markers in Northern Ireland.
2. Our assessment of the contentious, stop-and-go implementation of the Belfast Agreement and of continued sectarian divisions is based on interviews, conducted in June and July 2003, with political and community leaders and knowledgeable academics in Northern Ireland, Dublin and London, supplemented by publications and position papers of the British and Irish governments, political parties, NGOs, commissions and councils, opinion polls and published and unpublished papers by experts and commentators. Our interviewees included elected political leaders from the UUP, DUP, SDLP, Sinn Féin, Women's Coalition, the Alliance Party, and PUP. The range of political views expressed to us in these interviews spanned the spectrum of views on the Belfast Agreement, from full support to rejection.

REFERENCES

Alcock, A. (2002) 'Religion and Conflict in Northern Ireland', CIFEM news, December, 14–18.
Barry, B. (1975a) 'The Consociational Model and its Dangers', *The European Journal of Political Research*, 3, 393–415.
—— (1975b) 'Review Article: Political Accommodation and Consociational Democracy', *British Journal of Political Science*, 5 (4), 477–505.
Bryan, D. (2001) 'Parade Disputes in the Peace Process', *Peace Review*, 13 (1), 43–9.
Hadden, T., Irwin C. and Boal, F. (1996) 'Separation or Sharing?'. Belfast: Fortnight Education Trust.
Horowitz, D. (2001) 'The Northern Ireland Agreement: Clear, Consociational, and Risky', in J. McGarry (ed.), *Northern Ireland and the Divided World:*

Post-Agreement Northern Ireland in Comparative Perspective. Oxford: Oxford University Press, pp. 89–108.

—— (2002) 'Explaining the Northern Ireland Agreement: the Sources of an Unlikely Consensus', *British Journal of Political Science*, 32 (2), 193–220.

Hughes, J. and Donnelly, C. (2003) 'Community Relations in Northern Ireland. A Shift in Attitudes?', *Journal of Ethnic and Migration Studies*, 29 (4), 643–61.

Irwin, C. (2003) 'Devolution and the State of the Northern Ireland Peace Process', *The Global Review of Ethnopolitics*, 2 (3), 71–91.

Lijphart, A. (1977) *Democracy in Plural Societies: A Comparative Exploration*. New Haven and London: Yale University Press.

Mallie, E. and McKittrick, D. (2001) *Endgame in Ireland*. London: Hodder and Stoughton.

Mitchell, G. (1999) *Making Peace*. Berkeley: University of California Press.

Northern Ireland Life and Times (NILT) 2002. Available at http://www.ark.uk/nilt.

O'Leary, B. (1999) 'The Nature of the British–Irish Agreement', *New Left Review*, 233 Jan/Feb 1999, 66–96.

Rose, R. (1971) *Governing Without Consensus: An Irish Perspective*. Boston: Beacon Press.

Schelling, T. (1984) *Choice and Consequences*. Cambridge, MA: Harvard University Press.

Shirlow, P. (2003) 'Who Fears to Speak: Fear, Mobility and Ethno-Sectarianism in the two Ardoynes', *The Global Review of Ethnopolitics*, 3 (1), 76–91.

Sisk, T. (1996) *Power Sharing and International Mediation in Ethnic Conflict*. Washington, DC: USIP.

Wilson, R. (2002) 'War by Other Means. Devolution and Community Division in Northern Ireland'. Paper read at the Boston meeting of the American Political Science Association.

Wilson, R. and Wilford, R. (2003) 'A Route to Stability: The Review of the Belfast Agreement'. Belfast: Democratic Dialogue Discussion Paper.

6

The Unintended Consequences of Consociational Federalism: The Case of Belgium

Kris Deschouwer

The modern Belgian state is a product of secession. It was created in 1830, when the Catholic and French-speaking elites of the southern provinces of the kingdom of the Low Countries seceded from the Protestant and Dutch-speaking north. In its early years, Belgium was not viewed as a society divided by two different language groups. French was simply accepted as the language of politics. The fact that a minority spoke Dutch rather than French was not considered an important issue. During the nineteenth century, however, a mainly urban and middle-class group of intellectuals tried to promote the use of Dutch, called for some specific language rights, and promoted the concept of bilingualism (Lorwin 1966; McRae 1986; Zolberg 1974). This group came to be known as the 'Flemish movement', after the mainly Dutch-speaking county of Flanders located in the north-western part of the new state.

The term 'Flanders' has gradually come to define all of the Dutch-speaking parts of Belgium, and it is common nowadays to use the term 'Flemish' to refer to the use of the Dutch language. Accordingly, in this chapter I will use the word Dutch to refer to the language, and Flanders or Flemish to refer to the northern part of the Belgian state and its inhabitants.

More specifically, this chapter will begin by exploring the complex historical divisions upon which the Belgian federal state came to be built: linguistic, territorial, economic and religious/party political. It will then show how more recent attempts to manage these divisions through consociational-style institutions like segmental autonomy, while helping to pacify the historical divisions, have at the same time led to a process of ongoing federalisation and a concomitant 'emptying' of centralised political power. Having considered how the complexities of decision making at the state level – and in particular the rigid institutionalisation of community veto powers – do little to facilitate the reversal of this trend, the chapter then considers a number of key difficulties that continue to beset Belgian political life. In sum, the chapter argues that Belgium's power-sharing institutions, while beneficial up to a point, are nevertheless based on a logic of ongoing devolution that has done little to bolster and sustain a uniquely Belgian national identity.

THE ORIGINS OF THE LINGUISTIC TENSIONS

When the Flemish movement began to mobilise in the nineteenth century, one issue became very prominent: the role and position of Brussels. As the capital city of Belgium, Brussels is situated close to the *de facto* language border, but is clearly to the north of it. As a centre of government and administration, and as a city close to the Francophone world, it had already been somewhat 'frenchified' prior to the creation of the state. After its creation, this process continued as a result of immigration from the south, the practical need to speak French to function in the public administration, and the desire of the middle classes for their children to be educated in the language of upward social mobility. As a result, not only did Brussels become a Francophone 'enclave' in the Dutch-speaking part of Belgium, it also gradually expanded, just like any other capital city. This expansion meant, of course, the growth of the Francophone enclave in Flanders.

The First World War heightened the significance of linguistic divisions. Flemish soldiers complained that they were expected to fight in defence of a state that did not communicate with them in their own language, whereas Flemish elites tried to obtain the right to organise classes in Dutch at the University of Gent (in Flanders). However, perhaps the most obvious and visible change that occurred was the 'territorialisation' of the language issue (Murphy 1998). Admittedly, territory was part of the problem from the very beginning; yet language laws passed in 1921 and in 1932 would make territory a far more salient issue. Although these laws provided for changes in the language border, they were premised on the idea that the best way to boost Dutch as a full and equal second language, without introducing Dutch as a new language in the south, was the division of the country into three linguistic regions: a Dutch-speaking north, a French-speaking south and the bilingual area of the capital city. This logic of division was further deepened by efforts on the part of Flemings who wished to see the then Belgian unitary state reformed into a decentralised or even federal state, which would grant the Flemish region the right to organise its cultural life itself. This bipolar view also led to a new perception of Belgium by the Francophones: the feeling that Belgium was gone and that the Belgians were no more. They had been transformed into Flemings and Francophones.

Matters were made even more complicated by the fact that the Francophones themselves were (and still are) divided. Those living south of the linguistic borderline – the Walloons – shared a language with the Francophones living in Brussels, but the latter found themselves in a different situation. They lived in a city that was claimed by Flemings as belonging historically to them, and hence had much to fear from a bipolar Belgium. As we will see in just a moment, the presence of Francophones in Brussels would make the solution of the Belgium problem a complicated affair.

The upshot of this brief (and admittedly truncated) overview is that today, Belgium contains four distinctive linguistic territories (one of which has been ignored up to this point simply for the sake of clarity). The first is the Dutch-speaking north, or the Flemish region. The second is the southern region of Wallonia, which is Francophone. However, Wallonia also includes an area in the east which was transferred from Germany at the Treaty of Versailles in 1918, and where the population (some 60,000 people) speaks German. It is today formally recognised as the German-speaking territory, but for regional matters it belongs to Wallonia. The fourth area is the officially bilingual Brussels, the limits of which were set and fixed in 1963. Complexities do not end there, however.

In addition to linguistic divisions, Flanders and Wallonia – the two largest of the four regions – are clearly divided along socio-economic lines (Van Dam 1997). A number of areas in what was to become Wallonia were the first in Europe to industrialise. The Flemish region remained for a long time mainly rural, except for some industry in the major cities. In other words, in the nineteenth century the economic centre of the country was concentrated in the Walloon industrial basins. However, from the end of the nineteenth century on, all that began to change – so much so that by the 1960s the economic balance between the two had noticeably shifted. As we will also see, this laid the foundations for a further layer of division, centred on the question of fiscal transfers between the two main regions.

Perhaps unsurprisingly, the different societal and economic composition of the two regions has given rise to different party-political landscapes: until very recently, Flanders has been the home region of the Christian Democrats. It was not only the largest party in Flanders, but also – given the demographic weight of Flanders – the largest party in Belgium. The Flemish Christian Democrats have therefore almost always governed (the exceptions being 1954–58 and since 1999) and, as a rule, have provided the Belgian Prime Minister. In Wallonia, the Socialist Party remains by far the largest party of the region. The north and the south of Belgium thus have a different party landscape and produce different ideological majorities. The party landscape in the capital city of Brussels is also different. Parties of both language groups are present here (see below), although generally the Liberal parties are stronger in Brussels.

1963–93: FROM A UNITARY TO A FEDERAL STATE

The divisions that characterise inter-communal relations in Belgium have been somewhat pacified in the course of the twentieth century by using the decision-making techniques that are typical of consociational democracies (Deschouwer 2002; Lijphart 1969, 1981; Huyse 1971). In essence, major decisions have either required some agreement between the communities or, alternatively, have been devolved on the basis of 'segmental' autonomy. A combination of these techniques has gradually been built into the political system and political culture of Belgium, partly as informal convention and partly as written constitutional rules.

The first constitutional reform, introduced in 1970, was a subtle and complex agreement between the two main language groups, and represented a fundamental compromise with respect to their diverging visions of the institutional future of Belgium. The agreement was reached after a long negotiation process, during which the two major political forces, the Flemish Christian Democrats and the Francophone Socialists, played the most crucial roles. The agreement of 1970 officially divided Belgium both in terms of distinct language communities – a demand made by the Flemish population – and in terms of defined regional entities – a demand made by the Francophone population. Accordingly, both language communities were officially recognised, as were the two regions, Flanders and Wallonia, along with the greater metropolitan area of Brussels. Moreover, a special dispensation was afforded to the German-speaking area in the southeast of the state. The fact that the two main language communities overlap by and large with the defined regions, has, in turn, allowed the devolution of political power simultaneously on both a functional and territorial basis. The Dutch-speaking or Flemish community can offer its services (like education) in the Flemish region and in Brussels. The French-speaking community can offer its services in Wallonia (but not in the German-speaking area) and in Brussels. The German-speaking community can offer its services in its own territory that is part of Wallonia.

At the central state level, the constitutional reform of 1970 also reflected many of the principles that underpin power sharing. For example, it was agreed that the government would have an equal number of French-speaking and Dutch-speaking ministers, while any further reforms and all laws implementing constitutional change were agreed to require the support of two-thirds of the members of parliament and, concurrently, a simple majority in each of the two major language groups within the legislature. As a consequence of these stringent power-sharing arrangements at the central state level, and the concomitant risk of political stagnation, almost all important political powers have gradually been devolved to the autonomous regions and language communities. In a series of qualitative leaps – in 1970, 1980, 1988, 1992 and 2002 – so-called 'personalised' matters like education, culture and welfare have been steadily transferred to the communities, while the various regions have received competencies related to territory such as economic policy, employment, environmental policy, public transport, public works, housing and agriculture. All the international powers related to these competencies were also devolved to the regions and communities (Alen and Ergec 1998).

Today, the evolving Belgian state is an example of ongoing federalism whereby the central authority has been almost completely emptied of any meaningful political power. The result of this 'emptying' is a clear duplication of the democratic party-political system at the regional level. Between 1968 and 1978, the three major Belgian parties – Christian Democrats, Liberals and Socialists – each divided into two separate and unilingual parties, each fielding candidates only in their own part of the state and in bilingual Brussels. In fact, even newer parties like the Greens have followed a similar trend, developing as two different parties in each of the two Belgian party systems. All parties thus appeal for support from an exclusive, single-language community. They represent only one part of the country, and only compete with the parties of their own language. Even in Brussels, where parties of both languages are present, each seeks the votes of the speakers of its own particular language. This produces a strongly centrifugal dynamic, since there is simply nobody who appeals for votes across the ethno-linguistic divide. There is not one single party attempting to mobilise Belgian public opinion, or appealing to a civic and inclusive Belgian national consciousness. As an obvious consequence, all of Belgium's political parties favour, in varying degrees, a greater amount of regional and functional autonomy.

The *de facto* duplication of the electoral system has yet a further negative impact on Belgian national identity and solidarity. Belgium is governed by parties that are internally riven by conflicts of interest. On the one hand, unilingual parties must forge a coalition government that makes collective decisions for the whole of society. On the other hand, unilingual parties hold substantial political power in the regional entities, and have a vested interest in representing exclusivist constituencies and in promoting further devolution. The way in which they respond to these competing demands – the need to govern the federation and the demands made by their particular constituencies – is by relying on an essentially consociational logic: politicians wait until there is a large number of problems to be solved. Then they agree that the best way to solve such problems is to let both sides make their own policy. In effect, this means institutionalising the inability to make decisions, or what in consociational language is referred to as 'granting segmental autonomy'. This granting of autonomy has resulted in a programme of rolling federal devolution that weakens the sustainability of a unified Belgian state. As the next section suggests, the complexities and rigidities of decision making at the federal level do little to reverse this trend.

THE STAGNATION OF DECISION MAKING AT THE FEDERAL LEVEL

We have already noted the constitutional obligation to share power in the federal government. The logic of decision making in the federal government is consensus (Frognier 1988), which, negatively defined, means that both sides have a veto power. In reality, this is much more important than the rather symbolic obligation to have an equal number of ministers for each language group, not least because of the range of veto devices that are in play. For example, at the federal level, the so-called 'alarm bell' can be activated when three-quarters of the MPs of one linguistic group declare that a proposal could harm them as a linguistic group. This obliges the federal government to produce a balanced solution. Since the federal government is composed of an equal number of Dutch speakers and French speakers, and since it decides by consensus, this can be an exceedingly difficult task.

Similarly, the institutionalisation of communal identities also complicates the judicial decision-making capacity of the Court of Arbitration, which is charged with resolving conflicts over the distribution of powers, or so-called 'conflicts of competence'. Once again, the problem here is that there is a clear possibility that veto powers will be enforced: the Court is composed of twelve judges, six Dutch-speaking and six French-speaking, all appointed by the federal government, on proposal of the Senate. Half of the judges are former politicians, and half of them belong to the judicial profession.

Conflicts of interest – that is, conflicts involving lack of agreement on the substance of laws – are more problematic, since they need a political solution in an institutional setting which is complex, full of subtle equilibria and full of potentially diverging interpretations (Jans and Tombeur 2000). In order to deal 'officially' with conflicts of interest, the Concertation Committee was created. Once again, however, this Committee is constituted in such a way that veto powers make decision making exceedingly difficult and encourage ongoing devolution.

The Committee is composed of the federal Prime Minister, five ministers representing (and chosen by) the federal government and six members representing the governments of regions and communities. It also needs to be perfectly linguistically balanced (six Francophone and six Flemish). Either the federal government or the government of one of the federated entities can signal a potential conflict to the Committee. This move suspends the debated decision for a period of 60 days. During that time the Committee can try to find a solution by consensus. If the issue is resolved, this can eventually lead to legal changes or to some kind of formal agreement between the regional governments (Poirier 2002). However, if a solution is not found after 60 days, the suspension is lifted and the conflict remains unresolved. It then remains on the table and will eventually resurface in a following round of negotiations, or, as is seemingly more likely, be passed to the regions for more particularised policy making.

Admittedly, this Concertation Committee is only an official way to deal with such problems and is, in fact, rarely pursued. In practice, the prevention of conflicts rests with the presidents of the governing parties, who meet regularly with the Prime Minister. The role of the governing parties is crucial. They have to play the role of 'prudent leaders'. They know that if they push the ethno-linguistic demands too far, the system as a whole will cease to function. So far the political parties have tried to keep the burden bearable by forming the same type of coalitions at all levels. That means, for instance, that if the federal government is composed of the two Socialist and the two Christian Democratic parties, the regional governments of Flanders and Wallonia will be governed by the same coalition of Socialists and Christian Democrats (Deschouwer 2004). This permanent cooperation of the governing parties is the cornerstone of the Belgian consociational federation.

Nevertheless, the stability of the system is always under threat. Both language groups continue to operate with a different view on the future of Belgium. Disagreements remain on the importance of regions versus communities, on the degree of autonomy to be given to them, on fiscal and financial solidarity mechanisms, on the use of language in Brussels and along the linguistic borderline. In order to keep the system going, the governing parties typically try to deal with such issues by avoiding them. Yet such issues cannot be avoided, despite frequent attempts to 'bank' them until some more opportune time.

The basic logic of Belgium's state institutions, therefore, is that of the mutual veto. It is consensus or gridlock. Both language groups either agree to move together, or do not move at all. The difficulty, however, is that, on the one hand, this logic keeps Belgium alive as a political project, while on the other, the Belgian state institutions are the source of deep frustration and dissatisfaction. In the following sections, a number of these recurring tensions will be discussed.

REMAINING AND RECURRING TENSIONS IN THE BELGIAN FEDERATION

The evolution of a Belgian federation, therefore, is partly the product of political stagnation at the central state level, and partly the product of constant attempts to manage the conflict between the two major language groups by devolving power as a means of pacification. This gradual transformation of the state allows us to identify a number of weak points. More specifically, it allows us to identify aspects of the federal system where the logic of ongoing devolution has done little to reduce inter-communal antagonism, but, in actual fact, has arguably served only to heighten intransigence and conflict. These weak points can be organised and analysed under four headings: the problem of financial transfers between the regional entities; the bipolar logic; the use of language in Brussels and its periphery; and the absence of federal political parties who appeal to a voter base across the linguistic and territorial divisions of society.

The financial transfers

The striking differences in economic performance between the north and the south of Belgium are noteworthy. The two regions have had very different historical experiences and today have very different economic structures. In short, the northern region of Flanders has a growing economy with a very low degree of unemployment, while the southern region of Wallonia is struggling with the legacy of a collapse in its traditional heavy industry and a relatively high level of unemployment. Wallonia needs the support, therefore, of the federal state and is somewhat financially dependent on the north (Verdonck and Deschouwer 2003).

Yet in Flanders, this situation – and especially the obligation to support the south – is resented. After struggling for the recognition of linguistic and cultural rights, Flanders now sees itself as hindered by the lack of economic dynamism in a Socialist-dominated Walloon region (Keating, Loughlin and Deschouwer 2003; Van Dam 1997). In the spring of 1999, the Flemish regional parliament voted a series of recommendations for a further reform of the state, in which demands for more financial and fiscal autonomy were very prominent, as were demands for more autonomy in employment policy and devolution of the social security system. Some fiscal and financial autonomy was granted to the regions in 2002, but Flanders would like more. Indeed, the right-wing populist party Vlaams Blok (now Flemish Interest) – polling 24 per cent at the regional elections of 2004 – even wants full independence for Flanders (including Brussels).

For the Francophone community and the Walloon region, these demands are unacceptable. Even if the Flemish regional parliament defends its demands by referring to a better and more logical organisation and distribution of competencies, that reasoning is perceived by the Francophones as a clear and deliberate attempt to reduce or even to break the financial solidarity between north and south and thus is viewed as a direct attack on the viability of the Walloon region. The Francophones' response to any proposal to change the current rules is a clear and loud 'no'. And this only serves to add to the frustration of the Flemings, who interpret the refusal for further devolution as a choice in favour of an easy solution for the Walloon region to continue living at the expense of Flanders' economic prosperity.

The bipolar logic

The tensions that develop between richer and poorer regions within a federation are not, of course, in any sense unique to Belgium. They are typical of federal regimes in general. Yet in Belgium, this type of conflict occurs in a bipolar ethno-linguistic federation, and that makes the situation much more difficult to manage. The recurring problem is that while Flanders clearly wants to proceed further along the road of devolution, the Francophones and Walloon region do not have any concrete proposals, other than to keep the current federal system intact.

There are a number of explanatory variables as to why the Flemish community continues to demand a greater amount of autonomy. The initial drive to reform the Belgian unitary state came from the north. Today, there is a stronger feeling of regional-linguistic identity in Flanders than in Wallonia (De Winter 1998). Significantly, this sense of Dutch linguistic and territorial solidarity has been reinforced by the new political institutions. Although Belgium's institutions are fairly complex, they are rather straightforward on the Flemish side: there is one parliament and one government working and speaking on behalf of Flanders as a regional entity. The Flemish region and the Flemish Community have been fused into one single institutional framework, including the regional competencies for Flanders and the community competences for the Dutch-speaking population in both Flanders and the greater metropolitan area of Brussels. By contrast, the institutional counterpart in Wallonia is much more divided along functional and territorial lines. Francophones have a community parliament and government (for the Francophone community of Wallonia and Brussels); a parliament and government for the regional entity of Wallonia; and their own separate institutions for government in the greater metropolitan area of Brussels. In sum, while the Francophones function in a complex and heterogeneous institutional environment, the Flemish environment is much more homogeneous. It is this distinction that partly explains the demands made by the Flemish for an increase in devolved competencies, especially with respect to fiscal and financial matters (Van Dam 1997).

The use of language: Brussels and its periphery

One perennial source of conflict concerns the use of language. The two major linguistic communities now officially have an equal status. Yet in practice French, as a result of historical developments, dominates. Moreover, Flemings often understand and can speak French, while the Francophones are more often unilingual. Official rules on the use of language that have been put into place to protect the minority (or lower status) Dutch language are therefore often at odds with public life. As a consequence, at least two points follow.

First, Brussels is the capital city and the capital region and therefore has a bilingual status. That means that all public services have to be offered in both languages. Yet today the Dutch-speaking population of Brussels (of Belgian nationality) amounts to only some 15 per cent of the votes (for instance, at the regional elections of 2004 there were 13.6 per cent votes for the Dutch-speaking parties). In some local municipalities it is even less. Accommodating this minority is quite a burden for many Francophones. The language laws of 1963 seem, therefore, to be constantly on the agenda.

The same goes for the municipalities in the periphery of Brussels (that is, in the region of Flanders) where Dutch is the official administrative language. In 1963, language 'facilities' were granted to the inhabitants of six local municipalities conjoining Brussels that would simply have been added to Brussels at that time if the old principle of the language census had continued to be followed. It meant that more than 30 per cent of the inhabitants were Francophones. Today, Francophones are a majority in all six municipalities, but officially they have to administer them in Dutch.

There are still very different views and interpretations of the meaning and extent of these language facilities. Among the Flemish, the language facilities are seen as a temporary exception to the principle of territoriality, a means of accommodating the linguistic minorities until they learn the language of the region sufficiently to be able to communicate with the public authorities. Because the use of language is constitutionally free, the language laws regulate only the languages used by the public authorities. There is no limit on the use of any language in any other sphere of life. Although the facilities have been entrenched in the Constitution (needing a double majority to be changed), Flanders regularly demands their removal because they are an exception to the general rule. The Flemish argue that the relation between the language groups has been settled by the federal organisation of the Belgian state, that is, by the protective devices built into the federal institutions. Indeed, within the existing system, the Francophone minority is protected at the federal level, and Dutch-speaking minorities are protected in Brussels.

Among the Francophones, opinion on the language facilities is fundamentally different. They regard the French speakers in Flanders as a minority in need of the same formal protection that the very small Dutch-speaking minority in Brussels has received. They vehemently reject the idea that the facilities should be seen as a transitional measure. On the contrary, they see the facilities as protecting fundamental rights that should not be limited to the minority groups that received them prior to 1963 on the basis of the last linguistic census. Belgium's Francophones refer to international law – particularly the Council of Europe's Framework Convention for the Protection of National Minorities – in demanding better protection in general for the Francophones in Flanders. They define the French speakers of Flanders as a minority that deserves due cultural protection, whereas the Dutch speakers argue that linguistic rights should be based on a clear link between territory and the use of language (Clement 2002). The Dutch speakers, therefore, do not agree that explicit linguistic or cultural rights should be given to minority groups living in the Dutch-speaking part of the country.

Somewhat ironically, the German-speaking minority does not take part in these discussions. Indeed, the Belgian conflict is one between the two larger language groups. The German-speaking minority is very small (0.6 per cent of the population) and has received extensive rights: the status of a community with all the powers given to the other language communities, a directly elected community parliament and an autonomous government. For regional matters, the German-speaking community belongs to the Walloon region, but for all matters related to language (especially education and culture) it can make its own decisions and implement them.

The absence of federal parties

Belgium no longer has any federal political parties who appeal to a voter base across the linguistic and territorial divisions of society. Instead, all of the political parties are fundamentally ethno-linguistic. For, as we have seen, federalism has encouraged political parties in Belgium to mobilise in only one of the two language communities within the regional entities. And yet, the same parties are expected to form a coalition at the central state level, advancing the interests of an almost mythical Belgian society. Clearly, this is a very difficult dilemma to manage. The two levels of decision making are very different, and advance very different political imperatives and demands.

Governing at the regional level – within Flanders and Wallonia – is much easier. There is no language cleavage to deal with, and the governments can be more focused and responsive. By contrast, the federal government in Brussels cannot be anywhere near as responsive because there are no real Belgian elections and there is no Belgian party-political system; moreover, it cannot avoid differences between the two language groups, because the two are equally represented in the government. Thus far the parties have tried to contain this kind of tension by keeping the coalitions at all levels congruent, that is, the same parties – Christian Democrats or Socialists – are either in government or in opposition at both levels. However, the perverse effect of this attempt to manage within the regional parties the problematic effect of the absence of federal parties is that the political autonomy of the regional parties is reduced. Regional parties in each region must form a government that is compatible with the federal government. For this reason, they cannot be responsive to the electorate: regional elections are organised and conducted, but the formation of regional coalitions must take into account the result in the other region.

CONCLUSION

There are two Belgian stories to be told. The first is the story of a divided country that has been able – by making use of institutional craftsmanship – to pacify the tensions and antagonism that existed between ethno-linguistic subgroups. There have been conflicts, but never any significant violence. The Belgian institutions are full of guarantees and mutual vetoes, avoiding the use of blunt, simple-majority rule. Granting autonomy to the language groups and building a consociational federal state has been the institutional solution to the tensions occurring when two language groups, with different ideological orientations, have to be kept together in one single political system. This is the success story of Belgium.

There is however another story. Although the institutions put in place do function, there have been some high prices paid. The institutions are extremely complex and are not fully understood by the population at large. Crucial notions like language rights and minority rights remain a matter of deeply-diverging definitions between the two language groups. The granting of autonomy to the language groups, and the duplication of the party-political system into two separate unilingual blocks has increased and deepened the differences between both communities and regional entities. There is no longer any real political centre within the state and there is no sense of Belgian national solidarity and public opinion. Holding political parties accountable to only one half of the state has lead to a dichotomy, whereby the interests voiced by those in positions of power are essentially contradictory. The parties cannot be responsive to their electorate and the system therefore lacks legitimacy.

REFERENCES

Alen, A. and Ergec, R. (1998) *La Belgique fédérale après la quatrième réforme de l'Etat de 1993*. Brussels: Department of Foreign Affairs, Trade and International Development.

Clement, J. (2002) *Bestuurstaal, Faciliteiten en de Resolutie-Nabholz van de Raad van Europa. Geen taal, Geen Vrijheid*. Brussels: Koninklijke Vlaamse Academie voor Kunsten en Wetenschappen.

Deschouwer, K. (2002) 'Falling Apart Together: The Changing Nature of Belgian Consociationalism, 1961–2000', in J. Steiner and T. Ertman (eds), *Consociationalism and Corporatism in Western Europe: Still the Politics of Accommodation?* Special issue of *Acta Politica*, 37 Spring/Summer, 68–85.

—— (2004) 'Political Parties and Their Reactions to the Erosion of Voter Loyalty in Belgium: Caught in a Trap', in P. Mair, W. Müller and F. Plasser (eds), *Political Parties and Electoral Change*. London: Sage, pp. 179–206.

De Winter, L. (1998) 'Etnoterritoriale Identiteiten in Vlaanderen: Verkenningen in Een Politiek en Methodologisch Mijnenveld', in M. Swyngedouw, J. Billiet, A. Carton and R. Beerten (eds), *De (in)redelijke kiezer. Onderzoek Naar de Politieke Opvattingen van Vlamingen. Verkiezingen van 21 mei 1995*. Leuven: Acco, pp. 159–80.

Frognier, A.-P. (1988) 'Belgium', in J. Blondel and F. Müller-Rommel (eds), *Cabinets in Western Europe?* Houndmills: Palgrave Macmillan, pp. 68–85.

Huyse, L. (1971) *Pacificatie, Passiviteit en Verzuiling in de Belgische Politiek*. Antwerpen: Standaard Wetenschappelijke Uitgeverij.

Jans, M.T. and Tombeur, H. (2000) 'Living Apart Together: The Belgian Intergovernmental Cooperation in the Domains of Environment and Economy', in D. Braun (ed.), *Public Policy and Federalism*. Aldershot: Ashgate, pp. 142–76.

Keating, M., Loughlin, J. and Deschouwer, K. (2003) *Culture, Institutions and Economic Development: A Study of Eight European Regions*. London: Edward Elgar.

Lijphart, A. (1969) 'Consociational Democracy', *World Politics*, 21 (2), pp. 207–25.

—— (ed.) (1981) *Conflict and Coexistence in Belgium: The Dynamics of a Culturally Divided Society*. Berkeley, CA: University of California Press.

Lorwin, V. R. (1966) 'Belgium: Religion, Class, and Language in National Politics', in R. D. Dahl (ed.), *Political Oppositions in Western Democracies*. New Haven, CT: Yale University Press, pp. 147–87.

McRae, K. (1986) *Conflict and Compromise in Multilingual Societies: Belgium*. Ontario: Wilfrid Laurier Press.

Murphy, A. B. (1998) *The Regional Dynamics of Language Differentiation in Belgium: A Study in Cultural-Political Geography*. Chicago, IL: University of Chicago Press.

Poirier, J. (2002) 'Formal Mechanisms of Intergovernmental Relations in Belgium', *Regional and Federal Studies*, 12 (3), 24–54.

Van Dam, D. (1997), *Flandre, Wallonie, le Rêve Brisé, Quelles Identités Culturelles et Politiques en Flandre et en Wallonie?* Ottignies: Quorum.

Verdonck, M. and Deschouwer, K. (2003) 'Patterns and Principles of Fiscal and Financial Federalism in Belgium', *Regional and Federal* Studies, 13 (4), 91–110.

Zolberg, A. (1974) 'The Making of Flemings and Walloons: Belgium 1830–1914', *The Journal of Interdisciplinary History*, 5 (2), 179–236.

7

Partial Implementation, Partial Success: The Case of Macedonia

Florian Bieber[1]

Upon independence in 1992, Macedonia was confronted by multiple challenges to its legitimacy. Internationally, it was challenged by Greece and Serbia. Domestically, the 1991 constitution defined Macedonia as the nation-state of Macedonians, thereby effectively marginalising the large Albanian minority community along with other smaller communities, including Turks, Roma, Serbs and Muslims. Since that time, the Albanian political parties, some of whom have participated in government since the first free elections in 1990, have argued for greater rights for the Albanian population, in particular in the educational sector and in terms of representation in the public administration, especially in the police force. However, these grievances were not alleviated and, divided by language, religion and a strong sense of national identity, communication across the two communities remained minimal.

The low-scale insurgency of the Albanian National Liberation Army (NLA) in the spring and summer of 2001 initially sought some degree of self-determination for the Albanian-dominated territories, and was later primarily aimed at addressing the grievances which mainstream Albanian parties had been unable to alleviate in the 1990s. Although the conflict was the least horrific of the wars in former Yugoslavia, at least in terms of the number of victims, it left the country deeply scarred and further soured inter-ethnic relations between Macedonians and Albanians (Ethnobarometer 2001). In part, the conflict came to an early end due to concerted international efforts, resulting in the Framework Agreement, signed in Ohrid on 13 August 2001, which sets out a substantial agenda for constitutional and legislative reform of the state and the disbandment of the NLA under international supervision. Both the normalisation of the security situation and the implementation of the legislative reforms (discussed in detail below) have been slow due to low levels of cross-communal trust.

The main goal of the Ohrid Agreement has been to accommodate the grievances of the Albanian community, while at the same time addressing the concerns of the Macedonian majority who fear a 'federalisation' of the country and its eventual disintegration. The Agreement introduces some features of power sharing, such as a system of double majorities requiring consent from minorities represented in parliament to key decisions of the *Sobranie* (parliament); a substantial degree of municipal decentralisation; proportional representation in public administration; as well as confidence-building measures to overcome the immediate consequences of the 2001 conflict. However, although the Agreement does go some way towards enhancing the participation of the Albanian community in the state, it neglects three crucial issues: first, the Agreement often enhances the rights of the Albanian community while neglecting the interests of the smaller minorities; secondly, the lack of cross-ethnic communication, much worsened as a result of the conflict, remains unaddressed; finally, the Agreement and the power-sharing institutions it set up underplay conflicts *within* the communities, especially with respect to both the potential for extremist out-bidding and the difficulties of advancing cross-community cooperation.

Accordingly, this chapter argues that the Ohrid Agreement has been only partly successful in addressing the root causes of the conflict. At the same time, however, the chapter also argues that some of the difficulties confronting Macedonia since 2001, such as increasing segregation between Albanians and Macedonians, have been less the result of the Ohrid Agreement and more a consequence of earlier antagonisms and the distrust resulting from the 2001 conflict.

TRANSITION FROM INFORMAL TO FORMAL POWER SHARING

The Framework Agreement, signed by the main Albanian and Macedonian parties under the auspices of international mediators from the EU and the USA, set out an ambitious process of legislative reform combined with security measures designed to end the uprising of the NLA. The Agreement outlined a series of constitutional amendments, passed in late 2001 and early 2002, by the Macedonian parliament. It granted languages spoken by more than 20 per cent of the population (which include Albanian) official status; introduced a system of double majorities (a majority of all deputies, as well as of the Macedonian community and of all minority communities jointly) for key areas of legislation; established equitable representation in public administration at the national and local level; instituted a programme of decentralisation; and cleared the way for a multiethnic, representative police force. The Agreement also provided for the organisation of a new census, subject to international supervision. The aim of this was to end disputes over the actual size of the Albanian population resident in Macedonia and, on this basis, to facilitate the introduction of proportional representation in significant areas of public life (Framework Agreement 2001).

While the Ohrid Agreement aims to protect the members of the different communities that live in Macedonia, it has largely avoided institutionalising ethnicity as deeply as some other peace agreements in the former Yugoslavia, such as the Dayton Peace Accords in Bosnia and Herzegovina (Bieber 2004). It did not introduce strict representative quotas for communities in the government or parliament, or establish substantial territorial self-government, and hence has allowed greater room in Macedonia for non-institutionalised, but nonetheless cooperative, politics. However, like so many other peace processes, the implementation of certain aspects of the Ohrid Agreement was delayed, such as the holding of post-Agreement elections and the census.

In shying away from explicitly referring to specific ethnic groups, the Ohrid Agreement reforms seek to enhance the civic nature of the state. At the same time, the Agreement institutes key elements of power sharing and elevates the status of Albanians as a community by affording them rights comparable to those of the Macedonian majority. Admittedly, the Agreement does not provide the same degree of protection for the smaller communities. But as an Agreement specifically concluded between Macedonian and Albanian parties against the backdrop of the NLA insurgency in 2001, it is perhaps understandable that it gave greater weight to enhancing the participation of the Albanian community. Read positively, the Ohrid Agreement can thus be seen to address the legitimate grievances of the Albanian population while at the same time facilitating the transformation of Macedonia into a bi-national state. Read negatively, however, this move towards bi-nationalism often neglects smaller communities and has at times actually served to harden the main ethnic division between the Macedonian majority community and the large Albanian minority community (Daskalovski 2002; Engström 2003, pp. 335–48).

The chapter will now turn to an examination of key aspects of power sharing in Macedonia – the electoral system, the voting mechanism in parliament, coalition government, public administration, and decentralisation – in order to evaluate the equivocal successes established under the Ohrid Agreement.

ELECTORAL DYNAMICS

As indicated above, Macedonia has not adopted group-specific rules in its electoral legislation to include (or exclude) minorities from parliament. Yet despite the absence of minority-related electoral provisions, inter-ethnic tensions between Macedonians and Albanians have nevertheless had a profound impact on the evolution of the electoral system. Between 1990 and 2002, the electoral system underwent a gradual transition from a majoritarian to a proportional system with a 5 per cent threshold. However, while Albanians have been represented in all parliaments, their numbers have been generally lower than their population share due to gerrymandering and the unequal distribution of single-member constituencies (ICG 1998, p. 6).

The system for parliamentary elections was amended as part of the general overhaul of the political system initiated in the Ohrid Agreement, although electoral reform was not specifically mentioned in the Agreement (Friedman 2004). In the debate over electoral reform in early 2002, Albanian parties supported the creation of a single countrywide constituency and strict proportional representation, which was thought to enhance the number of Albanian deputies; by contrast, Macedonian parties favoured smaller constituencies and the maintenance of some seats elected according to the first-past-the-post system. Finally, the electoral law was amended to introduce proportional representation in six electoral districts. Further discussions focused on the language of the ballot and the composition of the electoral commission, discussions in which ethnicity did not constitute the only line of division, as opposition parties – both Macedonian and Albanian – feared undue government influence on the elections (Constitutional Watch: Macedonia 2002b, pp. 33–4).

The benefits of the new electoral system were identified by the OSCE Office for Democratic Institutions and Human Rights (ODIHR) as consisting in the cutting of costs by restricting parliamentary elections to a single round and in reducing the danger of inter-ethnic tensions by having larger electoral districts. In addition, PR was considered to ensure better representation of smaller minorities than the majoritarian system in use during the first democratic elections (OSCE/ODIHR 2002, p. 4). The reform also eliminated some of the disadvantages to Albanian parties implicit in the previous electoral system, such as the larger size of Albanian single-member districts.

The reform did not, however, address the concern of smaller minorities over entry into parliament: since 1990, only a few members from non-Albanian minorities have won seats. Roma have been represented in every legislative period, but only by one deputy per period. Other minorities have been represented even less. This is largely a consequence of the relatively small size of the individual minorities and the nature of the electoral system. Both the majoritarian system and the proportional system with a 5 per cent threshold constituted an insurmountable hurdle for the representation of virtually all smaller minorities, since these minorities either number less than 5 per cent of the population of eligible voters, or are not sufficiently geographically concentrated to directly elect deputies to parliament. As a result, smaller minorities, such as Roma and Turks, remain dependent on pre-election coalition pacts with the two larger Macedonian parties.

In addition to the marginalisation of smaller communities in parliament, a second feature of the electoral system unaddressed by the Ohrid Agreement has been intra-communal outflanking, in particular among the Albanian parties. The Party for Democratic Prosperity (PDP) – the longstanding coalition partner of the largest Macedonian party, the Social Democratic Union of Macedonia (SDUM) – was beaten in 1998 by the more 'nationalist' Democratic Party of Albanians (DPA), which in turn was defeated by the Democratic Union for Integration (DUI), the party which emerged from the National Liberation Army in 2002. Similar outflanking has been attempted by the Macedonian opposition party with varying degrees of success.

While voting in Macedonia's parliamentary elections mostly follows ethnic lines, voting in presidential elections has involved substantial cross-ethnic voting, both prior to and after the Ohrid Agreement. While Albanian candidates have stood no chance of winning the presidential race, the two-round system has resulted in two cases (1999 and 2004) in which the Macedonian parties had to rely on their respective Albanian coalition parties to secure the necessary support among the Albanian population to win the elections (Mehmeti 1999; *Dnevnik* 2004). This trend has strengthened the reliance of the Macedonian parties on their Albanian coalition parties, thus reinforcing the coalitions. Once again, however, there are significant negatives. The support generated by the Albanian coalition partners has been somewhat undermined insofar as it has depended on serious voting irregularities such as ballot stuffing, proxy voting and intimidation among Albanian voters (OSCE/ODIHR 2004, p. 7). In short, voting in presidential elections has encouraged voting irregularities, not moderation.

As the Ohrid Agreement was only partly implemented prior to the 2002 elections, no conclusion can be drawn on whether the reform process initiated in Ohrid will reduce intra-communal out-bidding. However, elections are crucial for understanding the way in which power sharing works or does not work in Macedonia, even if not directly connected to the Ohrid Agreement per se. Thus, despite the success of DUI in its efforts to further implement the Ohrid Agreement since 2002, the party has been criticised by the opposition DPA, which has abandoned support for the Ohrid Agreement and at times argues for a separation of the Albanian-inhabited areas. As the Agreement does not change either the mechanisms of government formation or the electoral process, the long-term impact of the Ohrid Agreement in terms of positively redressing nationalist out-bidding is likely to be limited.

LEGISLATIVE VETO RIGHTS

Whereas the electoral system has remained largely unaffected by the Ohrid Agreement, the introduction of greater consensus requirements constitutes one of the core innovations of the Agreement. And yet, the system of a double majority, while formally extended to all minority communities, appears to allow only the Albanian minority to block legislation, while smaller communities remain marginalised.

The constitutional amendments prescribed in the Ohrid Agreement and passed by the *Sobranie* in November 2001 stipulate that consent of a majority of the deputies representing all non-dominant groups is required in a number of areas of legislation (culture, use of languages, education, personal IDs, use of symbols) (Amandman X 2001) and local self-government (Amandman XVI 2001). In all other areas of legislation, minority support is not required to pass laws. This system constitutes a compromise between the original demand of the Albanian parties for a fully-fledged veto right and its rejection by the Macedonian parties (Daftary 2001, pp. 300–1). The advantage of such a relatively delimited veto system is that it can limit the danger of blockage or immobilism with respect to certain areas of legislation. Nevertheless, it contains the inherent danger that other decisions, which might have a profound impact on minorities, such as decisions in economic policy, cannot be influenced by minority communities through the double-majority rule because these do not require a double majority.

In order to further prevent blockage of the legislative process, the largely ineffectual Committee for Inter-Community Relations was reformed to include seven Macedonians and seven Albanians, and one representative from all other communities represented in the Macedonian parliament (or, if not represented in parliament to be nominated by the Ombudsman). In theory, this body is charged with deliberating on inter-ethnic issues and, more specifically, with resolving any disputes arising from the double-majority system. In practice, however, the reformed committee has to date been of only marginal significance, as evidenced by the fact that it was not established until September 2003 and met only six times between its formation and May 2004; in real terms, this was a small number of meetings, considering that the key issue of decentralisation and local self-government reform was at the top of the parliamentary agenda during this period. Instead, the key mediating body has been the government, both before the elections of 2002 and since (Arifi 2003). As it includes the SDUM (the largest Macedonian party) and the DUI (the largest Albanian party), any government proposal is likely to already have sufficient support in parliament.

One of the key critiques of both the double-majority rule and the Committee has been the reinforcement of the bi-national nature of the state, highlighted above. The double-majority system at first appears to restrain the bipolarity of the political system by requiring a majority of all minority communities rather than only the Albanian minority. But bearing in mind that the representation of non-Albanian minorities in the *Sobranie* has fluctuated between one and four MPs, their influence is rather marginal. Admittedly, due to their small size and limited parliamentary representation, the extension of the double-majority requirement to minorities separately, as opposed to collectively, has not been feasible. Nevertheless, this has created further asymmetry between the Albanian minority and all other minorities. Little attention has been paid to ameliorating the political inclusion of these communities, a problem that is exacerbated by virtue of the fact that in the Committee only Albanians receive equal representation with Macedonians, while all others remain represented by only one deputy.

EXECUTIVE POWER SHARING

Macedonia has been governed by broad coalitions – including Macedonian and Albanian parties, as well as occasionally parties of other smaller minorities – since the first free elections in 1991. This system of government formation, although not a constitutional requirement but a tradition which has developed since the end of one-party rule, has not been directly affected by the Ohrid Agreement.

In the first democratically elected government constituted in 1991 – comprising 23 ministerial posts – the main Albanian party at the time, the PDP, held the posts of deputy prime minister, the labour ministry and a minister without portfolio. Subsequent governments under the leadership of the SDUM (1992–98) had between four and six Albanian ministers, holding portfolios such as economy, labour, development, culture and transport and finance. During this period, however, Albanian ministers never controlled what were considered the more sensitive portfolios, such as security and internal affairs.

After the transference of power in 1998 to the coalition of the Internal Macedonian Revolutionary Organisation (IMRO) and the Albanian DPA, the pattern of Macedonian-Albanian coalitions was continued with five Albanian ministers (Chiclet and Lory 1998, pp. 157–9). However, the Albanian coalition partner held less important ministerial posts than had its equivalents in the last governments of the SDUM. The share of ministries held by Albanian ministers and their significance increased sharply with the formation of the current SDUM and DUI coalition in 2002. In the 18-member government, the junior partner in the coalition presently holds five ministerial portfolios, including health, justice, communication and education. While in contemporary Macedonia these ministries are less sensitive than defence or internal affairs, they yield considerable financial resources and carry weight in areas important to the Albanian community. In addition to ministerial portfolios, the practice has been that deputy ministers would be drawn from a different ethnic community to that of the nominated minister. Such an allocation symbolically emphasises the participation of the respective Albanian coalition partner in all aspects of government; in reality, however, it has often had no influence on the work of the respective ministries. The deputy ministers have generally been denied both basic information and access to the decision-making process (ICG 2003, p. 28).

As with the electoral system, however, a striking feature of this system of coalition governments encompassing minorities and majorities has been the regular outflanking by Albanian opposition parties. In Macedonia during the 1990s the defeat of Albanian government-coalition parties has been closely linked to their inability either to secure the broader inclusion of the Albanian community in the state or to in other ways substantially improve the community's economic or social status. Once again, the impact of the Ohrid Agreement on this aspect of power sharing has been both limited and equivocal.

The Ohrid Agreement does not offer any specificities on the inclusion of Albanians in government. At the same time, the way in which the state has been reconstructed since 2001 suggests that the Albanian community has been elevated to a status that makes them quasi-constituent – some have even described Macedonia as a 'bi-national' state – which suggests a reinforcement of the governmental participation of Albanian parties. In addition, the (limited) post-Ohrid governmental practice suggests that the share of the Albanian parties in power has increased to reflect the community's share of the population as a whole and is gradually extending to more sensitive ministries than it did in the period prior to the conflict. Unlike in Bosnia and Herzegovina or other divided societies where power sharing between the dominant communities is constitutionally prescribed, the informal nature of the Macedonian power-sharing executive allows for greater flexibility in terms of numbers of ministerial positions and specific portfolios (ICG 2003, p. 28). At the same time, however, the informal nature of the arrangement carries the risk of inadequately protecting against parties willing to break with this tradition. Furthermore, the informality has also meant that smaller communities are not officially included and thus may only incidentally be involved in the executive.

PUBLIC ADMINISTRATION

A key concern specifically addressed in the Ohrid Agreement has been the under-representation of Albanians in public administration (and in state-run enterprises). In sensitive areas of public administration in particular, such as the police, the number of Albanians remained low throughout the 1990s. The reform of public administration was thus deemed crucial in order to enhance a sense of joint-ownership of the state for the Albanian community. The reform has, however, been burdened with difficulties.

Prior to the Agreement, Albanians filled only some 7 per cent of positions in the public, mixed and cooperative employment sector. Similarly, most other minorities, in particular Turks and Roma, have also been under-represented in this sector. In contrast, Albanians and other communities have played a disproportionate role in private businesses, partly in response to low employment rates in the public sectors (HCHRRM 1999). The causes of this phenomenon have been manifold and cannot be reduced to discrimination alone. However, a number of confrontations between members of the Albanian community and the authorities – linked to the establishment of the unrecognised University of Tetovo and the hoisting of Albanian flags over town halls in Gostivar and Tetovo in the mid 1990s, as well as to a pattern of police harassment and administrative neglect – had alienated many in the Albanian community from the state. The 'ownership' of the state and its administration by the majority Macedonian community made employment in public administration unattractive to Albanians, who feared being ostracised by their community. As a consequence, Albanians primarily sought employment in the private sector.

A key aspect of the Ohrid Agreement, therefore, has been the requirement 'to ensure equitable representation of communities' (Annex B, Art. 5). A particular focus was on recruiting Albanians and members of other minority communities into the police force with the goal of ensuring that it 'generally reflect the composition and distribution of the population of Macedonia' by 2004 (Annex C, Art. 5.2). An international programme carried out by the United States Ministry of Justice and subsequently by the OSCE trained over 1,000 new police officers from minority communities, substantially increasing the Albanian and other communities' share in the police force (OSCE/ODIHR 2002). However, this massive effort has highlighted some of the difficulties associated with aggressive affirmative-action programmes. The rapid training of new police officers has, according to observers, resulted in a multiethnic police force that lacks the skills to carry out its task effectively (ICG 2003, pp. 4–5). While it has been noted that the building of a multiethnic police force has increased trust by minority citizens in the policing, survey data from early 2003 suggest substantial deficiencies. For example, while 81.2 per cent of Macedonians view the police as a protector, only 25.9 per cent of Albanians view them in the same way (UNDP/Kapital 2003, p. 34).

Considering the low starting point – there were around 2.5 per cent of Albanians in the Ministry of Interior in 2001 – an increase by mid 2003 to 10–11 per cent could be considered a substantial success (Ristovski 2003). Since 2001 the recruitment of Albanians has extended beyond the requirements stipulated in the Ohrid Agreement. For example, the army was excluded from equitable representation requirements, but has nonetheless begun to include Albanians to a greater degree. By 2004 the share of Albanians among the officers of the army reached 5 per cent, with the government's stated aim being to establish a proportional representation by 2007 (*Koha Ditore* 2004).

That said, a key official of the ruling SDUM identified the reform of public administration as one of the most difficult aspects of the Ohrid Agreement since it requires satisfying the IMF conditions for governmental spending on public administration, the minority communities' expectations for employment, as well as the Macedonian workers who will lose their positions in the course of the reform (Ivanovski 2003). Furthermore, efforts at establishing equitable representation (together with the decentralisation discussed below) have been estimated to be the most costly aspect of the Ohrid reforms (Report on the Costing 2002, pp. 14–16). Moreover, the equitable representation project has remained much in dispute with Albanian opposition parties who argue that the increase has been insufficient and has not satisfactorily addressed the exclusion of Albanians from decision-making processes, especially in the security forces (PER 2004, pp. 14–15).

While equitable representation is a key reform mandated by Ohrid, the goals and means of accomplishing this policy are rarely examined separately. Prior to the reforms, public administration in Macedonia was both (a) unrepresentative of and (b) unresponsive to minorities. The policy of equitable representation was adopted to accommodate both aspects, which meant that the goal has been not just countrywide equitable representation, since at the municipal level it was also meant to ensure that citizens from minority communities are able to interact with civil servants from their own community. However, the policy of equitable representation has placed little emphasis on the interaction *between* the majority and minorities and assumes that the equitable representation of one community equals equitable representation *within* the community.

TERRITORIAL SELF-GOVERNMENT

Perhaps the most ambivalent aspect of the Ohrid Agreement has been the reform of municipal self-government. This reform seeks to offer limited autonomy to Albanians, compatible with many other power-sharing systems. At the same time, it shies away from allowing for full or formal autonomy and in fact replicates some of the state power-sharing mechanisms at the local level. While the Agreement itself emphatically declares that '[t]here are no territorial solutions to ethnic issues' (Art. 1.2.), it foresees substantial local-government reform. This reform has been largely de-ethnicised and framed to conform to European standards (and especially to the principle of 'subsidiarity') rather than facilitating fully-fledged self-government for the Albanian community (Art. 3.1.). Indeed, the law on self-government reverses the centralist tendencies of local government reforms in the 1990s (Todorovski 2000, pp. 246–7).

In addition to the municipalities' participation in the appointment of local police chiefs, their ability to cooperate and establish joint public agencies and shared administrative bodies can be considered a crucial aspect of the Ohrid reforms. These aspects of the reform allow for municipalities with an Albanian majority to constitute a form of community self-government (albeit one that falls short of the ability to pass legislation). During the Ohrid negotiations, the Albanian parties had advocated the right of municipalities to merge in order to allow for the creation of larger Albanian municipalities in Western Macedonia. Such a proposition was, however, rejected by Macedonian parties who saw local-government reform as a guise for the creation of Albanian territorial autonomy. In the final version of the Law on Local Self-Government, municipalities are allowed to cooperate and form joint bodies and institutions, but are not allowed to formally merge with adjacent municipalities as a means of increasing their overall power (Constitutional Watch: Macedonia 2002a, pp. 27–8).

At the same time, the law also institutes more generous power-sharing rules at the local level. While the 1994 Law on Local Self-Government stipulates the creation of a commission for inter-ethnic relations composed of the different communities along with proportional representation in appointments, little power sharing or cooperation took place in mixed municipalities. A notable exception was Kumanovo, which saw strong cooperation between the then mayor and the head of the commission for inter-ethnic relations in preventing the spread of the conflict to the city. This degree of cooperation was, however, more the result of personal ties than of institutional incentives for cooperation (Latifi 2003, pp. 120–5). The new law stipulates that decisions pertaining to the fundamental structure of the municipality and those affecting particular communities (such as culture, use of languages, coats of arms and flags) require a double majority of the majority community's councillors and those representing the smaller communities together (Zakon za lokalnata samouprava 2002). Such a mechanism not only secures the rights of smaller communities – if substantial in number in the municipality – but also allows members of the Macedonian majority – if in a minority in the municipality in question – to block certain decisions.

While falling short of substantial territorial autonomy, the local self-government reform does establish an opening for a weak form of territorial self-government for the Albanian community. In addition, the introduction of Albanian (or other minority languages) in municipalities where the community is larger than 20 per cent constitutes a form of enhanced minority inclusion. However, the introduction of minority languages has been hotly contested. The government proposal of July 2004, reorganising the country into 76 municipalities (from 123), wherein approximately 27 municipalities contain one or more minorities larger than 20 per cent, has been rejected by the Macedonian opposition parties and by a number of Macedonian NGOs (*Utrinski Vesnik* 2004). In particular, the creation of fewer, but larger, municipalities may, in certain areas, mean subsuming formerly Macedonian-dominated municipalities into ones which will now be Albanian-dominated. The resistance to the redrawing of municipal boundaries suggests that, as happens frequently with the drawing of territorial boundaries in multiethnic settings, this process is primarily perceived as one of negotiating the regional dominance of one community. Despite protective mechanisms for non-dominant communities, losses of numerical dominance under these proposals constitute a status-reversal hard to accept for many Macedonians. By contrast, in the absence of other types of autonomy, municipal reform has been viewed among many Albanians as a key means of ensuring self-government for the Albanian community.

CONCLUSION: CHALLENGES TO OHRID AND THE DANGERS OF SEGREGATION

While an overwhelming majority of Albanians support the Ohrid agreement, support among Macedonians has waned since 2001

(UNDP/Kapital 2003, p. 42; Jovanovski and Dulovi 2002, p. 67). This lack of popular support from the majority community had been expressed and instrumentalised by the governing IMRO–DPA coalition, in power until the general elections in September 2002, which sought to delay the implementation of some reforms as it continued to pursue an agenda of sectarian self-interest (Friedman 2003). In fact, a common critique of the Ohrid Agreement and its trajectory since 2001 has been the increasing segregation of society (see Zhelyazkova 2003, pp. 277–92). As a commentary for the Macedonian daily *Dnevnik* suggests:

> [p]eople are now [after Ohrid] convinced that it is safer for them to be part of the ethnic community that offers them greater opportunities, especially in areas where it makes up the majority population. If this is not possible, then they believe that it is wiser for them to sell their property and move somewhere where they may be better off. Unfortunately, that other place is currently somewhere beyond the borders of their fatherland. (Geroski 2003)

The informal nature of power-sharing institutions has given the Macedonian institutional framework a degree of flexibility absent in most other post-conflict power-sharing arrangements. This flexibility offers greater opportunities for reducing the significance of ethnic belonging in the political system and, perhaps in the long run, preventing the dominance of collective over individual identities. At the same time, the lack of institutionalisation of some aspects of power sharing has had a number of negative effects on politics in Macedonia. First, it fails to provide the same degree of security for both Macedonians and Albanians. Secondly, it provides insufficient protection for the smaller communities. Thirdly, the informal approach has at times linked government reform, such as decentralisation, with ethnic representation and power sharing. Such an approach was intended to help build cross-communal support for some aspects of the power-sharing system insofar as it could have been described as a general reform benefiting all communities. Yet rather than helping to depoliticise communal identity, government reforms have become increasingly 'ethnified'.

NOTE

1. I would like to thank Eben Friedman, Židas Daskalovski and the editors of this volume for their useful and constructive comments.

REFERENCES

Amandman X (2001) Art. 69, Ustav na Republika Makedonija, 16 November.

Amandman XVI (2001) Art. 114, Ustav na Republika Makedonija, 16 November.

Arifi, T. (2003) Vice-President of BDI, Interviewed by the author, 21 July.

Bieber, F. (2004) 'Power Sharing as Ethnic Representation in Post-Conflict Societies: The Cases of Bosnia, Macedonia and Kosovo', in A. Mungiu-Pippidi and I. Krastev (eds), *Nationalism after Communism. Lessons Learned.* Budapest: CEU Press, pp. 229–46.

Chiclet, C. and Lory, B. (eds) (1998) *La République de Macédoine.* Paris: L'Harmattan.

Constitutional Watch: Macedonia (2002a) *East European Constitutional Review,* 11 (1–2), 27–9.

—— (2002b) *East European Constitutional Review,* 11 (3), 32–5.

Daftary, F. (2001) 'Conflict Resolution in FYR Macedonia: Power-sharing or the "Civic Approach?"', *Helsinki Monitor,* 4, 291–312.

Daskalovski, Ž. (2002) 'Language and Identity: The Ohrid Framework Agreement and Liberal Notions of Citizenship and Nationality in Macedonia', *Journal on Ethnopolitics and Minority Issues in Europe,* 1. Available at: http://www.ecmi.de/jemie.

Dnevnik (2004) 'DUI mu donela 142.000 glasa na Crvenkovski', 30 April.

Engström, J. (2003) 'Multiethnicity or Binationalism? The Framework Agreement and the Future of the Macedonian State', *European Yearbook of Minority Issues* 2001/2, 1. The Hague/London/New York: Kluwer Law International, pp. 335–48.

Ethnobarometer (2001) *Crisis in Macedonia.* Available at: http://www.ethnobarometer.org.

Framework Agreement (13 August 2001) Available at: http://www.president.gov.mk/eng/info/dogovor.htm.

Friedman, E. (2003) 'The Spectre of Territorial Division and the Ohrid Agreement', *ECMI Brief,* 9. Available at: www.ecmi.de/doc/public_issue.html.

—— (2004) 'Party System, Electoral Systems, and Minority Representation in the Republic of Macedonia (1990–2002)', *European Yearbook on Minority Issues* 2003, 2. The Hague/London/New York: Kluwer Law International.

Geroski, B. (2003) 'Popis na etnički predrasudi i frustracii', *Dnevnik,* 6 December.

Helsinki Committee for Human Rights in the Republic of Macedonia (HCHRRM) (1999) Report on Minority Rights in the Republic of Macedonia, September.

International Crisis Group (ICG) (1998) *1998 Elections in Macedonia,* 9 October. Available at: http://www.crisisweb.org.

—— (ICG) (2003) *Macedonia: No Room for Complacency,* 23 October. Available at: http://www.crisisweb.org.

Ivanovski, I. (2003) International Secretary of the SDSM. Interviewed by the author, 21 July.

Jovanovski, V. and Dulovi, L. (2002) 'A New Battlefield: The Struggle to Ratify the Ohrid Agreement' in Institute for War and Peace Reporting (ed.), *Ohrid and Beyond: A Cross-Ethnic Investigation into the Macedonian Crisis*. London: IWPR, pp. 59–72.

Koha Ditore (2004) Macedonia Afternoon Press Review, 12 May.

Latifi, V. (2003) *Macedonian Unfinished Crisis: Challenges in the Process of Democratisation and Stabilisation*. Skopje: Konrad-Adenauer-Stiftung.

Mehmeti, I. (1999) 'Presidential Elections and Interethnic Relations', *AIM*, 2 December. Available at: www.aimpress.ch.

OSCE/ODIHR (2002) 'Former Yugoslav Republic of Macedonia, Parliamentary Elections 15 September 2002', *Final Report*, 20 November.

—— (2004) 'Former Yugoslav Republic of Macedonia, Presidential Elections – Second Round. 28 April 2004', Statement of Preliminary Findings and Conclusions. 29 April.

Project on Ethnic Relations (PER) (2004) 'Macedonia's Interethnic Coalition: The First Year, 13–14.12.2004, Mavrovo, Macedonia', Conference Report. Available at: http://www.per-usa.org/per.html.

Report on the Costing of the Implementation of the Framework Agreement (12 February 2002). Available at: http://www.seerecon.org/macedonia/documents/fa_implementation_cost.htm.

Ristovski, L. (2003) Head, Unit for Co-ordination of the Implementation of the Framework Agreement, Government of Macedonia. Interviewed by the author, 22 July.

Todorovski, I. (2000) 'Local Government in Macedonia', in E. Kandeva (ed.), *Stabilisation of Local Governments*. Budapest: LGI, pp. 241–88.

UNDP/Kapital (2003) *Early Warning Report*, 1. Available at http://ew.undp.sk/.

Utrinski Vesnik (2004) 'Skopje dvojazično, Struga so selata', 15 July.

Zakon za lokalnata samouprava (2002) Služben vesnik na RM, 5.

Zhelyazkova, A. (2003) 'Macedonia in April 2003. Diagnosis: "Cancer with Galloping Metastases"' in G. Bašić (ed.), *Democracy and Multiculturalism in South East Europe*. Belgrade: Centar za istraživanje etniciteta, pp. 377–92.

8

The Dichotomy of International Mediation and Leader Intransigence: The Case of Bosnia and Herzegovina

Marie-Joëlle Zahar

On 21 November 1995, Serb, Croat and Muslim leaders initialled a peace agreement at Wright-Patterson Air Force Base in Dayton, Ohio. *The General Framework Agreement for Peace*, commonly known as the Dayton Peace Agreement (DPA), was to form the basis for conflict resolution in Bosnia and Herzegovina. In keeping with recent wisdom among policy analysts, who identify the insecurity of warring communities as a serious threat to political stability (Posen 1993; Snyder and Jervis 1999; Walter 2002), the makers of the DPA sought to devise a number of reforms at the local, regional and state levels (Bieber 2004, pp. 5–8). To this effect, the DPA established a complex web of power-sharing institutions to underwrite the peace process.

The DPA, like many other agreements before it, was not the result of inclusive and open negotiations between the representatives of opposing communities. Indeed, of the three Bosnian warring factions, only one – the Bosniak community – was a full partner to the peace talks. Presidents Slobodan Milošević and Franjo Tudjman stood for the Bosnian Serbs and Bosnian Croats, respectively, although it is to be doubted whether these two men truthfully represented the interests of these communities. During the negotiations, participants played a game of 'chicken', in which the fear of failure and its consequences drove decisions. This was particularly so in the case of President Milošević, who had to contend with the threat of North Atlantic Treaty Organisation (NATO) air strikes and the weight of economic sanctions imposed by the international community.

Not only were two of the three concerned parties absent from the negotiating table but, moreover, ordinary people were not particularly supportive of the DPA when it was signed. At Dayton, participants of the talks were isolated from their constituencies. Had ordinary people been allowed to influence the decisions of their leaders, it is doubtful that the DPA would have been concluded. When the agreement was made public, the Bosniak population was highly critical of the decision to recognise Republika Srpska as one of the two 'entities' of Bosnia and Herzegovina. This, they felt, vindicated the Serbs in spite of their responsibility for ethnic cleansing. Bosnian Serbs, on the other hand, strongly objected to those aspects of the DPA relating to the unification of Sarajevo under Bosniak–Croat control. From the outset of the war, Serbs had claimed ownership of the Bosnian capital and were therefore extremely unhappy to see the city in the hands of their wartime enemies, especially since this involved massive Serb displacements from the Sarajevo suburbs (Zahar 2004).

Despite these difficulties, some commentators suggested that, of all the recent cases of peace implementation, that of Bosnia and Herzegovina was the most likely to succeed (King et al. 1998; Van Evera 1997). In their view, this particular region had a number of favourable conditions which suggested that a successful resolution might be possible. First, it had prior experience of power sharing. Secondly, unlike civil wars that end in one side's victory, and which therefore do not bode well for compromise, the conflict in Bosnia and Herzegovina ended in a negotiated settlement (Licklider 1995). Thirdly, the DPA was endorsed by a number of major regional and international actors whose commitment to stay the course was clearly signalled.

While peace settlements are notoriously prone to failure, many analysts agree that the credibility of foreign commitment helps such agreements overcome the security dilemmas that often create hurdles to full implementation. This chapter argues that irrespective of foreign support, Bosnia's power-sharing institutions – where power-sharing institutions are defined as those capable of securing sustainable peace *without* foreign intervention – are nevertheless ineffective. More specifically, the chapter begins by providing an account of the current state of play in Bosnia and Herzegovina, before proceeding to argue that the conjunction of two factors in particular accounts for the failure of Bosnia's power-sharing institutions to achieve the objective for which they were originally designed: (1) elite intransigence and (2) foreign intervention in favour of the 'status quo'.

POWER SHARING AND THE STABILITY
OF THE BOSNIAN TRANSITION

A necessary condition of successful power sharing *without* foreign intervention is that all concerned factions must be guaranteed an adequate and effective say in the running of affairs of state. This, analysts suggest, reduces the inclination of protagonists to retain their weapons as a guarantee of their political relevance and renders them less likely to resort to violence in pursuit of their objectives. Accordingly, in war-to-peace transitions, power-sharing institutions often aim to address the insecurity of the parties and the subsequent problem of credible commitment (Walter 1997, 2002) by ensuring 'inclusive decision-making, partitioned decision-making, predetermined decisions, or some combination of these' (Roeder and Rothchild 2005). This was, in case of point, the spirit behind the crafting of Bosnia and Herzegovina's post-war institutions at Dayton.

Decision making in a deeply divided society can be partitioned either territorially or functionally. Either way, the purpose is to assign exclusive jurisdiction to groups on matters of specific concern to them (Lapidoth 1996; Rothchild 2002). The DPA sought to partition decision making by giving the warring factions autonomy in a number of specified policy realms. Annex 4 of the DPA outlined a new national constitution for Bosnia and Herzegovina (General Framework Agreement, Annex 4, 'Constitution of Bosnia and Herzegovina'). Under its terms, Bosnia is a democracy consisting of two entities: the Federation of Bosnia and Herzegovina (which is also known as the Bosniak–Croat Federation) and the Republika Srpska. While the Republika Srpska is a centralised territorial entity, the Bosniak–Croat Federation is a federated entity that is, in turn, divided into ten cantons.

To ensure inclusive decision making, the Bosniak–Croat Federation and the Republika Srpska share a set of central governing institutions. Known as the Parliamentary Assembly of Bosnia and Herzegovina, this set of institutions consists of a House of Representatives, a House of Peoples, and a three-member collective Presidency. Members of the Presidency (one Bosniak, one Croat and one Serb) are directly elected from the Bosniak–Croat Federation (Bosniak and Croat members) and from the Republika Srpska (Serb member). The House of Peoples is comprised of 15 delegates, two-thirds of which come from the Bosniak–Croat Federation (five Croats and five Bosniaks), while the other third (five Serbs) comes from Republika Srpska. Similarly, the House of Representatives comprises 42 members, two-thirds elected from the Bosniak–Croat Federation (28 members) and one-third from the Republika Srpska (14 members).

The new constitution does not specify how members of the House of Representatives are to be elected, only that they 'shall be directly elected from their Entity in accordance with an election law to be adopted by the Parliamentary Assembly' (Constitution of the Republic of Bosnia and Herzegovina, IV-2 (a)). As things have turned out, however, the two entities initially adopted a proportional party list system which requires voters to choose a political party rather than an individual candidate, although there are now open lists which allow people to vote for individuals as well. Following elections, the creation of legislation requires the approval of both chambers voting by simple majority rule (of those present and voting). The constitution also stipulates, however, that members must attempt to ensure that the majority includes at least one-third of votes of members from both the Bosniak–Croat Federation and the Republika Srpska.

Power-sharing arrangements also typically set some issues outside of the decision-making powers of government. Thus, predetermined decisions often put matters such as the allocation of resources or positions within the bureaucracy and the military outside of the realm of contentious politics. In Bosnia and Herzegovina, a number of issues were set aside by negotiators. For example, Bosnia's constitution recognizes the 'rights and freedoms set forth in the European Convention for the Protection of Human Rights and Fundamental Freedoms and its Protocols' (GFAP, Annex 6, Agreement on Human Rights). These rights not only apply directly in Bosnia and Herzegovina but take precedence over domestic law.

Power-sharing institutions in Bosnia and Herzegovina are an example of Arend Lijphart's consociational model – a model that is based on four key characteristics: grand coalition, mutual veto, proportionality and segmental autonomy (Lijphart 1977). Advocates of consociational power-sharing argue that the stability of divided societies requires a decrease in the level of competition and contact among the members of constituent groups, communities or 'segments', so that the bulk of the political interaction and decision making takes place at the elite level (Lijphart 1969, 1977; McRae 1974). To this end, they argue that the consociational model permits elites to build upon and reinforce existing socio-political pillars of group support, so that necessary institutional mechanisms and procedures can be designed that guarantee cross-community decision making on issues of society-wide concern along with self-government on issues of particular concern to the different communities.

While this last claim may not reflect the reality of many consociational societies where there is as much horizontal interaction between members of different communities as there is interaction at the elite level, it does accurately describe the situation in Bosnia and Herzegovina at the time the DPA was signed. While many Bosnians did not necessarily think of themselves as exclusively or even partially Bosniak, Croat, or Serb before the war, these identities had grown so entrenched by 1995 that they became the basis of the post-war political order. Having said this, it is important to point out that ethnic polarisation in Bosnia and Herzegovina cannot be solely blamed on the war. To do so would be to fail to adequately understand the legacies of Yugoslavian federalism. The Yugoslav system under Tito could also be described as a system of institutionalised ethnicity (Pupavac 2000, pp. 3–8; USIP 2000, p. 3), albeit a system of control where 'Communist officials of the different nations were primarily charged with monopolising the only legitimate expression of national identity and opposing real and supposed nationalism within their own community' (Bieber 2004, p. 4).

Between 1992 and 1995, the polarisation of Bosnian politics was heightened by the 'success' of war elites in establishing exclusive zones of control over which they exercised absolute dominion. Some, such as the Republika Srpska and the Croat-controlled canton of Herceg-Bosna, had become akin to quasi-states, with all the trappings of statehood but without *de jure* legitimacy (Kingston and Spears 2004). The experience of ethnic cleansing during the war, which forced people to seek refuge within essentialised Bosniak, Croat and Serbian identities, was also instrumental in entrenching this polarisation (Zahar 2004). In theory, the nature of societal cleavages in post-war Bosnia and Herzegovina, the prior experience of the country with power sharing and the extent of international commitment to see the country through its peace building and post-conflict reconstruction periods seemed initially to augur well for the success of power-sharing institutions. In practice, however, these institutions and the role of the international community have not worked as well as predicted.

LEADER INTRANSIGENCE AS AN OBSTACLE TO SUCCESSFUL POWER SHARING

As already remarked, some theories that present power sharing as a stabilising device for divided societies hinge on the notion of elite accommodation. This, many argue (Lijphart 1977; McGarry and O'Leary 2004), is a prerequisite of successful power sharing since power-sharing institutions, inclusive decision making and mutual vetoes tend to carry with them the risk of 'immobilism' or state paralysis which can only be countered by the concerted action of responsible leaders willing to compromise in order to maintain stability (Lijphart 1997; Tsebelis 1990). Bosnia and Herzegovina is an illustrative case of such immobilism, largely due to a provision in the DPA that gives extensive veto powers to the parliamentary representatives of the three main ethnic groups on matters deemed destructive to a vital interest of the Bosniak, Croat, or Serb people (Zahar 2005). These veto rights allow members of the three groups to block the enactment of contested legislation. In such instances, a joint committee including three members of each ethnic group reviews the legislation; if this committee fails to reach agreement, the matter is forwarded to the Constitutional Court, a nine-member institution with exclusive jurisdiction to resolve disputes between the three main communities. A similar veto exists within the Presidency. However, while veto rights are quite extensive in Bosnia and Herzegovina, the nature of issues subject to veto is unclear. What constitutes a vital interest is open to extensive interpretation and misuse, so much so that observers have recently suggested that the scope of veto rights may need to be specified more clearly in order to avoid undue immobilism (ESI 2004).

In Bosnia and Herzegovina, the reality is that elite intransigence or unwillingness to cooperate are more often than not the norm. This intransigence is heightened by intra-communal out-bidding and by the ability of nationalist leaders on all sides to remain entrenched in positions of political power. To understand the dynamic underpinning elite intransigence, several factors can be invoked: the nature of electoral institutions; the balance of power between the central government and the entities; the causes and consequences of intra-communal out-bidding; and the impact of ethnic polarisation.

The nature of electoral institutions

It should be noted first that, of the many electoral exercises in Bosnia and Herzegovina, none is truly society-wide in scope. Elections at different levels of the state do not follow the same rules. Some representatives in the House of Peoples and House of Representatives are directly elected from the territory of the Bosniak–Croat Federation and the Republika Srpska, while others are selected from members of those two entities' regional parliaments. In other instances still, elections are restricted to members of a specific community to the exclusion of others. Thus, for example, Bosniaks and Croats living in the Republika Srpska, or Serbs living in the Bosniak–Croat Federation, cannot be elected to the office of regional president, while any person unwilling to identify with one of the three main groups is effectively excluded altogether.

The electoral system used for the appointment of parliamentarians at the central state level is proportional representation by party list. This system ensures a balance of parties but it has worked to 'penalise moderate parties and candidates at the expense of parties with a vigorous ethnic identification' (ICG 1999, p. 7). It is for these kinds of reasons that some analysts have suggested that communally based power-sharing institutions in general, and the DPA in particular, work to reify and strengthen narrow communal identities, and may produce ethnic out-bidding where two or more politicians compete for the support of the members of the same ethnic group (see, for example, Horowitz 1985; Reilly 2001; Sisk 1996).

The balance of power between the central government and the entities

Elite intransigence is further exacerbated by the weakness of the central institutions relative to the entities. The imbalance in power between the centre and the two entities has enabled representatives of the three ethnic groups to deadlock important decisions. Although the constitution clearly defines the functions and powers of the central government,[1] the entities nevertheless retain large residual powers, including the power of taxation. According to the constitution, the Republic of Bosnia and Herzegovina depends entirely on the entities for its financial needs; as such, Republika Srpska and the Bosniak–Croat Federation are responsible for providing the central institutions with resources necessary to meet the budgetary requirements of the state. This has serious consequences for the nature of relations between the central government and the entities. The latter are stronger than the former and they provide ethnic leaders with institutional bases to entrench their power and further stymie efforts at inter-entity cooperation.

In Bosnia and Herzegovina, the DPA put wartime nationalist leaders at the helm of the post-war political institutions, in effect giving them access to, and control over, entity financial and symbolic resources. These have been used to reward supporters and punish dissenters. For example, a report on the 1996 election stated that 'the ruling nationalist parties, the Serb Democratic Party (SDS), Croat

Democratic Union (HDZ) and Party of Democratic Action (SDA), hold a vice-like grip over the economy and all aspects of society in the particular territory under their control, they are almost always exerting covert intimidation'. In Republika Srpska, members of the opposition Socialist Party of Republika Srpska (SPRS) were 'dismissed from their jobs or threatened with dismissal in the course of the electoral campaign' (ICG 1996, p. 14). When and where possible, they have also been held back from the central government.

The causes and consequences of intra-communal out-bidding

Elite intransigence is also a function of intra-communal out-bidding which has mostly worked in favour of extreme nationalists at the ballot box. This out-bidding can only partially be blamed on the electoral system since, as often happens, it is also the result of wartime processes: (i) war-battered and ethnically polarised populations are more likely to vote for a party that is seen to represent their interests than one that seeks compromise with yesterday's enemy; (ii) this phenomenon is even more marked where nationalist parties also command the (scarce) resources of the state and use them to reward supporters with such essentials as access to jobs or housing (ICG 1998, 1999); (iii) war weariness can also have an effect as civilians may actually vote for extremists out of fear that the latter may disrupt the peace process in the event of a defeat at the polls (Wantchekon 1999).

In Bosnia and Herzegovina, these factors help account for political dynamics in the post-war society. They explain, for example, the consistent electoral successes of the more intransigent Croat and Serbian elites between 1995 and 1999, in contrast with the gradual yet consistent intra-group competition among Bosniak parties and the resulting erosion of the SDA's electoral dominance. Croat and Serb leaders were perceived as potential spoilers of the DPA, whereas voters in the Bosniak–Croat Federation knew the attachment of the Bosniak SDA party to the peace process. Fear might therefore have played a role in maintaining potential spoilers of the peace in power.

The impact of ethnic polarisation

Ethnic polarisation has also exacerbated the weight of nationalist considerations at the ballot box. When compromise is seen as treason, intransigence pays on election-day and intra-communal out-bidding can often be a winning strategy. The fate of former Republika Srpska president Biljana Plavšić illustrates this dynamic. Plavšić was ousted from power in the September 1998 elections because the majority of the Bosnian Serb population resented her pro-Western stance. She was punished for offering concessions to the international community that voters considered too numerous and inappropriate. Nikola Poplašen, a nationalist who adopted an intransigent discourse, replaced her. Polarisation is thus invoked by intransigent elites seeking to justify their 'inability' (read unwillingness) to compromise.

Perhaps the best illustration of this dynamic in Bosnia and Herzegovina is the debate over refugee returns. In an attempt to reverse the impact of ethnic cleansing, Annex 7 of the DPA provides for the return of refugees to their former towns and villages. Consecutive Republika Srpska governments have invoked lack of control at the ground level and fear of incidents involving refugees returning to their homes in Republika Srpska to justify their failure to comply fully with the provisions of Annex 7. Meanwhile, Bosnian Serb elites have also attempted to curry favour with the electorate by pointing to their position on refugee returns as proof of their commitment to faithfully representing the Bosnian Serb voters' interests. A further illustration comes from the Croatian community. In early 2001, the Croat nationalist party, HDZ, sought to renegotiate the terms of Bosniak–Croat association in order to increase its share in the broader power-sharing arrangement. It aimed to do this by capitalising on the dissatisfaction among Croat voters and arguing that it needed to remain responsive to the electorate.

FOREIGN INTERVENTION: A BLESSING OR A BANE?

The government structures established at Dayton were designed with an eye to reassuring all the Bosnian factions about their role in a future Bosnia and Herzegovina. And yet, these power-sharing institutions combined with the ethnic polarisation of Bosnian society have allowed the nationalist parties to entrench themselves at entity level and to refuse compromise at the central state level. Since 2000, reform efforts have tried to redress this entrenchment by reinforcing central state institutions.

In particular, such endeavours have involved considerable effort and intervention on the part of the international community. For example, the Office of the High Representative (OHR) of the international community in Bosnia was initially mandated to 'facilitate' the implementation of the civilian aspects of the DPA. However, because entity authorities dragged their feet in establishing the central political institutions called for by the DPA, the Peace Implementation Council – meeting in Bonn in 1997 – authorised the High Representative to take certain key decisions. These new 'Bonn powers' covered the 'crucial areas of institutional reform, substantial legislation, and the personnel of public office' (Knaus and Martin 2003, p. 63). They were to be used in support of the implementation of the DPA, either to force an issue in cases of deadlock or to forcibly remove elected officials who refused to implement the agreement. And used they were: in the course of his mandate as High Representative, Wolfgang Petritsch passed 246 decisions using the 'Bonn powers'. In fact, '[i]n the three days leading up to his departure ... Petritsch imposed a total of 43 laws, amendments, or regulations that had failed to receive approval in the state and entity legislatures, compared with only 19 made in the previous five months' (Zahar 2004; Constitution Watch 2002).

Clearly, the purpose of these new OHR powers was directly related to the issues of immobilism and leader intransigence. Up to a point, this policy has been successful in countering the paralysis of decision making at the central, federal level in Bosnia. It has resulted in such achievements as agreements on a single currency and licence plates. Both policies were highly symbolic in restoring a semblance of unity within the state. During the war, the Republika Srpska and Herceg-Bosna had adopted the currencies of Serbia and Croatia respectively. This strengthened their ties to ethnic kith-and-kin across the border and weakened the cohesiveness of Bosnia and Herzegovina. As for the single licence plate, its adoption and implementation in 1998 allowed free movement throughout the state. Until this point, many Bosniaks and Croats would not travel to Republika Srpska, nor would many Serbs travel to the Federation for fear that their licence plates would betray their ethnic origin and subject them to harassment and ill-treatment.

In the long term, however, this delegation of decision-making power to the OHR must surely undermine political-capacity building, given that local politicians and public officials do not have to wrestle with key political issues or to arrive at compromises. Indeed, as it stands, the most difficult of decisions continue to be taken by the High Representative rather than locally elected officials. These range from imposing a law on citizenship and modifying the constitutions of the entities to bring them into line with the DPA, to forcing the members of the collective presidency to meet 'after a long break' (OHR decision of April 15, 1999). As a result, political leaders can 'choose intransigence and delay when a decision would be unpopular with constituents or colleagues', secure in the knowledge that if the decision needs to be taken, the High Representative will step in (Woodward 1999, p. 9). There are few incentives for Bosnian politicians to be conciliatory because they can hold their ground and gain support with their respective electorates, whilst simultaneously remaining safe in the knowledge that no return to conflict is likely given the decision-making capacity of the international community.

Post-DPA nationalist leaders have capitalised on the benefits of cooperation without incurring the domestic cost of compromise. Goods and public services have been delivered to the population but the leaders have not had to back down on their intransigent positions in the process. Consider, then, the following evaluation:

> Bosnia's joint institutions did eventually come together in January 1997. However, it is no exaggeration to state that to date they have failed to function, that every issue has been viewed in zero-sum terms, and that almost all 'breakthroughs' have required disproportionate, indeed often ridiculous, amounts of time, effort and concessions on the part of the international community. (ICG 1998, p. 8)

The international community has a stake in preventing a return to hostilities in Bosnia and Herzegovina – not least because it has made a substantial investment in the peace process, has the reputation of NATO to consider and uphold, and must review and justify the enormous financial expenditure involved in support packages and military intervention. Not only has the international community been crucial in avoiding and breaking deadlocks, but it has also contributed to keeping power sharing stable by keeping potential spoilers at bay. NATO's Stabilisation Force (SFOR) has demonstrated its willingness to use military action and move against would-be spoilers. For example, SFOR troops intervened during the 1997 internal crisis in Republika Srpska between the extremist supporters of Radovan Karadžić and supporters of the then president, Biljana Plavšić. Ever since that time, SFOR's presence in Bosnia and Herzegovina has been used as a deterrent when serious crises threaten the stability of the DPA.

And yet, the absence of war should not be misread as the presence of sustainable peace. Indeed, as I have argued, a close reading of the situation suggests that the current stability of Bosnia depends in large part on international intervention rather than on the actual power-sharing structures established under the DPA. Bosnian elites remain intransigent and refuse to cooperate in spite of extensive power-sharing arrangements that should have given them a stake in the political system. But while international intervention may be useful in warding off short-term crises, it may also be detrimental to peace and stability in the long term. In short, the recent experience of power sharing under the DPA shows that Bosnians have yet to learn the virtues of compromise and to acquire the leadership skills necessary to take difficult and controversial decisions on their own.

ASSESSING THE LEVERS OF STABILITY IN BOSNIA AND HERZEGOVINA

Eight years after the signing of the DPA, observers are doubtful that the Bosnian power-sharing institutions could survive an abrupt pull-out of the European Union (EU) mission which has now taken over from the NATO Stabilisation Force (SFOR). Optimists do not question the ability of the power-sharing institutions established under the DPA institutions to endure; but they suggest that this ability has less to do with their intrinsic ability to stabilise the country than with the impact of the Bonn powers. These analysts credit consecutive High Representatives with using their powers to remove 'obstructionist' leaders from office and thus open the way for new moderate elites. Contributing to this trend were international successes in the realm of refugee returns and in the redefinition of entity citizenships from an exclusivist ethnic to a more inclusive civic mode of belonging (ICG 2002).

In spite of the victory of nationalist parties, the October 2002 elections indicate a recent decrease in popular support for the Croat Democratic Union (HDZ) and the Serb Democratic Party (SDS). The vote of successfully returned refugees has allowed parties based in the Bosniak–Croat Federation to gain 17 per cent of the seats in the National Assembly of Republika Sprska. The current High Representative, Lord Paddy Ashdown, is also trying a new approach to break the hold of intransigent elites on their electorates. Claiming to be responsive to the people, he has urged governments to pass economic, legal and governance reforms. Forcing nationalist leaders to shoulder responsibility for reform might be the best strategy to ensure the stability of power sharing in Bosnia and Herzegovina. Whether they will do more than pay lip service to it remains to be seen (ICG 2003, pp. i–ii).

Under the DPA, Bosnia and Herzegovina has adopted the characteristics of a power-sharing system: inclusive decision making, partitioned decision making and predetermined decisions, including a number of constitutional mechanisms to institutionalise decision-making procedures and prevent intransigence. These safeguards have proven insufficient, however, in securing a sustainable commitment from nationalist parties to the peace process. The fragility and inefficiency of post-conflict power-sharing institutions have often resulted in deadlock, prompting the OHR to intervene. The sustained military presence of SFOR has also played a role in stabilising the country. The repeated threat or actual use of force and sanctions to ensure compliance further suggests that external actors, not domestic political institutions, are the determining factor in understanding why a return to violence has been prevented.

At the same time, external intervention and internal procedural mechanisms have, nevertheless, also resulted in somewhat perverse outcomes. By allowing leaders to display mutual intransigence without necessarily shouldering responsibility for the consequences, these two factors have also increased the frequency, though not necessarily the intensity, of inter-segmental conflict. Thus, in spite of hopeful signs indicating that the international community might ultimately be able to reshape elite–follower interactions, observers suggest that peace remains a function of the continued international presence and involvement in the domestic affairs of the state, rather than of the institutions created at Dayton per se (Gurr et al. 2001).

NOTE

1. Central institutions are responsible for: foreign policy and trade; customs; monetary policy; finances of the institutions and international obligations of Bosnia and Herzegovina; immigration, refugee and asylum policy and regulation; international and inter-entity criminal law enforcement; the establishment and operation of common and international communications facilities; regulation of inter-entity transportation; and air traffic control (Article III-1).

REFERENCES

Anonymous (2002) 'Constitution Watch – Bosnia and Herzegovina, 2002', in *East European Constitutional Review* 11 (3) (Summer). Available at http://www.law.nyu.edu/eecr/vol11num3/constitutionwatch/bosnia.html.

Bieber, F. (2004) *Institutionalizing Ethnicity in the Western Balkans: Managing Change in Deeply Divided Societies*. ECMI Working Paper No. 19. Flensburg, Germany: European Centre for Minority Issues (ECMI).

European Stability Initiative (2004) *Making Federalism Work: A Radical Proposal for Practical Reform*. http://www.esiweb.org.

Gurr, T. R., Marshall, M. G. and Khosla, D. (2001) *Peace and Conflict 2001: A Global Survey of Armed Conflicts, Self-Determination Movements, and Democracy*. College Park, MD: Center for International Development and Conflict Management

Horowitz, D. (1985) *Ethnic Groups in Conflict*. Berkeley, CA: University of California Press.

International Crisis Group (1996) *Elections in Bosnia and Herzegovina*. Sarajevo: ICG.

—— (1998) *Doing Democracy a Disservice: 1998 Elections in Bosnia and Herzegovina*. Sarajevo: ICG.

—— (1999) *Breaking the Mould: Electoral Reform in Bosnia and Herzegovina*. Sarajevo: ICG.

—— (2002) *The Continuing Challenge of Refugee Returns in Bosnia and Herzegovina*. Balkans Report No. 137. Sarajevo and Brussels: ICG.

—— (2003) *Bosnia's Nationalist Governments: Paddy Ashdown and the Paradoxes of State-Building*. Balkans Report No. 146. Sarajevo and Brussels: ICG.

King, G., Keohane, R. O. and Verba, S. (1998) *Designing Social Inquiry: Scientific Inference in Qualitative Research*. Princeton, NJ: Princeton University Press.

Kingston, P.W.T. and Spears, I. (eds) (2004) *States Within States: Incipient Political Entities in the Post-Cold War Era*. Houndmills: Palgrave Macmillan.

Knaus, G. and Martin., F. (2003) 'Lessons from Bosnia and Herzegovina: Travails of the European Raj', *Journal of Democracy* 14 (3), 60–74.

Lapidoth, R. (1996) *Autonomy: Flexible Solutions to Ethnic Conflicts*. Washington, DC: United States Institute for Peace.

Licklider, R. (1993) *Stopping the Killing: How Civil Wars End*. New York, NY: New York University Press.

—— (ed.) (1995) 'Memory and Reconciliation After Civil Wars: The US and Nigerian Cases'. Unpublished manuscript.

Lijphart, A. (1969) 'Consociational Democracy', *World Politics*, 21, 207–25.

—— (1977) *Democracy in Plural Societies*. New Haven, CT: Yale University Press.

McGarry, J. and O'Leary, B. (2004) 'Stabilising Northern Ireland's Agreement', *The Political Quarterly*, 75 (3), 213–25.

McRae, K. (1974) *Consociational Democracy: Political Accommodation in Segmented Societies*. Toronto: McClelland and Stewart.

Posen, B. (1993) 'The Security Dilemma and Ethnic Conflict', in M. Brown (ed.), *Ethnic Conflict and International Security*. Princeton, NJ: Princeton University Press, pp. 103–124.

Pupavac, V. (2000) 'Socialist Federal Republic of Yugoslavia's Multiethnic Rights Approach and the Politicisation of Ethnicity', *Human Rights Law Review*, 5 (2), pp. 3–8.

Reilly, B. (2001). *Democracy in Divided Societies: Electoral Engineering for Conflict Management*. Cambridge: Cambridge University Press.

Roeder, P. and Rothchild, D. (2005). *Sustainable Peace: Democracy and Power-Dividing Institutions After Civil Wars*. Ithaca, NY: Cornell University Press.

Rothchild, D. (2002) 'Settlement Terms and Postagreement Stability', in S. J. Stedman, D. Rothchild and E. M. Cousens (eds) *Ending Civil Wars: The Implementation of Peace Agreements*. Boulder, CO: Lynne Rienner.

Sisk, T. (1996) *Power Sharing and International Mediation in Ethnic Conflicts*. Washington, DC: USIP Press.

Snyder, J. and Jervis, R. (1999). 'Civil War and the Security Dilemma', in B. Walter and J. Snyder (eds), *Civil Wars, Insecurity and Intervention*. New York, NY: Columbia University Press.

Tsebelis, G. (1990) *Nested Games: Rational Choice in Comparative Politics*. Los Angeles, CA: UCLA Press.

United States Institute for Peace (2000) *Bosnia's Next Five Years: Dayton and Beyond*. Special Report No. 62. Washington, DC: USIP.

Van Evera, S. (1997) *Guide to Methods for Students of Political Science*. Ithaca, NY: Cornell University Press

Walter, B. (1997) 'The Critical Barrier to Civil War Settlement', *International Organization*, 51 (3), 127–56.

—— (2002) *Committing to Peace: The Successful Settlement of Civil Wars*. Princeton, NJ: Princeton University Press.

Wantchekon, L. (1999) 'On the Nature of First Democratic Elections', *Journal of Conflict Resolution*, 43 (2), 245–59.

Woodward, S. (1999) 'Transitional Elections and the Dilemmas of International Assistance to Bosnia and Herzegovina', in S. Riskin (ed.), *Three Dimensions of Peacebuilding in Bosnia*. Washington, DC: USIP Press: pp. 5–13.

Zahar, M-J. (2004) 'Republika Srspka', in T. Bahcheli, B. Bartmann and H. Srebrnik (eds) *De Facto States: The Quest for Sovereignty*. London: Routledge, pp. 32–51.

—— (2005) 'Bosnia and Herzegovina', in A. L. Griffiths (ed.), *Handbook of Federal Countries*. Montréal and Kingston: McGill/Queen's Press and The Forum of Federations, pp. 116–29.

9
Power Sharing and National Reconciliation: The Case of Lebanon

David Russell and Nadim Shehadi

The 'Document of National Understanding', referred to hereafter as the Ta'if Accord, was signed on 22 October 1989 and affirmed through a constitutional amendment approved on 21 August 1990. It is the product of negotiations between 62 Lebanese parliamentarians – one half Christian and the other half Muslim – who were last elected in 1972 prior to the outbreak of the Lebanese civil war. The politicians responsible for this agreement were familiar with a range of institutional options that could have been adopted in order to try to promote durable peace and stable democracy within a divided society. Lebanon has a long history of power sharing that stretches back to the period of Ottoman rule, specifically to the existence of an autonomous Druze Muslim/Maronite Christian emirate from the end of the sixteenth century, and, in the nineteenth century, the development of an autonomous province known as the *Mutassarrifiyya*, governed by an Ottoman Christian governor and protected by a concert of Western powers (Akarli 1993). More recently, from independence in 1943 until the onset of sectarian violence in the 1970s, the state was governed in accordance with an informal and unwritten power-sharing arrangement commonly referred to as the 'National Pact' (Hanf 1993, p. 71; Lijphart 1977, pp. 147–50).

In an important sense, then, the Ta'if Accord was nothing new. Rather, it amounted to the formal acceptance and institutionalisation of a philosophy that had already been largely established by practice until it was disrupted by the onset of inter-communal hostilities. The document itself represents the political conclusion to a period of history that cost somewhere in the region of 150,000 lives (approximately 5 per cent of the population), left more than 300,000 people injured, and rendered approximately 750,000 people (a quarter of the population) internally displaced (Zahar 2002, pp. 572–3). Underpinning the Accord is a longstanding view that simple majority rule is an unsuitable basis for democracy, given Lebanon's social and political character. The assumption is that democratic decisions in a divided society cannot derive from a crude aggregation of competing communal interests, but instead require a strong commitment to collective decision-making as the product of a generally accessible and inclusive process of deliberation between the representatives of different communities, each of whom assured an equal political voice and veto.

Power sharing in Lebanon is, in many respects, similar to the other examples considered in this volume. And yet, the agreement that underpins Lebanese power-sharing is notably distinct in the way it seeks to address the source of inter-communal antagonism. The Ta'if Accord is explicitly concerned to look strategically far beyond the passive acceptance of institutionalised sectarianism as a means of managing civil strife on a permanent basis. Although the recognition and protection of the main communities is accepted as necessary in the short term, there is also an envisaged process that promises to allow for the phased elimination of sectarianism at the political level and throughout society more generally over the longer term (Dagher 2000, p. 175). The text of the document refers to this objective as 'national reconciliation', understood to involve the bridging of sectarian divisions by prioritising the common citizenship of the Lebanese people. The question this chapter is concerned to address is whether the goal of national reconciliation can be adequately promoted under the terms of the Ta'if Accord. As such, it asks whether a power-sharing agreement that enshrines communities within the institutions of the state can subsequently lend itself to the creation of public policies that will encourage citizens to look beyond these communities.

INSTITUTIONS AND DECISION-MAKING PROCEDURES

In order to try to reduce inter-communal conflict, the Lebanese have created a power-sharing political system that is more-or-less consociational. The agreement takes a pillarised view of society and calls for internal cross-community power sharing between Christian and Muslim groups; vetoes to assure the communities that important decisions will only be made with their consent; proportionality rules applied throughout government and the civil service; and a high level of cultural and legal autonomy for 18 religious sects. Although much has been written about consociational power sharing, perhaps the most salient consideration for this discussion is that the model is itself an instance of a broader conceptual approach to dealing with the challenge of sectarian divisions: namely, that political accommodation and peaceful coexistence is best secured within a divided society through extensive institutional provisions which guarantee people will be treated as members of distinct communities (McGarry and O'Leary 1993, pp. 35–7).

In Lebanon, seats in both the legislative Chamber of Deputies and the executive Council of Ministers are predetermined. That is to say, the communities which are to act as partners in power sharing are named in advance, while the positions, or number of seats, to be held by them are rigidly fixed on a permanent basis (Lijphart 1995, pp. 275–87). According to convention, the top three public offices, that of the President, Prime Minister and Speaker of Parliament, are reserved for the Maronite Christian, Sunni Muslim and Shi'a Muslim communities respectively. Representation in the 128-member Chamber of Deputies is divided equally between Muslims and Christians, with the 64 seats in each communal block allocated proportionally to the Sunni, Shi'a, Druze and Alawite (Muslim), the Maronite, Greek Catholic, Greek Orthodox, and Armenian Orthodox (Christian) and a number of smaller named denominations (Article 24). The task of executive formation, the distribution of portfolios in the government, or Council of Ministers, is not strictly defined but is agreed nonetheless in relation to the number of seats held in the legislature by the various religious sects (Hudson 1997, p. 113; Rigby 2000, p. 176).

Unlike a standard case of presidentialism, the incumbent Maronite politician who acquires the top public office is not elected by the citizens, but must instead achieve support from a weighted majority of two-thirds of the Chamber of Deputies (72 parliamentarians) (Article 49). While the President is then responsible for nominating a Sunni candidate as Prime Minister, there is an obligation upon both to consult the Chamber of Deputies and to win support from the Shi'a Speaker of Parliament prior to making the appointment (Article 53). Since the Speaker is also subject to parliamentary approval, the net result is that only those politicians who appeal for support across party political lines and across the communal divide stand a chance of being elected to one of the top three posts (Article 44).

A significant consequence of this particular system is that instead of returning the most representative person of a group to one of three principal positions of power within the state, candidates are sometimes promoted and secure political office on the basis of being the least objectionable to other groups. The same applies to seats in parliament. Since most constituencies in Lebanon are mixed, candidates are often returned having been accepted as the most moderate by the other groups within a given constituency, rather than on the basis of being the most representative of their own group interests. The Lebanese electoral system is similar to a common role system in that voters can choose individual candidates from a number of different lists, or might vote for an independent candidate. In any case, the freedom of choice is restricted by the fact that seats are predetermined according to communities. Voters must choose a set number of candidates from Muslim and Christian groups. A positive reading of this arrangement suggests that the Lebanese political system has a built-in electoral mechanism to dilute sectarian loyalties and promote inter-communal collaboration and civic leadership. Yet, simultaneously, a negative reading suggests that the power sharing upon which the Ta'if Accord is premised has been distorted by the absence of actual sectarian political opinion. In other words, the cost of moderation is that of inclusion. Those returned to power may not represent the opinion of the community whose seat in parliament they hold. Indeed, they might have been returned to power by a majority of the electorate from a community other than their own. For power-sharing arrangements premised upon embracing the sectarian divisions in society, this situation may raise a difficult issue of democratic representation (see also Wolff, chapter 4 in this volume).

The Lebanese system is such that virtually any political decision requires in addition to the President's signature that of the Prime Minister and another minister – usually the Speaker of Parliament (McLaurin 1992, p. 31). Nowhere are these restrictions more visible than when it comes to the task of creating a government. The formation of a cabinet, or Council of Ministers, is dependent upon the joint signatures of the President and Prime Minister. In addition, the Council as a collegial body must present its 'general statement of policy' to the Chamber of Deputies, and cannot exercise any executive functions before it 'gains the Chamber's confidence' through a parliamentary vote (Article 64). In sum, the constraints placed on the allocation of executive portfolios mean that it is difficult to envisage a scenario whereby those who are unwilling to engage in cooperative behaviour might obtain seats. In fact, it is almost guaranteed that the President, Prime Minister, Speaker of Parliament and Council of Ministers will come together as a cross-community coalition of moderates. Once again, there are both positive and negative aspects to approaching politics in this way. On the one hand, the coalition-type system demands and often facilitates coalescent behaviour among political leaders. On the other hand, however, there is also an inherent danger that a demand for so much compromise may result in political paralysis, stagnation and perhaps the collapse of government during times of crisis.

The underlying rationale of the Ta'if Accord is to recognise that citizens may have competing aspirations, and that democracy should enable them to deliberate their way beyond these aspirations in order to arrive at a workable compromise. The principal aim of power sharing is to transform sectarianism from being the foundation of antagonism and negative engagement to being the foundation of cooperative politics and positive engagement. Predetermination in the Lebanese Chamber of Deputies allows us to see exactly how many seats the major communities hold. By resolving the issue of communal participation in parliament in this way, it aims to bracket this issue and thus encourage non-sectarian agendas to develop. Being able to identify the particular loyalties of political representatives in such a way is perhaps a good thing. Knowing how many seats different communities hold allows for the creation of institutional procedures like weighted majorities on what are classified as 'basic national issues'.[1] A decision made on such issues is subject to various restrictions: for example, constitutional amendments proposed by the executive require the support of two-thirds of the Chamber of Deputies (Article 77). Even where this high threshold does not apply, the Chamber must endorse legislation by a simple majority of its membership. In practice, therefore, any issue of debate can be interpreted as one that requires cross-community consent. However, it is also subject, and at risk from, the same problem of potential stagnation during times of crisis as already detailed above in relation to the President, Prime Minister and Speaker of Parliament.

A PROGRAMME FOR CIVIC UNITY

A workable power-sharing agreement demands, at some level, a suitable process of deliberation between the members of contending communities through which democratically legitimate decisions can be reached. The assumption is that sharing power will encourage moderation on issues underpinning differences in identity; that it will counteract the centrifugal thrust created by sectarianism and thereby reduce the destructive tendencies of inter-communal antagonism (Sisk 1996, p. 30). In addition to these aims, there is the anticipation that the choice of political institutions and decision-making procedures will help citizens reconcile their fundamental differences and build a sense of civic unity that will strengthen and provide support for sustainable democracy and peaceful coexistence.

Where communal divisions are prevalent, the tendency has therefore been to try to shift the balance within the self-identity of people over time, so that being a citizen will take precedence over any other loyalty which may exist – an objective referred to in the Ta'if Accord as 'national reconciliation'. As a first step in achieving this objective an agreement was reached on the constitutional status of the Lebanese state (Máiz 1999, p. 37). The state has been declared:

> sovereign, free and independent ... It is a final homeland for all its citizens. It is unified in its territory, people and institutions ... Arab in its identity and in its association ... is a parliamentary democratic republic based on respect for public liberties, especially the freedom of opinion and belief, and respect for social justice and equality of rights and duties among all citizens without discrimination ... There shall be no constitutional legitimacy for any authority which contradicts the pact of communal coexistence. (Preamble a, b, c & j)

Apprehension that Islamic overtones could eventually lead to a Muslim hegemony has often been sufficient cause for Lebanese Christians to deny their Arab heritage. The Accord intends to allay this fear and aims to strengthen any developing civic unity by separating the concepts of Arabism and Islam. It begins by unequivocally proclaiming the democratic and parliamentary character of the republic and asserts that 'the people are the source of authority and sovereignty' (Preamble d). All of the agreement's signatories, and subsequently elected Members of Parliament, are duty bound to defend an independent and unified state. Thus, according to a Shi'a government minister, there is a realisation by Muslims that the 'Christians need guarantees ... and we are accepting to give them these guarantees'.[2] The Muslim population has conceded that there can be no Islamisation of Lebanon and that Arabism must be rendered consistent with the principle of religious pluralism, both for the sake of political stability and for the future prospect of inter-communal reconciliation (Hamdan 1990, p. 22).

For their part, the Christian population has accepted that in all domains – and with no exceptions – foreign and domestic policies should be made on the basis of Lebanon's Arab identity (Maila 1992, p. 14; Tueni 1991, p. 23). The Ta'if Accord demands a real sense of Arab belonging. In short, it makes the concepts of secular Arabism and an independent state interdependent. Thus, although some citizens may view the declaration that Lebanon is a founding and active member of the Arab League as an opportunity to stress their identity, others may emphasise the fact that this affirms state sovereignty within the regional order (Preamble b). What is important from the perspective of power sharing is that the two positions are equally valid and inextricably linked; they have been recognised by the communities as such, and can be proclaimed openly without coming into conflict with one another. The agreement effectively renders the inter-communal dispute between Christians and Muslims obsolete, having reached a central compromise that enables them to affirm their constitution, albeit in different ways.

Beyond the resolution of Lebanon's constitutional status and the commitment to 'national reconciliation', the Ta'if Accord envisages a rolling programme of political reforms aimed at encouraging civic unity. There is a clear attempt to construct an 'exit strategy' that might allow politics as a whole to move in a new direction, away from the institutionalised divisions that were viewed as a necessary condition for peace in the short term (Hudson 1997, p. 117). The agreement places a statutory obligation on politicians following election to:

> take the appropriate measures to realise the abolition of political sectarianism according to a transitional plan. A National Committee shall be formed headed by the President of the Republic, including, in addition to the Speaker of the Chamber of Deputies and the Prime Minister, leading political, intellectual, and social figures. The task of this Committee shall be to study and propose the means to ensure the abolition of sectarianism, propose them to the Chamber of Deputies and the Ministers, and supervise the execution of the plan. (Article 95)

The content of this article, like the concept of power sharing itself, is not new. The abolition of political sectarianism had been provided for within the Lebanese constitution even prior to the civil war. What is important about the Ta'if Accord, however, is that it elaborates upon this commitment and details how it should be implemented. The amended Article 95 advocates a staged process that will lead people away from the segregationist mentality of institutionalised divisions towards a more integrationist concept of society where diversity is celebrated in an inclusive manner (Gemayel 1992, p. 14). That is not to say, of course, that the abolition of political sectarianism is expected to happen overnight. The negotiators of the Accord were not so naive as to think that they would be able to remove the sources of the Lebanese conflict in one grand move. Yet, crucially, nor were they averse from the outset to the idea of introducing policies that might challenge traditional community politics.

From the initial signing of the agreement we are told that members of parliament 'shall represent the whole nation. No restriction or stipulation may be imposed upon their mandate by their electors' (Article 27). There is, in other words, a duty on public representatives to consider the common or greater good, and to make sure that their deliberations and decisions reflect the collective interests of everyone in society, irrespective of differences in identity. The allocation of parliamentary seats prior to any election is partly intended as a facilitator of this requirement. Since the issue of communal representation is settled in advance of any election, the hope is that Lebanese politicians will have the opportunity, and be encouraged, to leave their sectarian baggage 'outside the door'. Hence, the aim is to lessen the influence of sectarianism among those responsible for developing public policy, thereby making it more likely that any subsequent decisions will reflect the concept of 'national reconciliation'.

In addition to the changes demanded in favour of removing sectarian divisions at the political level, there are also a number of practical requirements provided for in the agreement. To help facilitate and create the kinds of background conditions against which the larger project of 'national reconciliation' might be brought about, the Accord called for the immediate creation of a number of institutions and procedures that would lay a foundation for civic unity. For example, there is a clear attempt to look beyond the narrow concept of government to a wider concept of governance by creating an Economic and Social Council. The Council was to be a new avenue of dialogue for a spectrum of interests from the public, private, community and voluntary sectors whose say might otherwise go unheard. Its task is to act as a civic forum and offer advice and suggestions to both the legislative Chamber of Deputies and the executive Council of Ministers in areas of public-policy formation. Perhaps more importantly, from the perspective of reconciliation, the Council provides an alternative to community-based politics. Put concisely: as a public body that stands outside the main political arena, the Economic and Social Council is intended to provide a space in which the barriers of sectarianism could, in principle, be broken down and replaced by cross-cutting social concerns. In this sense, the Council is meant to help prevent sectarian lock-in, and is supposed to open up alternative avenues of discourse from the antagonistic politics that so often characterise inter-communal contact (Maila 1992, pp. 68–9).

At the level of daily interaction between individuals, and with the aim of increasing social cohesion, the agreement called for two further significant developments. First, it affirmed the need to ensure the return of displaced persons. Although briefly addressed, the Ta'if Accord upholds the right of every Lebanese citizen to live in any part of the state they choose. It also insists that there should be no 'segregation of people on the basis of any type of belonging, and no fragmentation, partition, or colonisation' (Preamble i).[3] The clear aim is to support the concept of a society of many different yet interdependent identities, where residential areas are mixed and good community relations promoted. Second, proposed educational reforms are also intended to complement and support this vision of a unified Lebanon. While the agreement guarantees communal autonomy by protecting the private education of Muslim and Christian schools, it also stipulates that educational programmes are to be re-examined and re-designed so as to strengthen national identification, to ensure spiritual openness, and to unify history and civic education (Maila 1992, pp. 69–71). Even prior to the civil war it was always the case that children attended religious but nevertheless integrated schools. The significant development of the Ta'if Accord, however, is that this mixing is now to be supported by mainstreaming an integrated ethos throughout the educational system.

THE CHALLENGE OF IMPLEMENTATION

Modern Lebanon is therefore premised upon a paradox. On the one hand, power sharing institutionalises the Christian and Muslim communities as the foundation of political life. On the other hand, the aim of 'national reconciliation' suggests that outspoken claims for one's own community by politicians are considered politically incorrect, and perhaps even unconstitutional. The question is whether the first of these requirements has had a positive or negative impact upon the realisation of the second. More specifically, the issue is whether the opportunities to pursue a programme for civic unity have been unduly constrained and stymied by the structures of power sharing and their subsequent outworking or whether, by neutralising communal agendas, the new constitution has created the opportunity for the emergence of a political disposition that transcends them. At present, is seems fair to conclude that Lebanon is in a period of transition with two political dynamics at work – one civic, the other sectarian. What remains to be seen, however, is which of these two dynamics is likely to dominate in the future, and whether the two are connected to each other, with one having an influence over the other.

Sectarianism has not been abolished in Lebanon in a positive sense by creating a secular, non-confessional citizenship and politics, but it may, nonetheless, have been weakened in a negative sense by strict guarantees of communal representation. Arguably, guarantees of representation have allowed politicians the freedom to develop a new set of non-sectarian political divisions that sit alongside, and in some instances supplant, traditional divisions. Recent political debates – for example, over French and United States intervention through the United Nations Security Council Resolution 1559 demanding the withdrawal of Syrian troops from Lebanon – have taken place on non-confessional grounds and probably have their roots in different interpretations of history and the causes of the civil war, as well as patron–client relationships that transcend communal ties (Blanford 2004). This clearly suggests that sectarian interests are giving way in some areas to ideologically-motivated divisions determined by broader social concerns, international agendas and so forth. The question to be answered, however, is should Lebanon as a consequence of this new dynamic declare 'sectarianism' over and move to abolish the current constitutional power-sharing arrangements? Or is it that those institutions need to be maintained in their current state if politics is to continue developing across communal lines?

Some commentators do not view the Ta'if Accord as a positive contribution to national reconciliation and have gone so far as to suggest that instead of reducing tensions, the enshrining of communal identities within the institutions of the Lebanese state has actually bolstered sectarian clientelism. Thus, it might be argued that while the agreement has undoubtedly reduced the worst manifestations of sectarian violence, it has also led to a deepening of communal divisions, especially at the political level (Hudson 1997, p. 117). More than 15 years have passed since the signing of the agreement, and yet little progress beyond the sectarian political system has been made. Although the word citizen 'appears in political speeches, official and unofficial, in actuality the Lebanese citizen', according to former President Amin Gemayel, 'does not exist'. The basic idea of citizenship, he goes on to argue, has not yet taken root in the political system. It is 'constantly challenged by the strength of community feeling. The Lebanese are first and foremost members of their community, not citizens of their state' (Gemayel 1992, p. 14). Moreover, the Economic and Social Council has had no noticeable success in introducing effective, non-sectarian opinions; the process of returning persons displaced during the civil war has 'been considerably slowed by the lack of state resources' (Zahar 2002, p. 584); and attempts to reform the educational system have encountered several problems, including failure to gain cross-community support for a new unified history curriculum.

Under these sorts of conditions, politicians often have little appetite for championing the cause of national reconciliation in the broad, society-wide sense. Despite the statutory obligation to implement policies favouring civic unity, there continues to be a substantial danger that such unity will prove to be a bridge too far for the politicians to cross. Circumstances appear such that political leaders tend to see sectarianism in society, whether overt or concealed, as a *fait accompli*. For many politicians, integrationist public policy is little more than vague aspiration, and they view the possibility of moving away from a political system that prioritises the interests of certain predetermined communities as an implausible fantasy. Behind the pluralising democratic facade of the agreement, little has been achieved in terms of changing mindsets. 'Political life in the new republic', according to one Muslim government minister, continues 'along an established historical precedent of sectarian rivalry. The same words are used by everyone. The same words. The same logic. The same phrases.'[4] This view is supported by a Christian minister who states, 'Now we use trenches, but without using guns.'[5]

The relation between consociational-style power sharing as communal politics and political issues is not clear cut. The predetermination of parliamentary seats in the Chamber of Deputies (half Christian, half Muslim) may give certain guarantees of protection for the members of the main communities. The electoral system may force politicians to form inter-communal coalitions and to appeal to a constituency beyond their own community. But, the role placed upon politicians by the power-sharing arrangements more generally to represent a particular identity is nonetheless detrimental to the promotion of a transitional process aimed at fostering civic unity among the citizens. The success of a negotiated power-sharing agreement, according to one prominent Christian member of the Lebanese Parliament, 'is to a large extent dependent on a unity of purpose among leaders who have the same outlook, and who hold the same aspiration to tackle sectarianism courageously'.[6] This unity of purpose appears absent in Lebanon. There are, admittedly, instances of politicians working together. Parliament and the state, for example, is currently divided between what is referred to as the 'opposition' and the 'loyalists' – respectively, those who are in favour of Syrian intervention and those who are against. This is a political division that has seen cross-community alliances forged and the transcendence of community politics achieved (Young 2005). Yet, despite such commendable changes, the dichotomy remains that the ethos of the reconstructed Lebanese system is firmly grounded, first and foremost, in an acceptance that citizens should live within a shared society, and yet, at one and the same time, in separate communities. Put succinctly: the worry is that the Ta'if Accord could well lead to a situation in which the citizens are guaranteed equality, but nevertheless remain fundamentally divided.

In a society where competition between the members of different communities is upheld as the principal basis of political life, elected representatives are all too often encouraged to see their own futures as being tied up with the perpetuation of the status quo, such that to do otherwise might risk threatening their individual self-interest and privileged position of power (Maalouf 2000, p. 122). To assume that politicians might promote civic unity because they are less ethnocentric than their supporters is often simply to misjudge the reality of politics. The aspirations of the negotiators of the Ta'if Accord, and those returned to positions of power in the years that have followed, are indeed ambiguous. However, what remains unclear is whether they were consolidating sectarianism or instead planning to abolish it. It is obvious that reform towards a more secular Lebanese civil society is not happening in any tangible sense. One example of this lack of progress concerns the position of women in politics, despite the fact that women's groups were often at the forefront of peace-building initiatives (Johnson 2001, p. 232). At present there are only three women in parliament and two female government ministers. The bulk of political representatives remain essentially sectarian, even though the coalitions being formed at present are reflective of much wider political agendas. How this tension might play out in the long run is uncertain.

CONCLUSION

In a very important sense, democracy in a society like Lebanon requires a dual foundation: an institutional framework that supports collective governance and the development of a set of working relationships between the members of society in the diversity of their interests, opinions and identities. The members of conflicting communities will not develop the working relationships necessary for peaceful coexistence if the political system underpinning the institutions of the state is deemed to be undemocratic. Hence, the justification for power sharing. Conversely, the political system will not function properly regardless of how power is shared, if there is no cooperation between the political parties and the individuals charged with the task of government, and, more generally, the citizen-body as a whole (Bloomfield 2003, pp. 10–11). The difficulty for those charged with the task of promoting both of these interdependent imperatives is that they need not be complementary – a point illustrated by the outworking of the Ta'if Accord.

According to some, by consolidating sectarianism, the Accord has risked reifying existing divisions. A critic might even suggest that the result is a cultural and political 'cold war' between competing traditions. This may not be all that surprising. The more explicitly a political system enshrines communities within the institutions of the state, the greater the risk that it will serve to reinforce the illusion among political representatives that they have no need, or responsibility, for enacting a programme of change. To paraphrase Giovanni Sartori, there is the worry in Lebanon that by rewarding divisions and divisiveness the negotiators of the agreement have only served to heighten such divisions and divisiveness (Sartori 1997, p. 72). The institutionalisation of the Christian and Muslim communities through power sharing has raised a palpable danger that in the long term communal separation could increase, while political parties and their leaders may be reduced to little more than the custodians of mutually exclusive sectarian interests. Developments on the ground, however, show that the issue is complex. Fifteen years is a short time in the development of a society emerging from an extended period of inter-communal violence, the trends are still barely visible and not easy to interpret precisely.

NOTES

1. Basic national issues include: 'The amendment of the constitution, the declaration of a state of emergency and its termination, war and peace, general mobilization, international agreements and treaties, the annual government budget, comprehensive and long-term development projects ... the review of the administrative map ... electoral laws, nationality laws, personal statute laws, and the dismissal of Ministers' (Article 65, subsection 5). These decision-making rules add a degree of certainty and predictability to politics. Essentially, they are the primary means by which mutual vetoes are put in place so as to ensure that one community cannot dominate the other.
2. Interviewed by David Russell 11 October 2002.
3. Removing the possibility of territorial division was a direct response to the concept of a federal Lebanon, as advocated predominantly by a number of Christian militias during the civil war. The reference to colonisation is a response drafted with particular mind to the Palestinian refugees living in Lebanon and displaced as a result of the Arab/Israeli wars.
4. Interviewed by David Russell 11 October 2002.
5. Interviewed by David Russell 14 November 2002.
6. Interviewed by David Russell 14 November 2002.

REFERENCES

Akarli, E. D. (1993) *The Long Peace: Ottoman Lebanon, 1861–1920*. Oxford and London: The Centre for Lebanese Studies and I. B. Tauris.

Blanford, N. (2004) 'Lebanese Voices Rise Against Syria's Dominance', *Christian Science Monitor*, 4 October.

Bloomfield, D. (2003) 'Reconciliation: An Introduction', in D. Bloomfield, T. Barnes and L. Huyse (eds), *Reconciliation After Violent Conflict: A Handbook*. Stockholm: International Institute for Democracy and Electoral Assistance, pp. 10–18.

Dagher, C. H. (2000) *Bring Down the Walls: Lebanon's Post-War Challenge*. New York, NY: St. Martin's Press.

Gemayel, A. (1992) *Rebuilding Lebanon*. Maryland, MD and Boston, MA: University Press of America.

Hamdan, K. (1990) 'A Lebanese Solution: The Only Way Out', *Afro-Asian Solidarity*, 3–4, 19–22.

Hanf, T. (1993) *Coexistence in Wartime Lebanon*. Oxford and London: The Centre for Lebanese Studies and I. B. Tauris.

Hudson, M. C. (1997) 'Trying Again: Power-Sharing in Post-Civil War Lebanon', *International Negotiation*, (1), pp. 103–22.

Johnson, M. (2001) *All Honourable Men: The Social Origins of the War in Lebanon.* London and New York: I. B. Tauris.

Lijphart, A. (1977) *Democracy in Plural Societies: A Comparative Exploration.* New Haven, CT: Yale University Press.

—— (1995) 'Self-Determination versus Pre-Determination of Ethnic Minorities in Power-Sharing Systems', in W. Kymlicka (ed.), *The Rights of Minority Cultures.* Oxford: Oxford University Press, pp. 275–87.

Maalouf, A. (2000) *On Identity.* London: The Harvill Press.

Maila, J. (1992) *The Document of National Understanding: A Commentary.* Oxford: The Centre for Lebanese Studies.

Máiz, R. (1999) 'Democracy, Federalism and Nationalism in Multinational States', *Nationalism and Ethnic Politics*, 5 (3&4), 35–60.

McGarry, J. and O'Leary, B. (eds) (1993) *The Politics of Ethnic Conflict Regulation: Case Study of Protracted Ethnic Conflicts.* London: Routledge.

McLaurin, R. D. (1992) 'Lebanon: Into or Out of Oblivion'. *Current History*, 91 (561), 29–33.

Rigby, A. (2000) 'Lebanon: Patterns of Confessional Politics', *Parliamentary Affairs*, 53 (1), 169–80.

Sartori, G. (1997) *Comparative Constitutional Engineering: An Inquiry into Structures, Incentives and Outcomes*, second ed. New York, NY: New York University Press.

Sisk, T. D. (1996) *Power Sharing and International Mediation in Ethnic Conflicts.* Washington, DC: USIP Press.

'The Constitution of Lebanon after the Amendments of August 21, 1990'. (1991) *Beirut Review*, 1, 119–72.

Tueni, G. (1991) 'Looking Ahead', in L. Fawaz (ed.), *State and Society in Lebanon.* Oxford: The Centre for Lebanese Studies and Tufts University, pp. 19–77.

Young, M. (2005) 'Give Assad More Reasons to Leave', *International Herald Tribune*, 5 January.

Zahar, M. (2002) 'Peace by Unconventional Means: Lebanon's Ta'if Agreement', in, S. J. Stedman, D. Rothchild and E. M. Cousens (eds), *Ending Civil Wars: The Implementation of Peace Agreements.* Boulder, London: Lynne Rienner.

Part III
Deepening Democracy

10
Overlapping Identities:
Power Sharing and Women's Rights
Rachel Rebouché and Kate Fearon

WOMEN AND POWER SHARING

Women 'as a group' are unlike most others. They continue to be the target of widespread and systematic discrimination; yet the fact that their identities cut across almost all social, political, economic and cultural groups makes them enormously difficult to protect. The need to redress discrimination while at the same time allowing for the fluidity of women's identity and experience creates a tension with which feminists – including contemporary feminists who look to the literature on multiculturalism for inspiration – have long struggled: how to take the position of women within a particular group seriously while at the same time accounting for the fact that women themselves are a diverse group across society as a whole.

Within the context of a divided society struggling to build a sustainable power-sharing democracy, this tension is often heightened and exacerbated. Although power sharing can be a crucial element in according due recognition to conflicting group identities, we contend that it can nevertheless damage cross-communal relationships by ignoring the complexities of individual identity. As other authors in this collection highlight, groups participating in power-sharing arrangements are not themselves monoliths. But, depending on how particular group identities are institutionalised, those institutions may create terms of political engagement that are ill-suited to meeting the diverse needs of individual group members. In short, the danger is that if we seek to protect a group by institutionalising its identity, we may stifle internal diversity; but if we strive to protect internal diversity, we may end up weakening our ability to protect the group. This is especially true with respect to women because diversity of the type that women express 'as a group' is often perceived as a threat to ethno-national group cohesion.

In order to explore why the institutionalisation of identity through power sharing can be problematic for the pursuit of gender equality,

155

this chapter will begin by examining two particular cases: Northern Ireland and Bosnia and Herzegovina. Against this background, we will then explore some of the difficulties that contemporary feminists have in trying to balance the need to recognise women as a group with the need to recognise the diversity particular to women. The chapter will then conclude by offering a number of suggestions as to how future research on these issues might avoid creating the false choice between feminism and group identity and instead seek to encourage institutions that recognise and accommodate the complexity of women's interests and experiences.

THE INSTITUTIONALISATION OF IDENTITY: TWO EXAMPLES

Power sharing in Northern Ireland and Bosnia illustrates the difficulty of protecting (1) women as a group and (2) the diversity of women's identities in contexts marked by longstanding ethno-national antagonism. While the Belfast Agreement and the Dayton Accords establish power sharing between conflicting ethno-national communities, they also make specific provisions for gender equality and rights to non-discrimination. Yet these documents do not provide guidance when identities overlap in ways that pose particular problems for women. On the contrary, the Belfast Agreement and the Dayton Accords value identity primarily in the singularised terms of ethnicity and nationality, and hence lack meaningful ways to realise their respective promises of gender equality and non-discrimination.

Northern Ireland

The first of our two examples, then, concerns the 1998 Belfast Agreement. Since much has already been written about this Agreement, we assume some familiarity on the part of readers with its mechanics (see, for example, O'Leary 1999). In what follows, we will highlight only those aspects that bind access to political decision-making to predetermined, institutionalised identities in ways that we regard as troubling from a gender perspective.

As already indicated, the Agreement refers to issues of gender, equality and non-discrimination independently of the issue of national identity. For example, against the background of 'the recent history of communal conflict', the Agreement affirms (*inter alia*) the 'right to equal opportunity in all social and economic activity, regardless of class, creed, disability, gender or ethnicity', as well as the 'right of women to full and equal political participation'

(Agreement 1998, Strand Three, 'Rights, Safeguards and Equality of Opportunity', para. 1). Moreover, it commits the British Government to pursuing 'broad policies' that promote social and political inclusion and contribute towards 'the advancement of women in public life' (Agreement 1998, 'Rights, Safeguards and Equality of Opportunity', para. 1). More generally, the Agreement announced the creation of a new statutory Equality Commission charged with 'mainstreaming' equality provisions across Northern Ireland, and with ensuring that all public bodies 'equality proof' their policies as required under the terms of Section 75 (1) of the Northern Ireland Act 1998 (see McCrudden 2001).

Despite these (significant) references to gender and equality, the Agreement is nevertheless primarily framed in terms of national identity, British unionist and Irish nationalist. Perhaps nowhere is this more obvious than in how the Agreement treats collective decision making. Although most decisions made under the terms of the Agreement, and in particular within the Northern Ireland Assembly that it established, are taken using a simple majority rule, the Agreement also contains arrangements to ensure that key decisions are taken on a cross-community basis. These key decisions include the election of the First Minister and Deputy First Minister and budget allocations, although standing orders allow that any pressing issue of concern can, in principle, also be decided on this basis. More specifically, important decisions may be passed under the 'parallel consent' rule, which requires both an overall majority of Assembly members and a majority of both unionist and nationalist members; or, alternatively, they may be taken under the 'weighted majority' rule, which requires, amongst those present and voting, at least 60 per cent of all members voting, plus at least 40 per cent of both nationalist and unionist members (Agreement, Strand One, para. 5(d); O'Leary 1999, p. 70).

In order for the cross-community nature of such decisions to be validated, Members of the Legislative Assembly (MLAs) are required, upon taking up their seats after election, to designate themselves as 'Unionist', 'Nationalist' or 'Other'. However, since the parallel consent and weighted majority rules effectively mean that the votes of the 'Other' are discounted on key decisions, MLAs actually must designate as 'Nationalist' or 'Unionist' if they are to have a meaningful say (see O'Flynn 2003, p. 144). It is interesting to note that this designation can have as much or as little meaning for MLAs as they or their party like. In the present context, one example stands

out as being particularly apposite. In November 2001, MLAs from
the Women's Coalition (NIWC) – a political party that aims to be
trans-national – changed their designation (and later changed back
to their 'other' designation) on a key vote that effectively helped
save the Assembly from collapse.[1] The NIWC's re-designation was
not proscribed at that time because no party had anticipated that
another party would *want* to do this. NIWC MLAs were subsequently
prevented from doing so again by a hastily added Assembly rule.
From the perspective of the NIWC at least, this new rule illustrated
how seriously the dominant unionist and nationalist parties view the
issue of identity and, more particularly, how committed they are to
its rigidity and continuance.

Bosnia and Herzegovina

In many senses, the position of women in public life in Bosnia and
Herzegovina is actually stronger – at least on paper – than that of
women in Northern Ireland. The 1995 Dayton Peace Accords, which
incorporate the European Convention of Human Rights (ECHR) into
domestic law as one of its provisions (*General Framework Agreement
for Peace* (GFAP), Annex 6, Agreement on Human Rights), does not
contain any reference to gender representation, to gender-specific war
crimes like rape, or the gendered impact of war policies like 'ethnic
cleansing'. However, subsequent to the Dayton Peace Accords, several
initiatives aimed at raising the issue of gender in a post-conflict,
transition context have been introduced.

For example, the Provisional Election Law (the law under which
the early elections were run) placed a requirement on political parties
to ensure that candidate lists have no less than one third of either
gender. This requirement is now part of the Permanent Election Law
(Article 4.19, State Election Law, Bosnia and Herzegovina). More
clearly still, Section 9 of the Bosnian Gender Law makes explicit
provision for gender inclusion in a very practical way. It states that
the 'state and local authority bodies, corporate management bodies,
political parties and other non-profit organisations shall ensure and
promote equal gender representation in management and the decision
making process', to which end 'the relevant authorities shall draw
up special programmes and plans to improve gender representation
in the bodies of governance at all levels' (Law on Gender Equality
in Bosnia and Herzegovina, Article 15 (2003)).

In explicitly recognising and making provision for gender
inclusion, the Gender Law implicitly acknowledges gender as a key

social and individual identifier – seemingly a legal admission that the ethno-national 'bias' of the Dayton Peace Accords does not reflect the multiple components of identity which may constitute an individual's sense of self. The trouble is, however, that there are no resources within the legal, civil service or NGO arenas in Bosnia and Herzegovina to actually oversee, implement and enforce the provisions of the Gender Law. Moreover, parliamentary elections have had little if any effect on altering the gender balance in political life. Currently, there are only 16.8 per cent women in the National Assembly of the Republika Srpska, 21 per cent in the Bosniak–Croat Federation House of Representatives and 14 per cent in the State Parliament. Nor, for that matter, has it served to alter the attitude of political party leaders. For example, in municipal elections to be held in October 2004, the position of Mayor was directly elected for the first time. Candidates for this position were subject to the same provision, presumably because parties only put forward one candidate each for the position. So, while most major parties have Women's Forums and relatively good paper policies on the position of women, only 33 out of a total of 803 candidates for Mayor were women.

In a sense, of course, none of this should come as a surprise. This concern for women's interests is set against a power-sharing backdrop that does not simply recognise the three main ethno-national groups, but embeds them deeply at almost every level of the state. There are, for example, three main legislatures, one each for the central state and the two entities (the Bosniak–Croat Federation and the Republika Srpska). The central state parliament is comprised of two Houses: a directly elected body and an indirectly elected body with representatives from each of the three main ethnic groups (Serbs, Bosniaks and Croats). The executives of the entity parliaments are also required to have ethnically proportional representation, as is the Executive Branch of the state parliament, referred to as the Council of Ministers (COM). While details could easily be multiplied, the basic point should be clear enough: the fundamental institutional emphasis of political life is firmly placed on the ethno-national communities, which is difficult to reconcile with issues of gender equality.

Shared issues and obstacles for overlapping identities

Power-sharing agreements, like those in Northern Ireland and Bosnia, must contend with what are often conflicting concepts: group accommodation and rights to non-discrimination. What, we might wonder, would happen if one identifier (ethnicity) were to come into direct competition with another (gender)? Or more concretely, what would happen if the Gender Law came into conflict with the Constitutional Court ruling on the constitutiveness of all three peoples?[2] These are not merely speculative questions but may well have crucial practical consequences. A well-qualified Bosniak woman could, for example, be rejected for a position with the newly established State Court because the Court had reached its quota of Bosniaks and is only seeking those from a Serb or Croat background. If this person sees herself primarily as a woman who happens to have Islam as her religion, it is not clear if this would amount to gender discrimination. The political answer to such questions, however, would probably be to side with the imperative of ethnicity, given that gender relations are not the attributed cause of the war. The legal answer, however, remains open.

While Bosnia and Herzegovina has the possibility of raising this interesting politico-legal question, at one important level the same is not true of Northern Ireland. The Belfast Agreement does not explicitly institutionalise communities by requiring representative quotas at the political level, throughout the civil service, the judiciary and significant public authorities. For this reason, the rights of women enshrined in the Agreement and the rights of communities seem much less likely to conflict with each other. It is notable, however, that on those few occasions where the Agreement does prescribe quotas – such as the Protestant/Catholic 50-50 recruitment policy within the police service – special legal dispensations have allowed these bodies to remain exempt from the Section 75 (1) equality duty alluded to above.[3] As a consequence, if a Protestant woman were to apply to the police and then be refused on the basis that the Protestant quota had already been achieved, she could not claim gender discrimination under Section 75 (1) of the Northern Ireland Act.

Viewed from the perspective of a gender equality agenda, special legal dispensations indicate a hierarchy that values group-based concerns over women's concerns. Admittedly, the goals of conflict management are such that prioritising national group identity may be necessary to stop ethno-political violence and encourage inter-communal reconciliation. But as currently organised, power-sharing institutions guarantee representation for ethno-national communities without ensuring that a commitment to gender equality is taken up by their representatives. They lack the additional mechanisms or institutional incentives for ethno-national parties to organise to contemplate different priorities. Within each national or ethnic camp there are a number of parties competing for the same role: to be the protector of the nationalist group as a whole. Any party making overtures to the 'other side' risks incurring severe electoral punishment from within its own group, who will present moderation as 'weakness' or 'failure', incompatible with 'standing up for the national interest'. Under these conditions, the question of discussing women's political participation is viewed as diverting attention from the 'real' issues at hand: promoting and protecting the national interest of the group. Crucially, this is exactly what creates the 'false dichotomy' that feminist theorists fear: an artificial choice between acting on behalf of 'women's interests' or being part of a group's political agenda.

GENDER, DIFFERENCE AND GROUP ACCOMMODATION

The Northern Ireland and Bosnia and Herzegovina examples provide a useful context for thinking about some of the problems that women in power-sharing contexts face. In particular, they serve to highlight the central tension that this chapter seeks to explore, namely, the tension between (1) the need to take the position of women within a particular group seriously and (2) the need to take seriously the fact that women themselves are always a diverse group (both within that group *and* across society as a whole). This tension is acute, especially, though by no means exclusively, in the case of divided societies trying to build a sustainable, power-sharing democracy. For while power sharing is now widely regarded as the most appropriate means of instantiating democracy in contexts marked by deep, ethno-national divisions, the tendency to opt for mechanisms that institutionalise group identities can impact adversely on within-*group* differences, making it all the more difficult to address within-*gender* distinctions. Under such conditions, women often find themselves in a double-bind. On the one hand, if they are to succeed politically, women may have to conform to an institutionalised identity that may be untrue to their particular experiences. On the other hand, this means that women may end up denying their own internal diversity as a distinctive group. As we argued above, this adverse impact is not mitigated by the often hollow impact that mainstreaming gender concerns in new power-sharing institutions produces.

Theorists, working within both the feminist and multiculturalist traditions, have sought to address this tension by looking to reform systems of governance in general. However, as we will now show, framing their suggestions and insights against a background of power sharing and ethno-national division does much to illuminate both the strengths and the weaknesses of their particular approaches.

The women's movement and fair bargaining

Feminists have long been concerned with how structures of governance relate to an equality agenda. The early Western women's movement was a response to what many women's rights activists saw as the masculine nature of formal politics that had traditionally excluded women, both in terms of participation and in terms of the types of issues discussed. More specifically, it was a response to the ways in which men and women were defined against each other and how those definitions led to social and political structures that rewarded masculine characteristics (Squires 1996, p. 627). Put more positively, those in the early women's movement emphasised the need to dissolve the infamous 'public/private' distinction and, correspondingly, to create a more collaborative, consensual style of decision making. Ideally, this meant adopting an 'intensely egalitarian approach' (Phillips 1991, pp. 121) that could transcend the things that differentiated women from one another in favour of a more 'universal' notion of woman's identity (Phillips 1993, pp. 67–70).

Contemporary feminist theorists have, however, criticised the early feminist movement on the grounds that it substituted one kind of devaluing for another: instead of the public/private distinction, the early feminists relied on a conception of women's rights that became seen as insufficiently sensitive to the diversity of women's experiences and, correspondingly, the sources of women's oppression (see Phillips 1991, pp. 106–11). Put in slightly different terms, contemporary feminists have argued that, although the public/private distinction was undoubtedly a source of oppression and subjugation, the early feminist movement could itself be exclusionary, simply because its notion of what it meant to be a woman was too narrowly construed. In this vein, for example, Anne Phillips has detailed the problems that women's movements have had with accountability and transparency in the making of decisions that supposedly represent 'women'. More specifically, she has considered the ways in which the intensely egalitarian ideals of the earlier feminist movement were often a source of disillusionment for those who were excluded from the movement's close-knit organisation and its prevailing notion of 'women's interests' (1991, pp. 133–46).

For contemporary feminists, making the women's movement more inclusive has therefore focused on the need to ensure greater recognition of the fluidity and contingency of women's identities. Significantly, the women's movement's desire to ensure that the diversity of women's interests and concerns were taken seriously coincided with, and in certain respects drew upon, the modern articulation of multiculturalism and its concern with protecting the identity of subjugated groups and communities. Perhaps unsurprisingly, the feminist model of multiculturalism has come to be characterised by a more pronounced focus on how procedures that facilitate the participation of under-represented groups might be created so as to ensure consistent access and transparency for all members of society, irrespective of their gender. This has translated into a demand for a 'proceduralist' model of democracy that is more inclusive of difference and that creates greater space for a diversity of different modes of participation and democratic communication (Squires 1996, pp. 627–8; Young 2000).

This latter development within the contemporary feminist movement has not, however, been systematically applied to the more specific challenges that power sharing in divided societies raises. In particular, feminists have not considered the ways in which power sharing – and, more specifically, the institutionalisation of group identities – impact on questions of in-group differentiation and cross-cutting identities. At the same time, it is important to acknowledge that there is significant overlap between the thinking behind many contemporary power-sharing arrangements and the more general concerns of contemporary feminist scholars: the Dayton Accords and the Belfast Agreement can be understood as mechanisms that amend the linear, traditional democratic process – and in particular majoritarian democracy (Lijphart 1984) – to take account of, to be inclusive of, difference (albeit difference narrowly defined in terms of ethno-national identity).

When it comes to recognising and protecting difference, it seems, then, that democracy can be more nuanced. However, when feminist scholars argue that systems of governance need to take account of women, for example through the provision of quotas, they have been met with criticism that such changes are antithetical to democracy. Particularly in divided societies, the charge has been that in claiming institutional recognition for women within particular ethno-national groups, they run the risk of undermining the coherence of such groups and, consequently, their ability to participate as such within the democratic process. We address this issue in the following sub-section.

Women in national and ethnic groups

Unlike the demands made by conflicting ethno-national groups for special group-based protections, the central tension with which feminists are concerned – that of accommodating and protecting women's diverse identities while assuring that the voices of women as minority groups will be heard – has not been systematically addressed at the institutional level. On the contrary, feminists continue to be concerned about how institutional arrangements that seek to protect ethno-national groups – such as ensuring group representation in politics, mutual vetoes, and so on – actually allow particular ethno-national groups to further their own sexist ideologies.

For example, some scholars have highlighted the ways in which feminism and nationalism collide under liberation movements, identity movements that are internal to societies, and decolonisation movements (see, for example, West 1992, p. 568). In nationalist movements, for example, there is usually a tension between the prioritisation of the struggle and women's concerns, where feminism becomes threatening to the perceived social order. This tension seems to be particularly acute when motherhood and the private dimension becomes an important signifier of group consciousness. In this context, Nira Yuval-Davis has highlighted how 'women are often the ones who are given the social role of intergenerational transmitters of cultural traditions' in groups who are fighting to preserve their religious, ethnic or national identity (1998, p. 28). In such groups, she contends, women are often the 'symbolic bearers of collective identity' such that departures from group norms are perceived as threats to the stability of the group taken as a whole (1998, p. 29).

Thus, as Susan Moller Okin and Yuval-Davis recognise, part of the problem with multiculturalism is the assumption that groups are homogeneous or that all members of a specific group or cultural collectivity are equally committed to that culture (Okin 1999; Yuval-Davis 1998). To the extent that the standard consociational power-sharing model (Lijphart 1977) also treats groups as if they are a homogeneous whole, it, too, cannot resolve the basic tension that this chapter addresses. For as Yuval-Davis also enables us to see, 'such a construction would have space for neither internal power conflicts and interest difference within the minority collectivity, nor conflicts along the lines of class and gender as well as politics and culture' (1998, p. 28).

As our analysis of the cases of Northern Ireland and Bosnia and Herzegovina suggests, power sharing is, or certainly can be, a mechanism that gives group leaders institutional reasons to preserve group identity without coming to terms with how the rights of an ethno-national group and the rights of women within that group might conflict. If women are popularly imagined as the transmitters of group identity, then efforts to encourage a feminist agenda can be seen to be at odds with the institutionalised promotion of group rights.

Women's role and identity within groups is therefore complicated by the duality of that role: an identity that is formed in part by group characteristics and an identity that is often subjugated because of a group's oppressive gender norms or because of group decisions that undervalue women's interests (see West 1992, p. 575). Yet, rather than try to address this duality through a more universalised notion of feminism – where women's rights are simplistically pitted against nationalist interests – contemporary feminists have sought alternative routes of redress.

Gendered citizenship and representation

As already noted, feminists have sought to develop their own style of participatory democracy, one that aims to be more inclusive of the diversity of women's experiences and less hierarchical in respect of them (Rouslton 1998, p. 26). More specifically, authors like Carole Pateman (1989) have argued that the task is no longer that of fighting for citizenship rights for women as such, but about challenging citizenship, particularly with respect to the invisibility of the domestic sphere, so that the differences that attach to gender can be debated in the public domain. Unfortunately, this debate has been somewhat stymied because women have not been able to consistently attain the kind of political profile that might enable them to highlight such issues publicly. As our examples demonstrated, a combination of gender bias, electoral process and selection process means that few women reach top positions within mainstream parties or are put forward for electable seats (see also Ward 2000). This predicament is further complicated by the nature of representation, at least in the sense that women elected to political office do not always advocate on behalf of women's interests.

These considerations have been highlighted by women disillusioned with the lack of participation options. In response, they have advocated a movement towards a politics that emphasises inclusion, shared ownership, and fairness in process – in other words, new ways of dealing with difference. To this end, scholars like Anne Phillips (1995) and Iris Marion Young (1990, 2000) have drawn from the civic republican tradition, communitarian politics and deliberative democratic theory. Young, for example, argues that although citizenship has already been translated into terms that are allegedly applicable to everyone, it is, in fact, levelling of difference on a more explicit level (1990, pp. 118–21). In response, she argues for differentiated citizenship and has defended separate institutions for particular groups, including women and indigenous peoples, within a broader system of federated government (1990, pp. 173–83, 2000, pp. 255–65). In other words, she has advocated the type of consociational arrangement that many scholars of power sharing argue make group meeting, discussion and policy making possible in divided societies. Yet as we have already suggested, the trouble is that to the extent that consociational forms of power sharing tend to freeze the experienced fluidity of women's interests and experiences, they tend to institutionalise identity in precisely the way that our paper rejects.

In contrast, Phillips focuses on a 'politics of presence' which goes beyond the institutionalisation of particular group identities and creates mechanisms of publicity and accountability by drawing heavily on deliberative democratic theory. More specifically, Phillips advocates a form of public debate that emphasises the accommodation of difference, both in terms of the contributions that might feed into that debate and in terms of its outcome (Phillips 1995). At the same time, however, Phillips recognises that a culture of deliberation might nevertheless favour some participants over others (1995, pp. 145–65; see also Young 1999, p. 155). This, she suggests, is particularly true for women, not simply because (as noted above) they continue to struggle to achieve the kind of political profile that could lend greater weight to their concerns, but because the full diversity of women's interests cannot always be easily expressed within the standard political rhetoric (see also Rouslton 1998, p. 36).

Thus, despite the excellent scholarship on these issues, we are still left with some fundamental questions about how identities are constructed and, more specifically, how overlapping identities like those of women should be valued. As Squires has noted, both feminism and multiculturalism fail to define what differences we will value, on what ethical basis and by what set of procedures we will assign this value (Squires 1996, p. 627).

WHERE DO WE GO FROM HERE?

Feminists are struggling to find new ways of responding to political structures that impact negatively on women – as members of particular groups, as in-group members, and as a gender category that reaches across society as a whole. By way of tentative suggestion, we argue that the reason why contemporary feminism seems to be in such a state is because it has failed to take seriously precisely the kinds of issues that power sharing in divided societies poses for women: institutionalised identities that reward certain kinds of political participation over others; political structures that effectively exclude women; rights legislation that does not satisfactorily address the particular heterogeneity of women's interests.

One approach might be to draw on the kinds of institutionalised models suggested by Young that support creating privileges of citizenship based on the characteristics of the group. This would suggest a new layer to power-sharing arrangements that could allow women to have their own distinctive voice within the democratic process. Considering the problems theorists and activists alike have encountered with trying to further a universalised notion of 'women', and given the already stifling effects of power sharing on intra-group identity, this option may not move us closer to valuing overlapping identities. Institutionalising identity may be a step in the right direction – and under certain sorts of empirical conditions may be the only viable approach to protecting groups – but it seems to fall into the trap of treating 'women' as a singularised identity.

Perhaps, then, what is needed is an approach that takes the commitments that some contemporary power-sharing arrangements have already made to gender equality much more seriously. This would mean treating gender as a legally cognisable category that deserves the same scrutiny as ethnic or national identity, particularly when thinking about questions of political representation. In particular, it would mean that the courts need to weigh gender and ethnicity concerns as equally valuable categories, and not simply assume that the one must necessarily trump the other. Attractive though this second approach may be, it does suffer from two fairly obvious drawbacks. Firstly, taken to its extreme, this approach seems tantamount to a quota system for women in power-sharing arrangements, and hence seems open to the same sorts of objections that we have just levelled at Young. After all, if women's rights are to have any positive effect, then the terms of those rights must be fixed in legislation and hence may not be flexible enough to account for the diversity of women's experiences and interests, both within particular groups and across society as a whole. Secondly, this approach also seems to overlook the fact that, in societies marked by longstanding ethno-national antagonisms, the project of creating mechanisms that could enable women to have a more effective voice in the democratic process may have to take its place behind the project of creating just and stable institutional relations between competing ethno-national groups (see O'Neill 2003, p. 387). And yet, it seems to us that herein may lie a third potential solution.

We accept, then, that under some conditions, it may be currently impracticable to create power-sharing arrangements that contain language that is equally weighted between the concerns of women and those of ethno-national groups. However, if divided societies are to succeed in their attempts to build a just and stable democracy, then that democracy must make room for everyone in society. Put in slightly different terms, the responsibility for making democracy work does not rest – nor should it rest – simply with the leaders of the various ethno-national parties, but with everyone in society, irrespective of how they choose to express themselves as democratic citizens (see O'Flynn 2004, pp. 556–7). This is especially so, given the rather obvious but oddly often neglected fact that women form half the population.

Women's overlapping identities give them a unique group characteristic, and a unique set of perspectives, that must be more thoughtfully provided for in the design of power-sharing institutions. What this suggests is a need to rewrite power-sharing mechanisms in a way that recognises the protection that disadvantaged groups *within* groups and *across* society require if they are to have an effective voice within the democratic system. From a gender perspective, what it suggests is the need for institutional incentives that reward progress in pursuing a women's rights agenda, and that encourage elected officials to consider the gender implications of their decisions much more comprehensively. Crucially, these are not mere utopian aspirations. If, as Donald Horowitz (2001, 2002), Benjamin Reilly (2001), Timothy Sisk (1996) and others have suggested, it is possible to design power-sharing mechanisms that reward moderates, then it is surely possible to design mechanisms that similarly create greater space for women and hence pre-empt some of the problems we posed in our case studies. They may even go some way in helping national leaders understand the ways in which gender is essential in understanding conflict itself, and indicative of national group diversity generally.

In conclusion, then, our primary intention in advancing these, admittedly tentative, suggestions is to highlight the need to think proactively and creatively about the unintended consequences of power sharing for women. These ideas are by no means fleshed out in ways that would suggest more concrete reform. But they do suggest approaches that might eventually enable women to deal just that bit better with the difficult issues that gender discrimination raises in general and in the case of divided societies in particular. If we are to succeed in fostering stable, post-conflict societies, we need to have frank conversations about the unintended consequences of power sharing for questions of gender equality and discrimination. This, we believe, is the underlying aim that power sharing ideally seeks to address. It is a goal, however, that cannot be obtained without a pluralistic and context-sensitive approach that takes its own commitment to protect group identity, with all of its complexity, seriously.

NOTES

1. Minutes of proceedings, Northern Ireland Assembly, 6 November 2001. Available at http://www.niassembly.gov.uk/minutes/proceedings/011102.htm.
2. Constitutional Court of Bosnia and Herzegovina, 'Request for evaluation of certain provisions of the Constitution of the Republika Srpska and the Constitution of the Federation of Bosnia and Herzegovina'. Case No. U 5/98-III, Third Partial Decision, 1 July, Paragraph 61, 1 July 2000. See also 'Implementing Equality: The "constituent peoples" decision in Bosnia and Herzegovina', ICG Balkans Report No.128, 16 April 2002.
3. Upon first forming, the Parades Commission did not have any female members. In *Re. White*, a female applicant lost her challenge in the High Court, failing to convince the court that the appointments were discriminatory and offended the principles of the Agreement. *In the Matter of an Application by Evelyn White for Judicial Review* (2000) NIQB.

REFERENCES

Agreement Reached in the Multiparty Negotiations (1998). Belfast: The Stationery Office.
General Framework Agreement for Peace (1995). Available at http://www.nato.int/ifor/gfa.

170 **Deepening Democracy**

Horowitz, D. (2001) 'The Northern Ireland Agreement: Clear, Consociational, and Risky', in J. McGarry (ed.), *Northern Ireland and the Divided World: Post-Agreement Northern Ireland in Comparative Perspective*. Oxford: Oxford University Press, pp. 89–108.

—— (2002) 'Explaining the Northern Ireland Agreement: The Sources of an Unlikely Constitutional Consensus', *British Journal of Political Science*, 32 (2), 193–220.

Lijphart, A. (1977) *Democracy in Plural Societies*. New Haven, NJ: Yale University Press.

—— (1984) *Democracies: Patterns of Majoritarian and Consensus Government in Twenty-one Countries*. New Haven, NJ: Yale University Press.

McCrudden, C. (2001) 'Equality', in C. Harvey (ed.), *Human Rights, Equality and Democratic Renewal in Northern Ireland*. Oxford: Hart Publishing, pp. 75–112.

Northern Ireland Act (UK) (1998). HMSO.

O'Flynn, I. (2003) 'The Problem of Recognising Individual and National Identities: A Critique of the Belfast Agreement', *Critical Review of International Social and Political Philosophy*, 6 (3), 129–53.

—— (2004) 'Why Justice Can't Have It All: In Reply to O'Neill', *Ethnicities*, 4 (4), 545–61.

Okin, S. M. (1999) *Is Multiculturalism Bad for Women?* Princeton, NJ: Princeton University Press.

O'Leary, B. (1999) 'The Nature of the Agreement', *New Left Review*, 233, 66–96.

O'Neill, S. (2003) 'Justice in Ethnically Diverse Societies: A Critique of Political Alienation', *Ethnicities*, 3 (3), 369–92.

Pateman, C. (1989) *The Disorder of Women: Democracy, Feminism and Political Theory*. Cambridge: Polity Press.

Phillips, A. (1991) *Engendering Democracy*. Cambridge: Polity Press.

—— (1993) *Democracy and Difference*. Cambridge: Polity Press.

—— (1995) *The Politics of Presence*. Oxford: Clarendon Press.

Reilly, B. (2001) *Democracy in Divided Societies: Electoral Engineering for Conflict Management*. Cambridge: Cambridge University Press.

Rouslton, C. (1998) 'Democracy and the Challenge of Gender: New Visions, New Processes', in R. Wilford and R. Miller (eds), *Women, Ethnicity and Nationalism*. London: Routledge, pp. 24–46.

Sisk, T. D. (1996) *Power Sharing and International Mediation in Ethnic Conflict*. Washington, DC: United States Institute of Peace Press.

Squires, J. (1996) 'Liberal Constitutionalism, Identity and Difference', *Political Studies*, 44 (3), 620–34.

Ward, M. (2000) 'The Northern Ireland Assembly and Women: Assessing the Gender Deficit', in *Women and the Local Government Elections: Briefing Papers*. Belfast: Democratic Dialogue.

West, L. (1992) 'Feminist Nationalist Social Movements: Beyond Universalism and Towards a Gendered Cultural Relativism', *Women Studies International Forum*, 15 (5/6), 563–79.

Young, I. M. (1990) *Justice and the Politics of Difference*. Princeton, NJ: Princeton University Press.

—— (1999) 'Justice, Inclusion, and Deliberative Democracy', in S. Macedo (ed.), *Deliberative Politics: Essays on Democracy and Disagreement*. Oxford: Oxford University Press, pp. 151–8.

—— (2000) *Democracy and Inclusion*. Oxford: Oxford University Press.

Yuval-Davis, N. (1998) 'Gender and Nation', in R. Wilford and R. Miller (eds), *Women, Ethnicity and Nationalism*. London: Routledge, pp. 23–35.

11
Below and Beyond Power Sharing: Relational Structures across Institutions and Civil Society

Manlio Cinalli

In this chapter, I analyse divisions in the public and institutional domains across specific cases of power sharing in order to intervene in the debate about the causal relationship between power-sharing implementation and inter-community segmentation. First, I focus on inter-community networks in the public domain, in order to assess the extent to which actors in civil society are embedded within a structure of linkages that extends beyond the limits of their own particular community, cutting across the main social cleavages. Secondly, I combine this 'horizontal' analysis of inter-community network patterns with an examination of 'vertical' networks that associations and organisations in civil society forge with political elites and state actors in the institutional domain. On the assumption that this 'vertical' pattern of networks will be impacted on by the kind of power-sharing institutions that are put in place, as well as by their degree of implementation, I formulate a four-part typology that can be used to analyse specific cases. I then move on to provide empirical support for these theoretical considerations that will demonstrate their relevance to rethinking power sharing. More specifically, I focus on the cases of Belgium, South Tyrol, Switzerland and Northern Ireland in order to illustrate a number of possible developments across the typology. In doing so, my aim in this chapter is to show that the prescription of institutional solutions cannot be separated from the empirical assessment of relationships and exchanges across institutions and civil society.

More specifically, then, this chapter begins by presenting the theoretical foundations of network analysis and systematically explains the idea of a 'relational structure' for those readers who might be unfamiliar with the approach. The main idea is that social and political actors are to be thought of as interdependent rather than independent units, across both the public domain and institutions of the state. It therefore becomes crucial to focus on the relations among actors, rather than on their more individualistic characteristics. Against this conceptual background, I propose a framework which, as I have already indicated, combines an analysis of inter-community networks in the public domain with an analysis of networks between different organisations and political elites across public and institutional domains. The aim of this analysis is to explore connections between civil society and power-sharing institutions. Following this introduction, I turn my to attention to identifying and comparing types of social and political processes that may occur in divided societies, testing the main hypotheses of power-sharing theory – and in particular its emphasis on democratic inclusion of both minority and majority groups – by reference to the four different empirical cases mentioned above. The main argument is that it is hardly possible to distinguish a straightforward causal relationship between the setting up of power-sharing institutions in contexts of deep divisions on the one hand, and decreasing inter-community antagonism between social and political actors across the public and institutional domains on the other hand, as is often assumed in the classical power-sharing literature. A final section sums up the main results of my study, emphasising the claim that empirical analyses of inter-community ties in the public and institutional domains should integrate, and in certain respects precede, prescriptive institutional design.

POWER SHARING AND RELATIONAL STRUCTURES

Scholars of power sharing exhibit considerable awareness of the range of possible institutional options when analysing contexts characterised by deep division and inter-community antagonism (see, for example, Sisk 1996). They have extensively examined the role of political and institutional arrangements to specify the contours within which political action is formulated and conducted, thus explaining and predicting the preference formation and strategies of the main political actors. Within this ongoing debate, special attention has been dedicated to the study of elites' behaviour (or the behaviour of leaders) and the processes of institutionalised decision making. For example, it is widely argued that political parties, bureaucracies, central governments and politicians need to forgo simple majority rule and embrace consensual, cross-community deliberation.

And yet, notwithstanding the valuable insights which have been provided by empirical investigations of conflict across deep cleavages of language, ethnicity, religion, nationality and so forth, it is notable that the policy focus and elite biases of the power-sharing debate have left the field weak in its appreciation of the independent role of specific configurations of relationships between conflicting communities in civil society and across public and policy domains. There has, in other words, been little concern given to civil society actors and networks that cut across divided societies and that, although politically significant, often stand outside the main decision-making institutions of the state (but see Lederach 1998; Varshney 2003). Thus, as I will argue, further advances in the study of divided societies and power sharing will depend, at least in part, on a better theoretical integration of power sharing and the structural analysis of actors within contexts of deep division, emphasising their correlation for explaining their strategies, values and behaviour. This linkage requires moving beyond vague references to the relationship between power sharing and network analysis. A robust theoretical framework is required that can integrate power sharing with the numerous studies of political participation found within the literature on network analysis in order to give more space to the role of civil society, which is frequently overlooked in the literature on power sharing, sometimes to the advantage of particular parties, elites and institutions (see Sisk 1996, p. 83). In sum, there is a need to integrate the analysis of formal decision-making institutions with the realm of social life, paying greater attention to the broader public domain, which is distinct from but nevertheless connected to formal decision-making institutions and the role of elites in the policy-formation domain. It is in the public domain, broadly conceived, that a wide range of actors exist and take action, potentially benefiting the development and consolidation of the democratic, power-sharing framework (Diamond 1994; Walzer 1992).

I propose, then, that this theoretical integration can be achieved by drawing on social-network analysis and, in particular, on the concept of relational structure. By 'relational structure' I mean the complex set of linkages in which actors are embedded within and across the public and institutional domains. By actors in the institutional domain, I have in mind, *inter alia*, the role of the main political and legal institutions, legislative decision makers and political elites, whereas I take the public domain to be comprised, again *inter alia*, of a wide range of actors such as interest groups, non-governmental organisations, political parties, churches, social movements and grassroots organisations. It is important to stress that relational ties between all these actors within and across institutional and public domains are not simply the channels for the flow of both material and non-material resources, such as the transmission of information, financial help, knowledge, and the formation of values and beliefs. Rather, they are also the means through which power-sharing institutions aim to include the members of different groups, organisations and communities within the political process. Viewed in this way, the idea of relational structure provides us with a powerful analytical tool to assess the extent to which communities (or actors within distinctive communities) can effectively access, and participate in, the institutional domain. Crucially, however, I maintain that it is not simply an analytical tool, but potentially provides for a fuller or more complete account of what power sharing involves. Power sharing does involve institutions, but it is also much more than this. It includes both the institutional and the social dimensions of political life, as well as the myriad linkages that may be formed within and across those dimensions.

Admittedly, these are ambitious claims. Yet it must be remembered that it is only relatively recently that social scientists have begun to fully engage with a research approach that evaluates political action starting from the appraisal of its relational properties. For example, scholars of social capital have emphasised the importance of resources embedded in social networks, which can be accessed by actors wishing to increase their likelihood of success in a purposive action, both at the individual (Lin 1999 and 2001) and at the group level (Bourdieu 1986; Coleman 1990; Putnam 1993 and 1995). The study of social networks has also found extensive application in a wide range of other research questions, and in particular on specific research questions of social-movement analysis and contentious politics, such as inter-organisational networks and overlapping memberships (Diani 1992 and 1995), processes of mobilisation and counter-mobilisation (Franzosi 1997 and 1999), the influence of individuals' relational contexts on their decision to mobilise (Klandermans 1990; Passy 2001), and the impact of whole communities' network structures on the development of their collective action (Gould 1991 and 1995). Admittedly, many of these latter projects have made use of social networks to determine the exogenous circumstances within which collective actors operate, and have thus offered a different perspective from theories of social capital (which consider social networks as an internal resource). But they have not extended this research to contexts that are aiming to deal with division through the establishment and consolidation of democratic, power-sharing institutions.

In sum, then, four central principles have to be emphasised to distinguish the network approach used in this chapter from 'standard' social science perspectives. First, actors are understood to be interdependent rather than independent units, and the relations among them are the principal focus of analysis. Secondly, the analytically relevant characteristics that can be identified for these actors can be explained as the effect of their structural and/or relational features. Thirdly, relational ties between these actors are indeed the channels for the flow of both material and non-material resources, but are also the channels through which power sharing includes different communities within the state's institutions. Fourthly, the complete network of actors, their positions and their linkages, provides opportunities for and constraints upon action. It is therefore assumed that each actor can be viewed as a node from which lines radiate to other actors/nodes within or across communities in the public and institutional domains. Figure 11.1 represents this assumption graphically: actors are structurally embedded not only in terms of their position within one of the constituent communities of a divided society, but also in terms of their relational structures *both* across communities *and* across public and institutional domains. They can be embedded in different patterns of relational structures across these positions. On the one hand, actors in the two communities (X and Y) can build linkages with other actors within the same community and hence establish intra-community networks (ties within the same community are drawn with dotted lines in Fig. 11.1). But they can also cut across social cleavages by establishing inter-community ties in the public domain.

On the other hand, civil society actors from both sides of the cleavage can be embedded in extensive relationships with policy elites and state actors more generally. This point is of crucial importance since, as already stated, the examination of linkages between community associations or organisations and institutional actors is a main focus of investigation, not least because these networks are considered to be a crucial indicator of the degree to which power-sharing institutions are genuinely inclusive (see Lijphart 1977).

Figure 11.2 utilises Cartesian axes to illustrate my distinction between political and social structures in contexts of deep division, presenting the results of their combination in a typology of

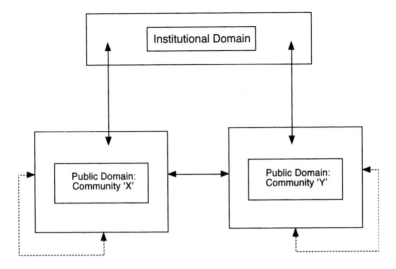

Fig. 11.1   Relational Structures in Divided Societies (Two Communities, X and Y)

network patterns across the public and institutional domains. More specifically, the Cartesian axes, which draw on network analysis for framing relations within a divided society, aim to model relations that majority (or dominant) and minority (or subaltern) communities establish both with one another and with power-sharing institutions. These axes represent the coupling of (1) a particular type of interaction (loose/dense) that characterises relational structures between majority and minority communities in the public domain, and (2) a particular type of interaction (loose/dense) which connects civil society actors from minority communities to policy elites and state actors in the institutional domain. Structures conducive to minority 'marginalisation' and majority hegemony are modelled in the bottom-left area, and are characterised by a combination of loose inter-community networks and loose exchanges between minority communities and state institutions. Where such structures dominate, minority organisations build only loose networks with state actors in the institutional domain, and tend to form loose relational structures within the public domain.

Structures conducive to 'integration' between conflicting minority and majority communities are modelled in the top-right area, and involve a combination of dense inter-community networks and dense exchanges between the minority community and the state's

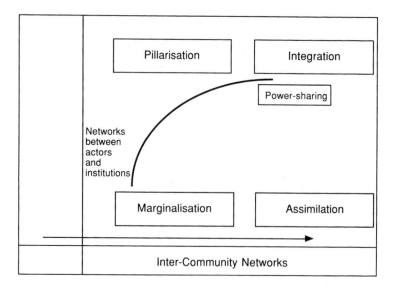

Fig. 11.2 Combinations of Political and Relational Structures

institutions. Under these conditions, both majority and minority communities find full representation in the institutional framework, while relational divisions are not reinforced within the public domain. 'Pillarisation' is found at the top left of the area, and is characterised by a combination of loose inter-community networks and dense exchanges between the minority community and the institutions. Where these structures dominate, majority and minority communities find full representation in the institutional framework, but only form loose ties with one another – as is often the case in states characterised by territorial federalism and/or high levels of group-based functional autonomy. Lastly, 'assimilation' is likely to occur at the bottom-right of the area, characterised by a combination of dense inter-community networks and loose exchanges between the minority community and state institutions. Here, the majority community holds a firm grip on the institutions, while relations between conflicting communities are made more dense by their interactions in the public domain.

At the same time, the Cartesian axes of Figure 11.2 provide meaningful conceptual space within which to situate what we might call a 'curve of segmentation' that models a trajectory posited by many scholars of power sharing, especially those in the consociational tradition. This curve shows that initial provisions for bringing minority organisations and representatives within the institutional domain are not immediately matched by decreasing tensions along the main societal cleavage. In fact, power sharing can often reinforce segmentation in the short run since communities become the main building blocks of politics (see Lijphart 1977, p. 42). Yet (or so the consociational argument typically goes), in the long run power sharing may reduce divisions so much that segmentation and inter-communal conflict lose their importance. According to this logic, power sharing itself is likely to become redundant since deep divisions and conflicts no longer need to be addressed. Hence, not only does Figure 11.2 integrate power sharing within a structural approach which furthers comparative investigation across real contexts of deep division through empirical measures of their relational properties; it also provides a conceptual framework which potentially allows us to test and challenge whether power-sharing institutions – and, in particular, those of the consociational variety – are sufficient to ameliorate or perhaps even transcend deep social and political divisions. As such, Figure 11.2 aims to advance empirically grounded answers to the main questions stated at the beginning of this chapter, namely, assessing whether a specific system of power sharing is working better than similar political experiences elsewhere, or whether there is an unequivocal causal relationship between the implementation of power sharing and decreased segmentation between conflicting communities. The next section aims to answer these questions, offering a broad analysis of inter-community networks and networks between community and institutional actors across a range of illustrative case studies.

ASSESSING RELATIONAL STRUCTURES ACROSS CASE STUDIES

While the typology outlined in the previous section provides a conceptual framework which models different possible empirical examples, network analysis is the actual analytical 'tool' that enables us to examine relationships within and across the public and institutional domains. More specifically, network analysis enables us to test the causal relation between institutional inclusion of constituent communities, on the one hand, and reduction of sectarian hostility as modelled in Figure 11.2 on the other. Since it can be assumed that all contexts where power sharing has been implemented have previously been characterised by strong inter-community conflict or perhaps hegemony of one community over the other(s), patterns of changing

relational structures can be graphically represented with arrows
starting somewhere from the bottom-left area of Figure 11.3.

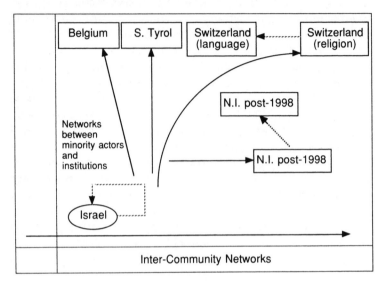

Fig. 11.3   Combinations of Political and Relational Structures

Although not a power-sharing democracy, Israel is a useful starting
point for this discussion insofar as it represents a contemporary
context characterised by sparse inter-community networks in a
context of predominant, majority exclusion of the minority from
the institutional domain. Some commentators argue that Israel is an
'ethnic democracy' (Smooha 2002; Yishai 2002), in no small measure
due to the fact that multi-party elections and democratic institutions
focus exclusively on the Jewish segment of the population. The
institutions of the 'Jewish' state, together with the presence of deep
inter-community divisions in the public domain, have forged a
relational structure between the state and its citizens that marginalises
the Arab, Muslim, Druze and Christian communities.

By contrast, Belgium provides a perfect example of a democratic
context that is characterised by both power sharing and deep divisions
(in this case, between two national-linguistic communities, namely,
the Dutch-speaking Flemings and the French-speaking Walloons).
Kris Deschouwer has already provided a detailed analysis of the
development of power sharing in Belgium in chapter 6 of this
volume. However, from the perspective of a network approach, the

point to pick up on from his argument is the fact that the inclusion of communities in the institutional domain has not been matched by the development of dense networks across the national-linguistic cleavage in the public domain. Indeed, the creation of a power-sharing system containing extensive provisions for both territorial and functional (community) autonomy, reinforced by the subsequent development of Belgian politics toward two separate monolingual party systems, has resulted in the formation of two distinct and predominantly unconnected public domains. Even claims on trans-national issues such as the environment have been made in different places and at different times by Green Dutch-speaking Flemings and Green French-speaking Walloons (Huan 1999). In short, the particular choice of power-sharing arrangements is in this case correlated with the reinforcement of community segmentation along the national-linguistic divide. The case of Belgium can thus be placed, in Figure 11.3, as an arrow moving with a negative inclination from the bottom-left to the top-left area. Increasing inclusion of communities within the institutional domain is in this case matched by decreasing inter-community networks in the public domain.

South Tyrol provides another example of power sharing in a context of deep national, territorial and linguistic divisions – in this case between German-, Italian- and Ladino-speaking communities. The full implementation of institutional, power-sharing reforms has had a significant stabilising impact on South Tyrol. Inter-community tensions have decreased and violence has come to a definitive end, while the German-speaking minority has been guaranteed political representation within the South Tyrol assembly and at the level of subnational government (Volgger 2001). Furthermore, in 1992 the Austrian government confirmed at UN level its satisfaction with the allocation of autonomy acknowledged by the Italian government to national-linguistic communities. Nevertheless, it should also be emphasised that inter-community networks in the public domain are still shaped along the national-linguistic cleavage. It suffices to emphasise that, within the party system, a deep division has separated the *Südtiroler Volkspartei* – which can rely on the almost unified support of the German-speaking community – from the other Italian political forces. The *Verdi-Grüne-Verc* have emerged as the only party actively engaged in recruiting members and leaders on both sides of the cleavage, while new social movements have rarely gained centrality within civil society and public debate. In sum, the case of South Tyrol can be drawn in our space as an arrow moving straight from the bottom-left to the top-left area, given the incorporation of communities as if they are homogeneous and pillarised blocks. The inclusion of these communities within the institutional domain has clearly brought about peace and stability, but it has nonetheless failed in fostering inter-community networks in the public domain.

Switzerland provides another example of power sharing, this time in a context of multiple deep divisions and cross-cutting cleavages. In particular, two main cleavages have been characterised by high salience, namely, language and religion. As regards religion, it is worth emphasising that the full implementation of power sharing in the 1950s did not mean a loss of salience of the religious cleavage, and each community continued to form a subculture of its own that was based on extensive intra-community networks. For example, two articles in the constitution discriminatory against Catholics (articles 51 and 52) were eliminated in 1973 with only marginal support from the Protestant community. However, over the past decades, the religious cleavage has lost much of its original salience, with intra-communal divisions becoming more apparent. For example, the (Catholic) Christian Democrats are today split on the abortion issue, with women's groups in particular taking a pro-choice position, while the religious composition of districts seems to have a marginal impact on referenda held at the federal level (Linder 1997). Viewed from this perspective, the case of Switzerland can be drawn in our space as a curved arrow which passes from the bottom-left to the top-left area before moving to the top-right area. This means that the inclusion of minorities in the institutional domain has not been matched initially by a weakening of segmentation; however, over time, it has reduced tensions across the religious divide. That said, the analysis of the language cleavage seems to complicate this pattern.

While it can be argued that power sharing has promoted integration across the religious divide, the language issue has recently gained increasing salience between French- and German-speakers, even after the definitive solution of the Jura problem, which historically has been the focus of their disagreement (Steiner 2001, pp. 111–12). The two linguistic communities have also taken different positions on the integration of their country within the EU, and taken distinct and conflicting positions on numerous referenda (Lehmbruch 1993). In sum, language segmentation appears to be growing, despite longstanding experience of power sharing between linguistic groups, thus offering another interesting pattern of development of relational structure. Arguably, Switzerland is currently moving from integration back to pillarisation, as inter-community networks decrease even as minorities continue to be firmly included within the institutional domain. From this point of view, it could be argued that the top-left area of pillarisation seems to exercise an outstanding power of attraction in the transformation of relational structures occurring across time in different cases of power-sharing implementation.

Finally, Northern Ireland exhibits another distinct pattern of relational structure that deserves attention. In this case, the extensive development of inter-community networks preceded (albeit at times sporadically) the institutional inclusion of the Irish nationalist minority under the terms of the 1998 Belfast Agreement. This web of inter-community ties was gradually forged during the era of British unionist rule from 1921 to 1972, the end of which was precipitated by the mobilisation of the civil rights movement that recruited its members mostly within the Irish nationalist community but, to some extent, also within the British unionist community (see, for example, McCluskey 1989). In the present context, the civil rights movement is interesting in that it arguably reflected the partial development of relational structures of 'assimilation', at least to the extent that the goal of many Irish nationalist representatives and organisations at this time was to achieve *British* rights in Northern Ireland. In more recent times, British unionists and Irish nationalists have, for example, cooperated in a wide range of 'new social movements', mobilising on environmental, peace and women issues (Cinalli 2002 and 2003; Fearon 1999; McWilliams 1993). But as the chapter by Anthony Oberschall and Kendall Palmer in this volume shows, the implementation of power sharing in 1998 seems to have encouraged rather than ameliorated community segmentation. Not only have the two political parties at the extremes, namely, the Irish nationalist Sinn Féin and the British unionist Democratic Unionist Party profited from (and arguably are partly the cause of) an increasing polarisation of political competition, but the new institutions seem to be unable to accommodate further claims to minority representation beyond the core network of the traditional communities. For these reasons, Northern Ireland can be represented in our space as following yet another trajectory – one which passes from 'marginalisation' to 'assimilation', before moving towards 'pillarisation' in the top-left area.

CONCLUSIONS

In this chapter, I have argued that the analysis of the relational structure can be valuable (1) to assess divisions in the public and institutional domains across specific cases of power sharing and (2) to intervene in the debate about the causal relationship, and its direction, between power-sharing implementation and decreasing segmentation. The elaboration of answers to these questions has been based on the examination of network patterns along two main lines of inquiry. On the one hand, I have focused on inter-community networks in the public domain, in order to assess the extent to which civil society actors are embedded within a structure of linkages which extends beyond the limits of their own distinctive community, cutting across the main divide. On the other hand, I have combined the analysis of inter-community network patterns with the examination of networks that organisations and representatives of minorities forge with policy elites and state actors in the institutional domain. Since it is possible to assume that this latter portion of networks will develop to one degree or another with the implementation of power-sharing arrangements (which are expressly designed to include minorities within the institutional domain), I have formulated a typology made of four main types of relational structures – namely, fragmentation, pillarisation, integration and assimilation. I have then applied this typology to the analysis of specific case studies of power sharing in Western democracies, thus opening space for further empirical investigation of social and political processes beyond prescriptive discussions of desirable institutional arrangements.

Up to a point, my findings are in line with the traditional teachings of power-sharing scholars. It is clear that where power-sharing arrangements are put in place to reduce antagonisms between competing communities, networks between institutions and communities can flourish, thus producing the crucial shift from instability to stability. The main concern of scholars of power sharing has traditionally consisted in producing this very shift, thus halting dominant majority-rule, ethnic conflicts, or processes of polarisation and civil strife. In other words, the aim has been to consolidate and bolster the transition to democracy. Nevertheless, the relational analysis presented in this chapter integrates power-sharing theories, showing not only that prescription of institutional solutions cannot be separated from the empirical assessment of relationships and exchanges in both the public and institutional domains, but also that the hypothesis of a causal, direct relationship between enhanced inclusion and increasing communication amongst conflicting communities does not always fit the empirical evidence, which turns out to be more complex and less predictable. For example, power sharing can be easily interpreted as a factor contributing to increasing exchanges between conflicting communities when we consider political-religious divisions in Switzerland; but the same cannot be said of the case of contemporary Belgium, where instability and inter-community competition is an ongoing concern. Furthermore, it is clear that power sharing, at the political, decision-making level, is not always the *cause* of inter-community agreement in and of itself, but can also follow a period of decreased segmentation within civil society, as was arguably the case in pre-1998 Northern Ireland.

Ultimately, then, this study draws on a structural approach to further cross-national and cross-regional comparative research on contexts of deep division, while showing that the correlation between inter-community segmentation and inclusion within institutions needs to be assessed case by case. Rather than being dependent upon particular political and institutional choices, relational structure is taken as an independent variable to be integrated with institutional structure for the appraisal of actors' strategies, values and behaviour. My network approach also emphasises the interdependency between concrete relationships, power sharing and shifts in inter-community network patterns. It demonstrates the potentialities of a research approach which examines political action and transformation starting from the evaluation of structural properties, thus opening space for further research, focusing for example on the distinct nature of specific cleavages and the relationship between relational structures and different types of power-sharing arrangements.

REFERENCES

Bourdieu, P. (1986) 'The Forms of Capital', in J. C. Richardson (ed.), *Handbook of Theory and Research for the Sociology of Education*. Westport, CT: Greenwood Press, pp. 241–58.

Cinalli, M. (2002) 'Environmental Campaigns and Socio-Political Cleavages in Divided Societies', *Environmental Politics*, 11 (1), 163–83.

—— (2003) 'Socio-Politically Polarized Contexts, Urban Mobilization and the Environmental Movement: A Comparative Study of Two Campaigns of Protest in Northern Ireland', *International Journal of Urban and Regional Research*, 27 (1), 158–77.

Coleman, J. S. (1990) *Foundations of Social Theory*. Cambridge, MA: Harvard University Press.

Diamond, L. (1994) 'Rethinking Civil Society: Toward Democratic Consolidation', *Journal of Democracy*, 5 (3), 4–17.

Diani, M. (1992) 'Analysing Social Movement Networks', in M. Diani and R. Eyerman (eds), *Studying Collective Action*. London: Sage.

—— (1995) *Green Networks: A Structural Analysis of the Italian Environmental Movement*. Edinburgh: Edinburgh University Press.

Fearon, K. (1999) *Women's Work: The Story of the Northern Ireland Women's Coalition*. Belfast: Blackstaff Press.

Franzosi, R. (1997) 'Mobilization and Counter-Mobilization Processes: From the Red Years (1919–20) to the Black Years (1921–22). A New Methodological Approach to the Study of Narrative Data', *Theory and Society*, 26 (Special Issue), 275–304.

—— (1999) 'The Return of the Actor. Interaction Networks among Social Actors during Periods of High Mobilization (Italy, 1919–22)', *Mobilization: An International Journal*, 4, 131–49.

Gould, R.V. (1991) 'Multiple Networks and Mobilization in the Paris Commune, 1871', *American Sociological Review*, 56, 716–29.

—— (1995) *Insurgent Identities: Class, Community and Protest in Paris from 1848 to the Commune*. Chicago, IL: University of Chicago Press.

Huan, Q. (1999) 'The Relationships between Green Parties and Environmental Groups in Belgium, Germany and the UK', Paper presented for the 27 ECPR workshop on 'Environmental Protest in Comparative Perspective', 26–31 March 1999, Mannheim, Germany, available at http://www.essex.ac.uk/ECPR/events/jointsessions/paperarchive/mannheim/w21/huan.pdf.

Klandermans, B. (1990) 'Linking the "Old" and "New": Movement Networks in the Netherlands', in R. J. Dalton and M. Keuchler (eds), *Challenging the Political Order: New Social and Political Movements in Western Democracies*. Cambridge: Polity Press, pp. 122–36.

Lederach, J.P. (1998) *Building Peace: Sustainable Reconciliation in Divided Societies*. Washington, DC: United States Institute of Peace.

Lehmbruch, G. (1993), 'Consociational Democracy and Corporatism in Switzerland', *Publius*, 23 (2), 43–60.

Lijphart, A. (1977) *Democracy in Plural Societies: A Comparative Explanation*. New Haven, CT: Yale University Press.

Lin, N. (1999) 'Social Networks and Status Attainment', *Annual Review of Sociology*, 25, 467–87.

—— (2001) *Social Capital: A Theory of Social Structure and Action*. Cambridge: Cambridge University Press.

Linder, W. (1997) *Swiss Democracy: Possible Solutions to Conflict in Multicultural Societies*. Basingstoke: Palgrave Macmillan.

Lipset, S. M. (1960) *Political Man: The Social Bases of Politics*. New York, NY: Doubleday.

McCluskey, C. (1989) *Up Off Their Knees: A Commentary on the Civil Rights Movement in Northern Ireland*. Galway: Conn McCluskey and Associates.

McWilliams, M. (1993) 'Women in Northern Ireland: An Overview', in E. Hughes (ed.), *Culture and Politics in Northern Ireland: 1960–1990*. Milton Keynes: Oxford University Press, pp. 81–100.

Passy, F. (2001) 'Socializing, Connecting, and the Structural/Agency Gap: A Specification of the Impact of Networks on Participation in Social Movements', *Mobilization*, 6, 173–92.

Putnam, R. D. (1993) 'The Prosperous Community: Social Capital and Public Life', *The American Prospect*, 13, 35–42.

—— (1995) 'Bowling Alone: America's Declining Social Capital', *Journal of Democracy*, 6 (1), 65–78.

Sisk, T. D. (1996) *Power Sharing and International Mediation in Ethnic Conflicts*. Washington, DC: United States Institute of Peace.

Smooha, S. (2002) 'The Model of Ethnic Democracy: Israel as Jewish and Democratic State', *Nations and Nationalism*, 8 (4), 475–503.

Steiner, J. (2002) 'The Consociational Theory and Switzerland revisited', *Acta Politica*, 37, 104–20.

Varshney, A. (2003) *Ethnic Conflict and Civic Life: Hindus and Muslims in India*. New Haven, CT: Yale University Press.

Volgger, F. (2001) *Manuale dell'Alto Adige*. Bolzano: Giunta Provinciale di Bolzano.

Walzer, M. (1992) 'The Civil Society Argument', in C. Mouffe (ed.), *Dimensions of Radical Democracy: Pluralism, Citizenship, Community*. London: Verso.

Yishai, Y. (2002) 'Civil Society and Democracy: The Israeli Experience', *Voluntas*, 13 (3), 215–34.

12
The Challenge of Reconciliation in Post-conflict Societies: Definitions, Problems and Proposals

Brandon Hamber and Gráinne Kelly

Most societies coming out of conflict are marked by competing understandings of the term 'reconciliation'. Correspondingly, the exact nature of the reconciliation process is also often contested. Some see it as a 'soft' concept used as a euphemism for the compromises made in fraught political processes; others narrow it to a basic level of tolerance and coexistence or, at best, the re-establishing of more workable relationships. Still others see it as a profound process intertwined with notions such as forgiveness and repentance. In contrast, there are yet others who are dismissive of the term and consider it to have little relevance in the world of *Realpolitik*. Yet no matter how it is perceived, there is no doubting that in recent years the concept of reconciliation has moved up the agenda of those devising, exploring and analysing power sharing in divided societies. There is increasing attention afforded to the establishment of so-called reconciliation processes aimed at supporting the overall peace-building strategy and the bedding down of political agreements.

The establishment of power sharing within previously contested societies can go some way towards addressing the legacy of the past at a political level. Power sharing can create a new dispensation based on equality, fairness and respect for difference and can even acknowledge the interdependence required between former enemies. However, it is also the case that power-sharing arrangements generally need to be supported by a reconciliation process to be rendered sustainable. In that regard, the process of reconciliation is not merely a goal which can be measured in agreements signed. Rather, it also involves a long-term and unpredictable process of deep change in attitude, in conduct, and in the quality of governance systems, socio-economic environment, structures and institutions. In an ideal scenario, those responsible for negotiating a power-sharing agreement should recognise the need to build in a comprehensive reconciliation process and to ensure that the necessary financial, institutional and structural arrangements are in place to ensure its effective delivery. However, in reality, negotiations between political adversaries are often time-bound, pressurised and fraught. There is often an over-emphasis on agreements being reached at the elite level with scant attention paid to the fundamental changes necessary at the societal, community and individual levels that are essential to holding the agreement in place.

Where new institutional structures are created to ensure fair and equitable accessibility to political power, the tendency is towards a 'coexistence view of reconciliation'. This is based on an assumption that political solutions alone can enable communities to coexist and function alongside one another without their past differences reigniting. Such an approach, although perhaps necessary and pragmatic in the short term, can result in an under-emphasis on the deep cleavages which may exist between communities. In the long term it can reinforce forms of parallel socio-cultural existence and fail to transform those relationships that have been at the root of the conflict. In this chapter we will argue that genuine reconciliation requires a deeper and more challenging process. It requires the involvement of all levels *of* society and is the responsibility of all *in* society. Ignoring these deeper levels, or creating pragmatic compromises to get to an agreement at the negotiation table, can create new problems for the future and has the potential to undermine the long-term stability of power sharing.

DEFINING RECONCILIATION

The literature on reconciliation, both academic and practitioner-focused, has increased as growing emphasis is placed on the challenges facing post-conflict societies. That said, there is not a comprehensive literature on the topic, empirical research is almost non-existent, and case studies are generally dictated by specific social or geographical contexts and the inherent political assumptions of practitioners and policy makers writing on the subject. Those definitions of reconciliation that do exist are useful and informative; however, there remains a notable lack of conceptual clarity. Motivated by a desire to present a set of simple, yet comprehensive, elements that make up reconciliation, we have devised our own working definition of reconciliation through which the practical application of power-sharing processes can be assessed (see also Hamber and Kelly 2004).

We contend that reconciliation is a necessary process in post-conflict societies. It is a process that must be entered into voluntarily and cannot be imposed on communities or individuals (see also Bloomfield et al. 2003). As such, a reconciliation process generally involves five interwoven strands. These are:

1. *Developing a shared vision of an interdependent and fair society.* The development of a vision of a shared future requiring the involvement of society as a whole, at all levels. Although individuals may have different opinions or political beliefs, the articulation of a common vision of an interdependent, just, equitable, open and diverse society is a critical part of any reconciliation process.
2. *Acknowledging and dealing with the past.* Acknowledging the hurt, losses, truths and suffering of the past. Providing the mechanisms for justice, healing, truth, restitution or reparation, and restoration (including apologies if necessary and steps aimed at redress). To build reconciliation, individuals and institutions need to acknowledge their own role in the conflicts of the past, accepting and learning from them in a constructive way so as to guarantee non-repetition.
3. *Building positive relationships.* Relationship building or renewal following violent conflict, addressing issues of trust, prejudice and intolerance; resulting in the acceptance of commonalities and differences, and embracing and engaging with those who are different to us.
4. *Significant cultural and attitudinal change.* Changes in how people relate to, and their attitudes towards, one another. The culture of suspicion, fear, mistrust and violence is broken down and opportunities and space opened up in which people can hear and be heard. A culture of respect for human rights and human difference is developed, creating a context where each citizen becomes an active participant in society and feels a sense of belonging.
5. *Substantial social, economic and political change.* The social, economic and political structures which gave rise to the conflict and estrangement are identified, reconstructed or addressed, and transformed.

Two points are worth noting in relation to any process of reconciliation. The first of these is that a reconciliation process always contains paradoxes and contradictions. It is not a neat or easy process, and can in itself seem incongruous. Lederach writes most eloquently about this, noting that:

> reconciliation can be seen as dealing with three specific paradoxes. First, in an overall sense, reconciliation promotes an encounter between the open expression of the painful past, on the one hand, and the search for the articulation of a long-term, interdependent future, on the other hand. Second, reconciliation provides a place for truth and mercy to meet, where concerns for exposing what has happened *and* for letting go in favour of renewed relationship are validated and embraced. Third, reconciliation recognises the need to give time and place to both justice and peace, where redressing the wrong is held together with the envisioning of a common, connected future. (1997, p. 20)

In accordance with Lederach's typology, we understand reconciliation to entail engaging in the process of trying to address these complex paradoxes.

A second point worth noting is that it is not possible to escape the fact that reconciliation is a morally-loaded concept and different people will bring their own ideological bias to the subject. Correspondingly, different ideologies of reconciliation can be identified. For example, a religious ideology often emphasises the rediscovery of social and individual conscience through moral reflection, repentance, confession and rebirth; a human rights approach might see reconciliation as a process achieved by regulating social interaction through the rule of law and preventing certain forms of rights violations from recurring; or an inter-communal understanding may see the process of reconciliation as being about bridging the divides between different cultures and identity groups (see Hamber 2002; Hamber and van der Merwe 1998; van der Merwe 1999).

Thus, if we are going to locate reconciliation within the power-sharing debate, we need to be cognisant of the fact that many people come to the debate with different ideological foci. Given that the term can be interpreted from different ideological perspectives, politicians may tend to be dismissive of it and see it as a 'soft' option laden with theological meanings. In our opinion, a more expansive view is therefore needed. Accordingly, having identified the five 'pillars' of reconciliation in our working definition, the challenge is to ground them in the practical realities of designing a reconciliation process. Although we recognise that there is significant overlap between each 'pillar', and similar processes may be applicable under more than one aspect, we will explore each of the five 'pillars' in turn.

Developing a shared vision of an interdependent and fair society

At a fundamental level, power-sharing arrangements aim to reconcile competing community interests, create new institutional structures and develop a new vision of the political future, based on agreed principles and practices within a shared democratic framework. The vision of the political future which is articulated, however, will greatly influence the type of reconciliation process which can be developed over time. While peace agreements may articulate grandiose statements in relation to 'building a new future', how this in operationalised on a society-wide level is often highly ambiguous. A coexistence model of power sharing, based on the view that keeping communities apart can be the best way of bringing them together at some future point, may well result in an underdeveloped form of social interaction and a failure of political stability in the longer term. By contrast, true reconciliation processes involve the development, and clear articulation, of a *common* vision by all of the stakeholders in society, from the highest political levels to the individual citizen.

Given that power-sharing arrangements are generally negotiated and devised at the leadership level, the primary onus is on political leaders to make that common vision public and to act as its champions. In many cases, however, leaders adhere to competing visions of the future and hence do little to further the cause of reconciliation. For this reason, we maintain that it is not enough for political leaders in a divided society to pay lip-service to the concept of reconciliation in their political rhetoric. Society at large will only accept the validity of their aspirations if they can see progress being reached at an institutional level and see the impact of subsequent political decisions made in favour of reconciliation at the local level. South Africa is an example of a society where a firm foundation was laid through the articulation of a new vision. Archbishop Desmond Tutu's often-criticised conceptualisation of the 'rainbow nation' is a case in point. Although such terms can be important in terms of their 'potential' value, Alex Boraine, for example, has highlighted the danger of talking about the 'rainbow nation' of South Africa as if it were already present when, in fact, it merely represents the potential for social harmony:

It may be that to speak of a nation being healed after deep wounds have existed for so long, or to speak of the uniting of a nation which has been so long divided, is to speak the language not of fact but faith. ... [W]e must never make the mistake of assuming we are talking about something which is already present. That is the danger of talking about South Africa as the 'rainbow nation'. When Tutu does this, he understands this as a potential, the promise, the hope, but sometimes the term is misunderstood and misinterpreted as a claim that is where we are now and dismissed as cheap rhetoric. (2000, p. 378)

In this sense, understanding reconciliation as an aspiration can help a divided society set a common goal, one which is the polar opposite of the goal of political conflict (Hamber 2003). Again, to use Boraine's terminology, 'the promise of what is possible in the future' (2000, p. 378) can be instrumental in moving divided societies forward and should be understood as being complementary to (and often the first step towards) the process of making concrete institutional and structural changes at the political level. This, of course, calls for a delicate balance because one needs to be aware of the potential gap that can be created between vision-based thinking and actual policy formation (Simpson and Rauch 1999).

At the same time, however, it is our contention that despite the difficulties in its articulation some sense of common vision is critical to building reconciliation and sustainable power sharing. The vision of the future may not necessarily be a joint-constitutional vision detailing the political status and identity of a defined territorial unit, but may instead be premised upon a common concern and commitment to democratic principles such as equality or human rights. In Northern Ireland, for example, one of the core difficulties in implementing the 1998 Agreement has been the failure on the part of politicians to articulate any genuine sense of common vision regarding even the most basic of principles that should underpin the Agreement. Human rights, for example – which, as a concept, is used in some societies as a way of articulating a common commitment to the future – is routinely seen as a 'political punching bag of groups that would describe human rights as belonging to only one community'.[1] In short, without the articulation of some set of common principles or vision, it remains very difficult to bed down the peace process in Northern Ireland. This is in part due to a very detailed and high-level focus on the intricacies of the Agreement at the expense of politicians and the media conveying and championing to the public the core principles and spirit behind the process.

Acknowledging and dealing with the past

The creation of a shared vision for the future can be significantly hindered if there is no shared understanding of what has happened in the past. While acknowledging and dealing with the past may not necessarily lead directly to reconciliation, and may even undermine power-sharing arrangements in the short term by reminding communities of painful memories or even by raising new areas of dispute, it is nonetheless imperative that some locally devised and context-specific processes are developed. Accordingly, there is a growing recognition of the importance of designing and implementing strategies for dealing with the legacy of violence in countries struggling to deal with the challenges that the transition to democracy inevitably brings (see, for example, Bloomfield et al. 2003; Hayner 2001; Minow 1998).

Although much of the available literature and research focuses on the growing field of transitional justice (see, for example, Teitel 2003), and more specifically on truth commissions, we maintain that dealing with the past involves a much broader process. It can entail a range of strategies for addressing the legacy of a conflict that aim at complementing the peace process. For example, trials, apologies, inquiries, truth commissions, reparations or compensation, victims telling their stories, museums, and the establishment of memorials. All such mechanisms, and more besides, can serve as vehicles through which interpretations of the past can be debated and hurts acknowledged. While political and financial exigencies may impose timeframes and other boundaries on such endeavours, the deeply layered history of relations between divided communities should be acknowledged and methods sought to explore them. Clearly, a realistic 'balance must be struck that takes into account all the conflicting claims on justice, all the differing demands for truth, and all the pain and suffering that may arise from the many layers of a complex social history' (Bloomfield et al. 2003, p. 41).

Space does not permit a thorough analysis of mechanisms for dealing with the past. Nevertheless, the important point is that it is improbable that the past can be simply bracketed out, since managing and dealing with damaged relationships lies at the core of many peace processes and no doubt remains vital to the building of positive relationships. In South Africa, for example, although other institutions were set up to facilitate the transition to democracy (for example, the Land Claims Court, the Human Rights Commission, the Gender Equality Commission), the Truth and Reconciliation Commission (TRC) played a pivotal role in political life for the first few years of this transition. Importantly, with the TRC came a vision of a new society with new values, reinforcing the importance of the notion of 'vision' outlined above. Leaving aside the specifics of the operations of the TRC – not to mention its shortcomings (see, for example, Hamber 2000; Hamber 2001; Lever and James, 2000) – the commission embodied a restorative and conciliatory spirit that broadly balanced a simultaneously backward-looking and forward-looking political agenda.

Thus, some basic level of acknowledgement of, and dealing with, the past is clearly important, for otherwise new power-sharing institutions risk being undermined over time. Arguably, one of the weaknesses in the Northern Ireland process at this point has been that new institutions have been constructed with very little public recognition of the past. Take, again, the example of the Northern Ireland Human Rights Commission. It is seldom argued that this commission is necessary due to human rights violations in the past; on the contrary, the commission is almost always portrayed as wholly forward-looking, which may help explain why its work has been perceived as unsatisfactory by so many people. Although more research is required, there is evidence, therefore, to suggest that power-sharing institutions in the present can be undermined by experiences in the past.

Building positive relationships

Although the depth of division between communities may vary, the nature of divided societies implies the absence of positive and functioning relationships between communities, particularly if the division has been prolonged over generations. The reality of divided societies, including the cases considered in this volume, is that citizens often live in separate residential, cultural and social worlds, based, for example, on their religion, ethnicity, nationality or political affiliations. These differences can result in patterns of behaviour and social interaction which are mutually exclusive (but see Cinalli, chapter 11 in this volume). Addressing relationship issues involves challenging those negative images, perceptions and stereotypes that have developed and which have helped to sustain divisions within society.

In order to build a peaceful, power-sharing democracy, it is not enough that contact is increased at the political elite level: meaningful contact must be created between citizens too. In apparent recognition of, and response to, the lack of real opportunities for interaction at the level of the ordinary individual, much relationship-building work within the peace-building sector has been dominated by Allport's (1954) 'contact hypothesis'. This hypothesis starts from the assumption that conflict arises from a lack of information about the other group. It then argues that conflict can be reduced, and hence sustainable power sharing bolstered, by bringing together individuals from opposing groups in the hope of fostering more positive attitudes towards one another. More specifically, Allport suggested four conditions which are necessary to support this contact and thereby reduce inter-communal conflict (Allport 1954). First, there should be equal status among the groups or individuals who meet. Secondly, the situation in which inter-communal contact occurs should require cooperation between groups or offer common goals to both groups. Thirdly, social competition among the communities involved should be avoided. Fourthly, the contact situation should be legitimised through institutional support (Pettigrew 1971).

This hypothesis has been further elaborated in past decades to explore issues such as the quality and quantity of contact, the issue of the individual's particular social identity being 'switched-on' and 'switched-off' in certain settings, and the extent to which an individual's contact with members of the opposing community can be generalised to the opposing community as a whole (Brewer and Miller 1984; Gaertner et al. 1993; Pettigrew 1988). To these ends, two approaches are commonly taken. The first is the bringing together of estranged communities on issues of common interest (for example, economic development, the environment, sports, the arts) and using these as building blocks of relationship formation. The second approach involves programmes and activities that set out to address issues of community division and political conflict (for example, justice, equality, dealing with the past) and that seek to actively engage individuals and communities in addressing these issues (Niens et al. 2003).

Although contact work is an essential component in reducing suspicion, stereotyping and prejudice between communities, we contend that it is only one of the many strategies that need to be adopted with respect to reconciliation. It is not the sole remedy for building positive relationships. Sustaining relations between divided communities will only be possible if appropriate structures, social conditions, political support, partnerships and alliances, as well as a conducive political context, are established which encourage such relationship building. This more 'holistic' process needs to be recognised and supported as a long-term endeavour. But this is not all, since attention must also be paid to the particular kind of power-sharing institutions that are put in place. Thus, while many power-sharing institutions have been founded on the belief that the best way to build a sustainable democracy is by institutionalising group identities through such protections as the mutual veto and group autonomy (see, especially, Lijphart 1977), reconciliation efforts tend to work in the opposite direction by encouraging ordinary individuals to engage with one another in order to find the common elements of identity that might bolster a common sense of solidarity. Competing imperatives are clearly at play here.

Significant cultural and attitudinal change

In divided societies struggling to build a sustainable democracy, cultural and attitudinal change will, by its very nature, be difficult to measure. Like all aspects of reconciliation, it is a process, not an act, and requires a series of initiatives which aim to support, strengthen and consolidate a new culture of peace within an interdependent, fair and just society. It is tempting, therefore, to pay less attention to these more intangible aspects of reconciliation, and to hope that, by focusing on institutional reforms, cultural and attitudinal changes will follow suit. At an individual level, attitudinal change is a voluntary process and people cannot be forced to change their opinions of others, or to develop respect for those with whom they share a conflicted past. Where people feel compelled to change, they may become more, rather than less, entrenched in their views.

Having said this, governments can encourage cultural and attitudinal change through appropriate policy decisions in the fields of education, housing or employment, for example. Naturally, resistance may be significant at the outset. Yet by encouraging contact and interaction between formerly divided communities – within the classroom, workplace or social settings – the hope is that the goal of an integrated and inclusive culture can become the accepted norm. This attitudinal change also needs to be mirrored in the relationships between politicians – and herein lies a major challenge for those who are to share political power.

As Anthony Oberschall and Kendall Palmer argue in chapter 5 of this volume, Northern Ireland provides an example of a society where, despite a power-sharing agreement containing a commitment to reconciliation initiatives, there has, to date, been a lack of consistent political support for fundamental attitudinal change. This is evident from an analysis of the Northern Ireland Life and Times Survey (NILT), which is conducted annually and which documents public attitudes on a wide range of social issues, including those under the banner of 'community relations'. In 1995, 56 per cent of people felt that 'relations between Protestants and Catholics are better than five years ago'. In 2003 this figure had dropped to 44 per cent. After 1999 (following a post-Agreement peak) a continually falling proportion of respondents felt that 'relations between Protestants and Catholics will be better in five years time'. Particularly worrying is the steady increase in the desire for single-identity neighbourhoods. In 1996, 83 per cent of people said they would prefer to live in a mixed-religion neighbourhood. By 2003, this figure had dropped to 72 per cent.

What is clear from the NILT survey results, therefore, is that attitudinal change does not necessarily follow an upward trajectory following peace negotiations. In fact, we concur with Oberschall and Palmer that, as far as Northern Ireland is concerned, attitudinal change has been undermined in no small measure by the failure of political leaders to articulate a shared vision of the future, as well as by the particular choice of power-sharing institutions established under the Agreement. Furthermore, there has been little external or civil society pressure on political parties to make or argue for policies of integration at the level of schooling or housing. Thus, the power-sharing process at this stage remains focused on the Agreement and, correspondingly, the attainment of power for particular sections of society, but with little focus on the future needs of the society more broadly conceived.

Substantial social, economic and political change

As noted above, an improvement in inter-community relations cannot be achieved merely by focusing on the personal interaction between individuals. Attention must be paid to the structural issues – including the power-sharing institutions – which can give rise to, influence, or maintain poor relationships. Increasingly, contact between the members of different communities may assist in developing new understandings and in building new relationships, yet this contact will be incomplete and may be ineffectual if the issues that underpin the conflict, such as inequality, disadvantage or injustice, are not tackled at the institutional, decision-making level. This is particularly true of minority communities who need to be included in the decision-making process for genuinely inclusive, and therefore democratic, power sharing to operate.

The nature of the political accommodation reached will have a significant impact on the manner in which subsequent reconciliation processes may unfold. The establishment of inclusive, democratic power-sharing structures should create a new atmosphere and momentum from which other processes can follow. Where opposing sides within a divided society have been willing to come together to reach a political accommodation some indication is provided of the potential for reconciliation. While power-sharing arrangements transform the nature of political engagement from antagonism to (incipient) democracy, the development of a new style of political leadership based on cooperation must also be cultivated.

Even after the transition to democracy has been made, the legacy of violence and conflict may continue to impact negatively on the social and economic fabric of divided societies. Such societies often have real economic difficulties, with low resource capacities and reduced investment opportunities. South Africa provides a good example here. The TRC was criticised for a narrow focus on reconciliation between so-called victims and perpetrators and consequently for under-emphasising conflicts rooted in economic injustices (van der Merwe et al. 1999). Social reconstruction or transformation and reconciliation are to be the flipsides of the same coin (Villa-Vicencio 2003), such that ongoing socio-economic difficulties are seen as a threat to sustaining reconciliation. Thus, before the rhetoric of reconciliation can translate into reality in South Africa, the process needs to move 'beyond formal political and constitutional change to tackle the deep-seated social imbalances that underlie the culture of violence' (Simpson 2002, p. 247).

At the same time, economic development in itself will not guarantee reconciliation in a linear way. While it is imperative to ensure a stable economic environment in which the opportunities for peace can be more completely realised, this needs to join up with other strands of reconciliation work. In Northern Ireland, the predominant emphasis of the European Union peace programme has been on economic development and employability – the assumption being that peace and reconciliation result from increased economic opportunity for all.[2] Although it is certainly important that substantial funds are injected into economic development, it is not sufficient to maintain peace in a deeply divided society. As the Northern Ireland case suggests, deep social and ethnic fissures may well remain, along with the possibility of a return to conflict. Clearly, therefore, economic and political progress is vital, but once again we argue that economic approaches need to be complemented by relationship building and attitudinal-change work, as well as by taking steps to acknowledge and deal with the past.

CONCLUSION

Reconciliation is only one of the many challenges which divided societies face in their efforts to deal with the new challenges that democratic power sharing brings. The establishment of power-sharing arrangements undoubtedly goes a long way in establishing the context and opportunity in which a reconciliation process can begin to take shape. However, it is important to recognise, first, that power sharing is unlikely without a prior modicum of reconciliation, and, secondly, that power sharing institutions have to be chosen very carefully so that they do not impinge on the potential for society-wide reconciliation. In short, reconciliation should be viewed as an integral part of any democracy-building process – as important as social reconstruction, governmental and constitutional reform, and economic rejuvenation – and should lead us to see why a much deeper and more far-reaching process is needed to sustain such arrangements over time.

It should not be assumed that the impact of new political arrangements based, in principle, on inclusiveness and cooperation will automatically trickle down to the societal, community and individual level. In addition, reconciliation should not be defined too narrowly as a *goal* or *outcome* as this will inevitably put it beyond reach. It is the *process* of addressing the dimensions of reconciliation that is critically important. This is the responsibility of political parties, but there is also a role for the non-governmental sector. Once awakened, reconciliation cannot easily be brought under the control of governments who later may find elements of it inconvenient (Porter 2003, p. 21). For example, mechanisms that deal with the past may reveal too many truths about the past activities of politicians. It is in this context that a strong and independent civil society may be necessary to further the acknowledgement and truth-recovery agenda.

In conclusion, then, reconciliation should be widely advocated, broadly supported and enthusiastically envisioned. At present, examples of best practice and case studies of success are not widely available. Reconciliation processes following the establishment of power-sharing arrangements require further reflection, debate and cross-fertilisation, as significant gaps in both knowledge and practice are evident. As we have argued, there is no one path to reconciliation, and no single model which can be transposed to multiple contexts. Any prioritisation of one aspect of reconciliation may lead to imbalances occurring in the reconciliation process as a whole. These may be difficult to redress later. A broad definition of reconciliation is needed if new power-sharing structures, agreements and institutions are to be supported and sustained into the future.

NOTES

1. United Kingdom Parliament, Joint Committee on Human Rights Written Evidence, 16. Memorandum from the Northern Ireland Women's Coalition (NIWC). Available at http://www.publications.parliament.uk/pa/jt200203/jtselect/jtrights/132/132we17.htm.
2. The EU Programme for Peace and Reconciliation (the second round of such funding is known as PEACE II) is a unique EU-funded programme for all of Northern Ireland and the Border Regions of Ireland (Cavan, Donegal, Leitrim, Louth, Monaghan and Sligo). Its main aim is to promote reconciliation and help to build a more peaceful and stable society as part of the ongoing peace process. Over €704 million was available under the Programme between 2000 and 2004. See http://www.seupb.org for more details.

REFERENCES

Allport, G.W. (1954) *The Nature of Prejudice*. Reading: Addison-Wesley.

Bloomfield, D., Barnes, T. and Huyse, L. (2003) *Reconciliation after Violent Conflict: A Handbook*. Stockholm: International Institute for Democracy and Electoral Assistance.

Boraine, A. (2000) *A Country Unmasked: South Africa's Truth and Reconciliation Commission*. New York: Oxford University Press.

Brewer, M. B. and Miller, N. (1984) 'Beyond the Contact Hypothesis: Theoretical Perspectives on Desegregation', in N. Miller and M. B. Brewer (eds), *Groups in Contact: The Psychology of Desegregation*. New York: Academic Press.

Gaertner, S., Dovidio, J. F., Anastasio, P. A., Bachevan, B. A. and Rust, M. C. (1993) 'The Common Ingroup Identity Model: Recategorization and the

Reduction of Intergroup Bias', in W. Stroewe and M. Hewstone (eds), *European Review of Social Psychology*, 4, 1–26.

Hamber, B. (2000) 'Repairing the Irreparable: Dealing with the Double-Binds of Making Reparations for Crimes of the Past', *Ethnicity and Health*, 5 (3/4), 215–26.

—— (2001) 'Does the Truth Heal? A Psychological Perspective on the Political Strategies for Dealing with the Legacy of Political Violence', in N. Biggar (ed.), *Burying the Past: Making Peace and Doing Justice after Civil Conflict*. Washington, DC: Georgetown University Press, pp. 131–48.

—— (2002) '"Ere their story die": Truth, Justice and Reconciliation in South Africa', *Race and Class*, 44 (1), 61–79.

—— (2003) 'Transformation and Reconciliation', in J. Darby and R. MacGinty (eds), *Contemporary Peacemaking: Conflict, Violence and Peace Processes*. Basingstoke: Palgrave Macmillan, pp. 224–34.

Hamber, B. and Kelly, G. (2004) 'A Working Definition of Reconciliation'. Occasional paper. Belfast: Democratic Dialogue. Available at http://www.seupb.org/consul_other.htm.

Hamber, B. and van der Merwe, H. (1998) 'What is this Thing Called Reconciliation?', *Reconciliation in Review*, 1 (1), 3–6.

Hayner, P. B. (2001) *Unspeakable Truths: Confronting State Terror and Atrocity*. New York, NY: Routledge.

Lederach, J. (1997) *Building Peace: Sustainable Reconciliation in Divided Societies*. Washington DC: United States Institute of Peace Press.

Lever, J. and James, W. (2000) 'The Second Republic', in W. James and L. Van de Vijvers (eds), *After the TRC: Reflections on Truth and Reconciliation in South Africa*. Cape Town: David Philip, pp. 191–200.

Lijphart, A. (1977) *Democracy in Plural Societies*. New Haven, CT: Yale University Press.

Minow, M. (1998) *Between Vengeance and Forgiveness: Facing History after Genocide and Mass Violence*. Boston, MA: Beacon Press.

Niens, U., Cairns, E. and Hewstone, M. (2003) 'Contact and Conflict in Northern Ireland', in O. Hargie and D. Dickson (eds), *Researching the Troubles: Social Science Perspectives on the Northern Ireland Conflict*. Edinburgh: Mainstream Publishing, pp. 123–39.

Northern Ireland Life and Times (1998–2003). Available at http://www.ark.uk/nilt.

Pettigrew, T. F. (1971) *Racially Separate or Together?* New York, NY: McGraw-Hill.

—— (1988) 'Intergroup Contact Theory', *Annual Review of Psychology*, 49, 65–85.

Porter, N. (2003) *The Elusive Quest: Reconciliation in Northern Ireland*. Belfast: The Blackstaff Press.

Simpson, G. (2002) '"Tell no lies, Claim no easy victories": A Brief Evaluation of South Africa's Truth and Reconciliation Commission', in D. Posel and G. Simpson (eds), *Commissioning the Past: Understanding South Africa's Truth and Reconciliation Commission*. Johannesburg: Witwatersrand University Press, pp. 220–51.

Simpson, G. and Rauch, J. (1999) 'Reflections on the First Year of the National Crime Prevention Strategy', in J. Maharaj (ed.), *Between Unity and Diversity:*

Essays on Nation Building in Post-Apartheid South Africa. Cape Town: David Philip Publishers, pp. 295–314.

Teitel, R. (2003) 'Transitional Justice Genealogy', *Harvard Human Rights Journal*, 16, 69–94.

van der Merwe, H. (1999) 'The Truth and Reconciliation Commission and Community Reconciliation: An Analysis of Competing Strategies and Conceptualizations'. Fairfax, VA: George Mason University.

van der Merwe, H., Dewhirst, P. and Hamber, B. (1999) 'Non-Governmental Organisations and the Truth and Reconciliation Commission: An Impact Assessment', *Politikon*, 26 (1), 55–79.

Villa-Vicencio, C. (2003) 'Reconciliation as Politics', *Reconciliation Barometer*, 1 (1), 1–3.

13
Towards a Civic Culture: Implications for Power-sharing Policy Makers

Robin Wilson

A TWENTY-FIRST CENTURY CHALLENGE

The early years of the new millennium have been marked by a sense of foreboding. 'September 11' and the events which followed have renewed concern – stimulated in the early 1990s when the world looked on as events in ex-Yugoslavia and then Rwanda unfolded – that violence driven by ethnic[1] rage is beyond the capacity of the international community to control. And yet, over most of the world, most of the time, multiethnic societies survive peaceably, if not free of tension, away from the media spotlight and academic scrutiny. We should thus beware of a distorted, 'overethnicised' view of the social world (Brubaker 2002, p. 168).

Multiethnic societies do not inevitably break down – by ethnic cleansing, partition or secession – into mono-ethnic entities. Indeed, mass migration is ensuring that even what have hitherto been relatively uniform populations are obliged to come to terms with growing ethnic diversity. The question thus becomes not whether, but how, we can live together. In particular, the question for policy makers – and all those in the NGO and academic communities who would seek to influence them – becomes one of how conditions can be established that set in train virtuous circles of tolerance and inter-communal confidence, where the default tendency is towards integration rather than separation, and where above all dialogue acts as an antidote to violence. As the editors of this volume make clear in their introductory remarks, this is not to say that integration can always be achieved in the short run. But where this is the case, those responsible for the design of power-sharing institutions and subsequent public-policy formation should nevertheless see integration as a goal that needs to be prioritised, actively pursued, promoted and resourced over the long haul.

Dealing with ethnic strife is not a matter of turning sinners into saints, but it is a matter of ensuring that saintly, rather than sinful, behaviour is encouraged and rewarded. What must be avoided above all is a climate of moral hazard – what Donald Horowitz calls an 'auction mentality' (2001, p. 341). This is where ethno-political entrepreneurs and military or paramilitary organisations are led to believe that force can be exercised with impunity, or that ethnic out-bidding or threats of violence may win recognition, even concessions, from those in the international community.

Realpolitik is an approach attractive to those seeking to broker settlements that bring an end to violence within a short timescale, especially under the intense but fickle spotlight of global media and with domestic electoral cycles in mind. But it risks saddling divided societies with governance arrangements which, whatever their short-term appeal, may have unintended consequences that imperil their long-term viability. Constitutional design matters. The fact that some or all of the contending parties endorse a draft accord is a necessary, but not sufficient, condition of success. A lowest-common-denominator agreement is never the only show in town. On the contrary, path dependence, particularly in enduring conflicts (Horowitz 2002), can lead policy makers to miss the obvious counterfactual: for every agreement a number of alternatives could have been written, and there is no guarantee that the one they chose is optimal.

PAVING WITH GOOD INTENTIONS

Contributors to this volume would offer no support for the idea that multiethnic societies can be governed in an assimilationist fashion, where persons belonging to minorities are forced either to give allegiance to a state whose apparatus is wholly coloured by the dominance of members of a majority ethnic group, or to accept ghettoisation and marginalisation. But this writer at least would dispute the contention by Arend Lijphart (2002) that non-majoritarianism and consociationalism are essentially coterminous.

Most working inter-ethnic democracies – most working democracies being inter-ethnic democracies nowadays – are governed by flexible arrangements which may or may not be explicitly power sharing but certainly are unlikely to be manifestations of Lijphartian theory. After all, as Lijphart has implicitly acknowledged (2002, p. 41), only Belgium and Switzerland currently conform to his consociational model (though he rather surprisingly suggests – accepting it is 'more controversial' – that India and South Africa are also power-sharing examples). Of his cases, however, only Switzerland is governed by a 'grand coalition' and the Swiss *Sonderfall* is otherwise very much the opposite of the basic consociational prescription – a grassroots democracy rather than an elite-dominated governance system.[2]

Although most of the world's multiethnic societies are not, therefore, governed by consociational arrangements, a 'common sense' commitment to consociationalism remains widespread among policy makers dealing with divided societies, based on an unquestioned acceptance of the essentialist conception of 'culture' – itself outdated in anthropological literature (Cowan et al. 2001; Wikan 2002) – that underpins the theory itself. This is the view that 'communal attachments' are 'primordial' and that in 'plural' societies people 'mix but do not combine' (Lijphart 1977, p. 17). Once again, Lijphart (2001) himself has now come to accept that primordialism is obsolete, but claims that his preference for 'self-determining' rather than 'pre-determined' communal 'segments' saves the model nevertheless. The trouble is, however, that this move still does not address the key danger attaching to consociational arrangements – however one deems its segments to be constituted – that they not only recognise but also entrench communal divisions.

It is as a result of unreflecting acceptance of the received wisdom that the road to policy hell can be paved with good power-sharing intentions. Ill-thought-through interventions may, as this volume has demonstrated, have unintended consequences. The rest of this chapter reprises the four sets of pitfalls set out in the introduction:

- perpetuating conflict by institutionalising division;
- inhibiting a transition from management to resolution of conflict;
- stifling internal diversity in reified ethnic groups; and
- failing to recognise cross-cutting identities and suffocating individual autonomy.

It concludes by suggesting how these might be avoided, by finding more innovative and progressive solutions to the genuine concerns about ethnic domination which power-sharing schemes, including consociationalism, seek to assuage.

WAR BY OTHER MEANS

In his book on 'constitutional engineering', Giovanni Sartori warns: 'If you reward divisions and divisiveness ... you increase and eventually heighten divisions and divisiveness' (1997, p. 72). The constitution of Cyprus introduced at independence is a perfect instance of such perils, based as it was on 'far-reaching consociational principles'. The Greek- and Turkish-Cypriot communities were treated as 'separate entities', with a 70–30 proportionality (the Turks being slightly over-represented) applying across the political system, producing 'extreme rigidity' (Ghai 2002, p. 146). Within this system, most Greeks came to believe that the Turks had acquired too much power, while most Turks baulked at the entrenched dominance of the Greeks. The results are well known (see, for example, Kyle 1997). In 2004, a last-ditch attempt by the United Nations to engender a similar deal in anticipation of European Union accession by Cyprus – or, in lieu, the Greek-Cypriot part of it – was also destined to fail.

The 1995 Dayton Accords are likewise premised on the view of 'ethnic communities as separate corporate bodies'. This means that politics in Bosnia-Herzegovina is 'entirely communal, and almost perforce all political parties are ethnically based' (Ghai 2002, p. 149). Moreover, as Marie-Joëlle Zahar's chapter shows, the political system functions only because of the protectorate role of the High Representative of the international community, Paddy Ashdown (whose predecessor Carl Bildt once complained that for most political leaders in Bosnia, 'peace was just the continuation of war by other means' (*Guardian*, 22 December 2000)). An open letter to Mr Ashdown in 2003 from the European Stability Initiative suggested that the political arrangements had merely perpetuated the dependence of Bosnia's political class: 'Successive High Representatives have tried to beg, cajole or bully Bosnian politicians into taking more responsibility. This is empty rhetoric, so long as an international institution is there to take the responsibility away from them' (*Balkan Crisis Report*, 23 July 2003).

Similar conclusions were drawn about Northern Ireland in an editorial in the British magazine *New Statesman* (27 October 2003). Under the heading 'Let Ulster's Leaders Grow Up', it declared:

> British ministers treat Ulster as though it were a nursery. The children are told to kiss and make up, only for them to start squabbling again within seconds, blaming each other and running to teacher to tell tales. But Ulster politicians are supposed to be adults. It is the British presence that infantilises them. They do not negotiate with each other but with Mr Blair, always in the hope that he can wrest one more concession from the other side.

Anthony Oberschall and Kendall Palmer show how this has worked to undermine inter-communal trust in Northern Ireland. From such instances, Ghai concludes: 'It is worthwhile to caution against reifying temporary or fluid identities, which are so much a mark of contemporary times. There is a danger of enforcing spurious claims of primordialism and promoting competition for resources along ethnic lines, thereby aggravating ethnic tensions' (2002, p. 169). And he adds: 'Constitutional recognition of cultures tends to sharpen differences between cultures ... [W]e need more inter-cultural than multicultural enterprises' (2002, p. 170).

DANGER OF SHORT-TERMISM

One of the unintended effects of consociational forms of power sharing is to inhibit political renewal and change. Even if this criterion is honoured more in the breach than in the observance, the 'grand coalition' of representatives of ethnic segments favoured by Lijphart would leave little room for an opposition and so an alternative government to emerge. Moreover, insofar as such segments are understood legitimately to monopolise the political space, it is very difficult for non- or inter-ethnic parties to develop. Yet, as Brij Lal remarks, the ability to change the government through elections is the 'very essence of a democratic system' (2002, p. 274).

Indeed, it is hard to imagine any power-sharing arrangement enduring unless there is a willingness over time – supported by explicit institutional provisions – for ethnic parties to moderate their identities in the name of a shared civic culture. As Stephen Gilliatt argues:

> In conditions where the identities are themselves constituted through conflict it is difficult to see what can guarantee a permanently successful outcome to the peaceful engagement with others unless participants are prepared to reconsider and perhaps sacrifice elements of what they have previously considered to be part of their identity ... Knowledge that over-commitment to an identity can obstruct the management of conflict does not only require moderation in the expression of those commitments and the willingness to be open to the views of others but ultimately some willingness to detach from the value of identity in order to guarantee peace. (2002, p. 24)

Stefan Wolff's concern that power-sharing arrangements should be inclusive as well as moderate seems, at first glance, difficult to reconcile with this argument. Yet while power-sharing governments must be of a moderate hue to succeed, inclusion of all strands of opinion in the democratic process is not the same as inclusion of all parties in the executive. The danger with the latter is of setting politics in stone, while the task of power sharing is to find a suitable balance. What is really key apart from moderation is not *inclusion in*, but *equality of potential access to*, government on the part of all elected representatives if violence is to be delegitimised. More positively, the requirement to construct inter-ethnic coalitions where no party's participation is guaranteed can be a means to encourage individual political figures reflexively to 'detach from the value of identity' and contribute to building inter-communal trust.

COMMUNAL CONFORMISM

One key mechanism for making inter-ethnic societies work is arrangements for personal cultural autonomy. The differentiated nature of such societies means that sensitive solutions to questions of language and education in particular have to be found, and the pioneering work of the Austro-Marxists in addressing this challenge in the then multi-national Habsburg empire still bears scrutiny. Ephraim Nimni (2000, p. xxv), who has brought this work into contemporary debate, argues that what differentiates this approach from the *millet* system characteristic of the Ottoman empire is a recognition that minority associations stepping forward as intermediaries between individuals and the state – for example, offering to supply schooling with a minority religious ethos – should in reciprocation ensure rights of voice and exit for members of the ascriptive groups on whose behalf such claims are made. Otherwise, as Ghai puts it:

> Cultural rights may ... put at risk human rights. The literature on group rights has highlighted how the rights of both certain members of the cultural community and outsiders may be infringed in this way ... Rules for cultural autonomy should be sensitive to the needs of individuals for more cosmopolitan identities, and, on the principle of self-identification, provide a reasonable basis for 'exit'. (2002, p. 169)

As Christian Joppke and Steven Lukes stress, cultural groups are not discrete, hermetically-sealed social entities. On the contrary:

in any cultural group whatsoever in the modern world, there will be at least the following: identifiers, quasi-identifiers, semi-identifiers, non-identifiers, ex-identifiers, cross-identifiers, and anti-identifiers. A multicultural politics of identity is angled exclusively towards the concerns and interests of the first group. (1999, p. 10)

Women are often the victims of such conformist pressures, as Rachel Rebouché and Kate Fearon emphasise in this volume. Their concern regarding the effective exclusion and disenfranchisement of women, both a distinct social category and one itself subject to internal diversity, is consonant with the work of the late Susan Moller Okin (1999, p. 24). In particular, it is consonant with Okin's claim that 'there can be no justification for assuming that the groups' self-proclaimed leaders – invariably composed mainly of their older and their male members – represent the interests of all of the groups' members'. A recent British example was an attack on the writer Monica Ali, following her celebrated first novel, *Brick Lane*, named after a famous mainly Bangladeshi street in east London. A protest by the Greater Sylhet Welfare and Development Council led to a telling *Guardian* (3 December 2003) headline: 'Brickbats fly as *community* brands novel "despicable"' (emphasis added). Another was the decision by the New Repertory Theatre in Birmingham to stop running a play written by a Sikh woman, by which local Sikh elders said they had been offended, following a violent protest outside the building (*Guardian*, 21 December 2004).

Consociational power-sharing arrangements can contribute to such an oppressive atmosphere by assuming that the only significant actors are the political elites. This risks an imbalance of state and civil society, with an invasive 'hypertrophy' of party politics (Sartori 1997, p. 190) and the associated 'Balkanisation' of civic life by competing demands for recognition. In such a context, 'rights' can easily become 'uniforms' (Wikan 2002, p. 142), and 'identity politics' the means by which people are denied 'the freedom to choose their own affiliations and associations' and instead bear the imposition of 'lifelong allegiance to a club which they never applied to join' (Wheen 2004, p. 75). The focus in many contemporary power-sharing institutions (as this volume clearly shows) on explicitly and publicly recognising certain 'communities' as the foundation of political life is illustrative of how negotiated constitutional arrangements can often become so prescriptive that they restrict future transformations toward pluralism. Thus, a potential move beyond sectarianism to a complex multi-faceted conception of citizenship – wherein the interests of those who wish to engage in political life as members of a distinct social group or community are not accorded greater (or lesser) weight than those who do not, or those who choose not to, politicise the collective aspects of their identity – is marginalised if not altogether refused.

FREEING-UP IDENTITY

Although one must be careful not to cast this claim in conspiratorial or functionalist language, the fact often remains that communalist politics in divided societies acts as a barrier to potential solidarities, such as that of social class. As Ghai remarks: 'Communal representation ... tends to obscure social and economic interests that sections of different communities have in common.' Thus, 'the interests of the wealthy elite tend to dominate' (Ghai 2002, p. 154). Northern Ireland is a good example: 'equality' is a word much bandied around in political discourse there. Yet recently generated data for the region suggest it has one of the highest Gini coefficients (a standard measure of income inequality) in the developed world (Hillyard et al. 2003, p. 42), although this has been contested by government officials. The explanation, here as elsewhere, is that it is 'parity of esteem' between 'two communities' which is constantly – and intractably – at issue, while growing socio-economic divisions across both communities have gone unchecked (Barry 2001, p. 3).

At bottom, the crucial point in all of this is that there is nothing 'essential' about our particular identities. Accordingly, Ziauddin Sardar (*New Statesman*, 25 February 2002) admonishes us to ask: 'how much of the Other is actually located within me? ... We need to move away from the politics of contested identities that heighten artificial differences and towards acceptance of the plasticity and possibilities of identities that focus on our common humanity.' Similarly, for Rory Conces, the potential of inter-ethnic dialogue lies in this: 'Not only is there an incorporation of others' views, which enlarges our perspective, but there is a recognition that the Other is not all that different in some ways and that a common ground exists between us' (Conces 2002, pp. 295–6).

Amin Maalouf has written an impassioned essay on identity which includes the eloquent sentence: 'My identity is what prevents me from being identical to anybody else' (2000, p. 10). Each one of us, he explains, is a unique synthesis of many elements, which, moreover, can change over time. On this basis, Bauman astutely argues that the most 'seminal of choices' is that between 'cultural variety' and 'variety of cultures' (2002, p. 176). For him only the former guarantees 'that cultural choice is a matter which should be left to the discretion of individual men and women and that the choice individuals make should be respected'. Far from being merely aspirational, this account of the nature of individual identity goes with the grain of an increasingly individualised world.

In today's world, as Steven Vertovec and Robin Cohen recognise, 'many individuals now seem to be, more than ever, prone to articulate complex affiliations, meaningful attachments and multiple allegiances' (2002, pp. 2–3). And thus they argue that in contrast to multiculturalism, 'cosmopolitanism is now increasingly invoked to avoid the pitfalls of essentialism or some kind of zero-sum, all-or-nothing understanding of identity issues'. Paradoxically, as Bauman points out, 'identity' has only (and very recently) become 'the loudest talk in town' because of our exposure to a range of 'communities' – allowing us to make a conscious choice, on a basis of affinity, to embrace the very 'traditions' the protagonists of identity politics contend are products of ascription (2004, pp. 17, 11). None of this is to deny that culture matters greatly to some people's sense of self. Rather, it is to emphasise once again that our identity is not based on a rigid, singularised set of 'essential' attributes to which we must inevitably keep true.

In the divided societies where power sharing is typically held up as a potential democratic solution, ethnic protagonists often win the day, by suppressing individual choice and condensing the complex determinants of identity into one simple definer, such as nationality, in which they can invest great significance and which they can represent as a boundary marker against the 'other' – represented via a similarly stereotypical and dehumanised enemy image. It is by rendering hegemonic this 'tribal' conception that 'fanatics of all kinds manage so easily to pass themselves off as defenders of identity' (Maalouf 2000, p. 25) and set former neighbours at one another's throats. Democratic political actors should do nothing – wittingly or unwittingly – to assist them.

TOWARD A CIVIC CULTURE

Critics of power-sharing arrangements premised upon a primordialist conception of identity must be able to offer cogent alternatives which address the realities of division. It is in the absence of a sense that these exist that with a heavy heart Bose endorses consociationalism in Bosnia and Herzegovina, *faute de mieux* (2002, pp. 247, 249). While recognising the risk of entrenching communal identities, he nevertheless and counter-intuitively hopes that over time these will wither away. The response, however, is to recognise that the fear of ethnic 'lock-in' to which consociationalism attends can (even if only over time) be met without resorting to its standard responses of grand coalition and mutual veto, allied in the theory to ethnic proportionality in public employment and segmental autonomy.

Sartori warns that in 'a polarised polity', coalitions are 'uncooperative, litigious and stalemate-prone' (1997, p. 60), a comment that can be taken alongside his further point that '[g]rand coalitions obscure responsibility to the utmost and are, as a rule, more heterogeneous and more easily gridlocked' (1997, p. 71). In other words, to expect all significant parties to come together and function successfully in government in the wake of a power-sharing agreement is to imply that the latter could instantly magic away decades of division – a herculean assumption. For example, far from ending antagonism through inclusion in government, the arrangements for executive formation in the Belfast Agreement emboldened the two ethno-nationalist poles – Sinn Féin and the Democratic Unionist Party – at the expense not only of the moderate middle but of power sharing itself.

By contrast, a cross-communal but not all-party coalition can in itself be one guarantee against ethnic oppression. Where the 'majority' component of the coalition is divided by intra-ethnic tension (but the ethnic out-bidding party is not included in government), the 'minority' component can be critical to government formation. For this to happen, mutual-veto arrangements – which are, in reality, more likely to be used against the minority than in its favour, owing to the balance of power – can be supplanted by mechanisms that prevent lock-in without reifying identities. For example, power-sharing accords may make provision for secular weighted-majority decision making on controversial issues, without the requirement of communal registration. International minority-rights declarations, such as those promulgated in the 1990s by the Council of Europe (1995), the Organisation for Security and Co-operation in Europe (Foundation on Inter-Ethnic Relations, 1996, 1998, 1999) and the United Nations, represent a supportive (if non-justiciable) set of external standards.

Furthermore, proportional representation in public, and indeed private, employment should be the product of equal-opportunity legislation, including scope for affirmative action as required. But this should not normally involve quotas and should arise from objective recruitment procedures, rather than the operation of communal patronage systems. The latter are not only inefficient but in the case of Austria's *Proporz* system, for example, gave Jörg Haider's xenophobic Freedom Party an easy stick with which to beat the 'red-black' establishment on its political rise (Fallend 2004).

Finally, in a divided society segmental autonomy is highly likely to be the starting point for reconciliation. Segregation is an inevitable counterpart of ethnic polarisation, especially where this spills into inter-communal violence. Yet in the final analysis, high fences do not make good, but rather mistrustful, neighbours. In this volume Manlio Cinalli rightly stresses the importance of horizontal relationships of interdependence within civil society if power-sharing arrangements are to go beyond ethnic pillarisation. It is for this reason that minority-rights conventions often stress the need for integration. A key document in this regard, the Council of Europe Framework Convention for the Protection of National Minorities (1994), commits the state to the promotion of 'a spirit of tolerance and intercultural dialogue' (a programme which the council itself has recently developed). In a similar vein, Jürgen Habermas stresses that tolerance is not 'a *one-way street* to cultural self-assertion by groups with their own collective identities'. He goes on: 'The coexistence of different life forms as equals must not be allowed to prompt segregation. Instead, it requires the integration of all citizens – and their mutual recognition across cultural divisions as citizens – within the framework of a shared political culture' (2004, pp. 17–18).

The security offered by separation *qua* segmental autonomy is illusory, as stereotyped enemy images risk perpetuating antagonism and ethno-political entrepreneurs maintain their dominance by sustaining an ever-present sense of insecurity. While 'community' has a warm and comforting connotation, what Bauman dryly calls the 'really existing community' (2001, p. 17) will always disappoint those who seek its solace:

[I]t will add to their fears and insecurity instead of quashing them or putting them to rest. It will call for twenty-four hours a day vigilance and a daily re-sharpening of swords; for struggle, day in day out, to keep the aliens off the gates and to spy out and hunt down the turncoats in their own midst.

And he concludes: 'Security is the enemy of walled-up and fenced-off community' (2001, p. 142).

Genuine security comes from the cultivation of cross-communal civic networks, whether these are business relationships, trade union or other voluntary organisations or ecumenical connections. On the basis of his comparative research on cities in India more or less prone to Hindu–Muslim riots, Ashutosh Varshney concludes: 'Vigorous associational life, if intercommunal, acts as a serious constraint on the polarizing strategies of political elites' (2002, p. 4). Segmented cities like Hyderabad, he found, offered no such buffers against the effect of nationwide ethno-political shocks: 'A multiethnic society with few interconnections across ethnic boundaries is very vulnerable to ethnic disorders and violence' (2002, p. 12).

Thus, Maria Hadjipavlou (2004, p. 197) argues that at the micro-level non-governmental 'conflict resolution' projects have been of value in Cyprus: 'The dualisms, bipolarity, and perceived homogeneity in each community are challenged as oversimplifications of a much more complex social landscape' (2004, p. 197). Writing in advance of the failed Annan plan of 2004, she contends that 'unless Cypriots have a well-developed, self-critical civil society committed to the peace-building processes, the best political agreement signed at the official diplomatic level will be very difficult to "sell" and will fail to crystallize in the long term' (Hadjipavlou 2004, p. 197). Thus, the balance of emphasis in securing power-sharing systems has to shift from political elites towards civil society.

CONCLUSION

For most people – including most people who see themselves as belonging to ethnic communities – integration is a much more attractive option than the subordination of assimilation on the one hand or the separatism of segregation on the other. Fundamentalism is the refusal of dialogue and where fundamentalists can secure political majorities, as increasingly appears to be the case on both sides of the Israel/Palestine conflict, the future is bleak. But, outside of such extreme situations, few find the appeal of fundamentalism compelling, given its associations with enforced isolation from the wider society. The secretary general of the Muslim Council of Britain, Iqbal Sacranie, gave a typical view to the *Guardian* (17 June 2002) when he said:

There is an overwhelming interest in the community in integrating but we need to be very clear what we really mean by integration. It does not mean assimilation – forgetting the culture and traditions you've been brought up with and adopting a culture that's alien to you. Integration involves understanding the English language, going to mainstream schools and having an interaction with mainstream society, developing better relations with people of different faiths and no faith.

More generally, Amin has rightly claimed that in a democratic multiethnic society the key challenge is 'striking the balance between cultural autonomy and social solidarity, so that the former does not lapse into separatism and essentialised identities, and so that the latter does not slide into minority cultural assimilation' (2002).

Negotiating a way around this Scylla and Charybdis is always high-risk and uncertain. It requires policy makers to engage in constant dialogue with non-governmental associations, voluntary networks, and others in the broader public domain, and a relentless pursuit of best practice through comparative example. In other words, it requires them to sustain ever-frail inter-cultural conversations both domestically and internationally. But the principles that should guide us through this ongoing dialogue are clear enough. With Chan Kwok-Bun we can 'look to the unspectacular, practical, everyday life activities that allow movement beyond group identities to the business of simply living together and solving practical problems collectively' (2002, p. 191).

NOTES

1. I am using this term in the now accepted broad sense of embracing any essentialist, ascriptive identity represented by its ideologues as a 'natural' boundary-marker between members of purportedly antagonistic social groups, whether this fault-line takes the form of religion, language or 'race' in the narrower sense.
2. I am indebted to François Grin for this point.

REFERENCES

Amin, A. (2002) *Ethnicity and the Multicultural City: Living with Diversity*. Report for the Department of Transport, Local Government and the Regions and the ESRC Cities Initiative. Durham: University of Durham.
Barry, B. (2001) *Culture and Equality: An Egalitarian Critique of Multiculturalism*. Cambridge: Polity Press.

Bauman, Z. (2001) *Community: Seeking Safety in an Insecure World*. Cambridge: Polity Press.

—— (2002) 'Cultural Variety or Variety of Cultures?', in S. Malešević and M. Haugaard (eds), *Making Sense of Collectivity*. London: Pluto Press, pp. 167–80.

—— (2004) *Identity: Conversations with Benedetto Vecchi*. Cambridge: Polity Press.

Bose, S. (2002) *Bosnia After Dayton: Nationalist Partition and International Intervention*. London: Hurst & Co.

Brubaker, R. (2002) 'Ethnicity Without Groups', *Archives Européenes de Sociologie*, 43 (2), 163–89.

Conces, R. J. (2002) 'Unified Pluralism: Fostering Reconciliation and the Demise of Ethnic Nationalism', *Studies in East European Thought*, 54, 285–302.

Council of Europe (1995) *Framework Convention for the Protection of National Minorities and Explanatory Report*. Strasbourg: Council of Europe.

Cowan, J. K., Dembour, M-B. and Wilson, R. A. (eds) (2001) *Culture and Rights: Anthropological Perspectives*. Cambridge: Cambridge University Press.

Fallend, F. (2004) 'Are Right-Wing Populism and Government Participation Incompatible? The Case of the Freedom Party of Austria', *Representation*, 40 (2), 115–30.

Foundation on Inter-Ethnic Relations (1996) *The Hague Recommendations Regarding the Education Rights of National Minorities in Public Life & Explanatory Note*. The Hague: FI-ER.

—— (1998) *The Oslo Recommendations Regarding the Linguistic Rights of National Minorities in Public Life & Explanatory Note*. The Hague: FI-ER.

—— (1999) *The Lund Recommendations on the Effective Participation of National Minorities in Public Life & Explanatory Note*. The Hague: FI-ER.

Ghai, Y. P. (2002) 'Constitutional Asymmetries: Communal Representation, Federalism, and Cultural Autonomy', in A. Reynolds (ed.), *The Architecture of Democracy: Constitutional Design, Conflict Management, and Democracy*. Oxford: Oxford University Press, pp. 141–70.

Gilliatt, S. (2002) 'No Surrender? The Attachment to Identity and Contemporary Political Thought', *Contemporary Politics*, 8 (1), 23–35.

Habermas, J. (2004) 'Religious Tolerance: The Pacemaker for Cultural Rights', *Philosophy*, 79, 5–18.

Hadjipavlou, M. (2004) 'The Contribution of Bicommunal Contacts in Building a Civil Society in Cyprus', in A. H. Eagly, R. M. Baron and V. L. Hamilton (eds), *The Social Psychology of Group Identity and Social Conflict: Theory, Application, and Practice*. Washington, DC: American Psychological Association.

Hillyard, P., Kelly, G., McLaughlin, E., Patsios, D. and Tomlinson, M. (2003) *Bare Necessities: Poverty and Social Exclusion in Northern Ireland – Key Findings*. Belfast: Democratic Dialogue.

Horowitz, D. (2001), *The Deadly Ethnic Riot* (Berkeley, CA: University of California Press).

—— (2002) 'Constitutional Design: Proposals versus Processes', in A. Reynolds (ed.), *The Architecture of Democracy: Constitutional Design, Conflict Management, and Democracy*. Oxford: Oxford University Press, pp. 15–36.

Joppke, C. and Lukes, S. (1999) 'Introduction: Multicultural Questions', in C. Joppke and S. Lukes (eds), *Multicultural Questions*. Oxford: Oxford University Press.

Kwok-Bun, C. (2002) 'Both Sides Now: Culture Contact, Hybridization, and Cosmopolitanism', in S. Vertovec and R. Cohen (eds), *Conceiving Cosmopolitanism: Theory, Context, and Practice*. Oxford: Oxford University Press, pp. 191–208.

Kyle, K. (1997) *Cyprus: In Search of Peace*. London: Minority Rights Group.

Lal, B. V. (2002) 'Constitutional Engineering in Post-Coup Fiji', in A. Reynolds (ed.), *The Architecture of Democracy: Constitutional Design, Conflict Management, and Democracy*. Oxford: Oxford University Press, pp. 267–92.

Lijphart, A. (1977) *Democracy in Plural Societies*. New Haven, CT: Yale University Press.

—— (2001) 'Constructivism and Consociational Theory', *Newsletter of the American Political Science Association Organized Section in Comparative Politics*, 12 (1), 11–13.

—— (2002) 'The Wave of Power-Sharing Democracy', in A. Reynolds (ed.), *The Architecture of Democracy: Constitutional Design, Conflict Management, and Democracy*. Oxford: Oxford University Press, pp. 37–54.

Maalouf, A. (2000) *On Identity*. London: The Harvill Press.

Nimni, E. (2000) 'Introduction to the English Reading Audience', in O. Bauer (ed.), *The Question of Nationalities and Social Democracy*. Minneapolis, MN: University of Minnesota Press, pp. xv–xlv.

Okin, S. M. (1999) *Is Multiculturalism Bad for Women?* Princeton, NJ: Princeton University Press.

Sartori, G. (1997 [1994]) *Comparative Constitutional Engineering: An Inquiry into Structures, Incentives and Outcomes*. Basingstoke: Macmillan.

Varshney, A. (2002) *Ethnic Conflict and Civic Life: Hindus and Muslims in India*. New Haven, CT: Yale University Press.

Vertovec, S. and Cohen, R. (eds) (2002) *Conceiving Cosmopolitanism: Theory, Context, and Practice*. Oxford: Oxford University Press.

Wheen, F. (2004) *How Mumbo-Jumbo Conquered the World*. London: Fourth Estate.

Wikan, U. (2002) *Generous Betrayal: Politics of Culture in the New Europe*. Chicago, IL: University of Chicago Press.

List of Contributors

Florian Bieber is Senior Non-resident Research Associate of the European Centre for Minority Issues, Belgrade. He teaches at the Central European University (Budapest), the University of Sarajevo and the University of Bologna. He has published extensively on nationalism and ethnic-conflict regulation in south-eastern Europe. His most recent publication is *Ethnic Structure, Inequality and Governance of the Public Sector: Bosnia-Herzegovina* (2005). He is the co-editor of *Southeast European Politics*.

Manlio Cinalli is Jean Monnet Fellow at the European University Institute, Florence, and Research Fellow at the University of Leeds. He has trained as a political scientist at the University of Florence and at Queen's University Belfast, where he was awarded a PhD in Politics and International Relations. His research interests are in comparative politics, ethnic relations, social movements and networks. His current work focuses on the relationship between political participation and policy outcomes in Europe.

Kris Deschouwer is Professor of Politics at the Vrije Universiteit Brussel. He has been involved in research on political parties, elections, consociational democracy, federalism and regionalism, and has published widely on these topics. He is the editor of the *European Journal of Political Research*.

Kate Fearon was a founder member of the Northern Ireland Women's Coalition, an adviser to its Northern Ireland Peace Talks negotiation team and adviser to its Assembly Members in the First Northern Ireland Assembly. She has previously published articles on the Belfast Agreement, peace processes, and gender and conflict. She has worked in democracy development in Bosnia and Herzegovina for the past three years.

Tom Hadden has taught both human rights and conflict resolution at Queen's University Belfast as a part-time Professor of Law. With his colleague Kevin Boyle, he has written extensively on the Northern Ireland problem. He is currently a part-time Commissioner of the

Northern Ireland Human Rights Commission and has recently completed a number of working papers for the United Nations Working Group on Minorities.

Brandon Hamber trained in South Africa as a Clinical Psychologist and currently works in Northern Ireland. He is a Research Associate of Democratic Dialogue, Belfast. He is a co-founder of the Office of Psychosocial Issues at the Free University, Berlin. Previously, he co-ordinated the Transition and Reconciliation Unit at the Centre for the Study of Violence and Reconciliation in Johannesburg. He has written widely on the psychological implications of political violence and processes of transition.

Gráinne Kelly is Research Associate of Democratic Dialogue, Belfast, having previously worked as a research officer with the organisation since 2000. She has worked in the field of community relations and reconciliation for the past decade, on projects including mediation of parades disputes, the role of storytelling in peace-building, the needs of victims of conflict and concepts and practices of reconciliation. She holds an MA in Peace and Conflict Studies from the University of Ulster.

Duncan Morrow is Chief Executive Officer of the Northern Ireland Community Relations Council, the body with primary responsibility for funding and development of community relations policy and practice. Previously, he was Lecturer in Politics at the University of Ulster and a Co-Director of Future Ways, an active learning agency focused on improving community relations. In 1998, he was appointed as a Northern Ireland Sentence Review Commissioner, the body responsible for implementing the early release of paramilitary prisoners agreed as part of the Belfast Agreement.

Anthony Oberschall is Emeritus Professor at the University of North Carolina, Chapel Hill. He is the author of *Social Conflict and Social Movements* (1973) and *Social Movements: Interests, Identities, and Ideologies* (1993), as well as many articles on ethno-national conflicts, conflict management, collective action and group violence. In 2003, he was a New Century Scholar in the Fulbright programme on ethnic conflicts and peace processes, for research on shared sovereignty and power-sharing governance in Northern Ireland.

Ian O'Flynn is Lecturer in Politics at the University of Newcastle upon Tyne. He is a former ESRC Postdoctoral Fellow at the Department of Government, University of Essex, and Visiting Scholar at the Center for European Studies, Harvard University. His current research aims to explore the normative implications of deliberative democratic theory for questions of institutional choice in divided societies.

L. Kendall Palmer is a PhD Candidate in Sociology at the University of North Carolina, Chapel Hill. His dissertation, entitled 'Power-sharing Extended: Policing and Education Reforms in Bosnia-Herzegovina and Northern Ireland', creates a framework to study the implementation of power sharing in grassroots institutions and applies this framework to policing and education in two post-peace agreement societies.

Rachel Rebouché is a *Juris Doctorate* Candidate at Harvard Law School. She received her LLM in Human Rights Law from Queen's University, Belfast. She is the co-author (with Eileen Fagan) of 'Northern Ireland's Abortion Law', *Feminist Legal Studies* 3, 221 (2003). She and Kate Fearon also co-authored the chapter, 'The Agreement's Promises and the Northern Ireland Women's Coalition', in M. Cox et al. (eds), *A Farewell to Peace?* (2004).

David Russell is Policy Officer at the Northern Ireland Community Relations Council, Research Associate, Democratic Dialogue, Belfast and Research Associate, The Centre for Lebanese Studies, University of Oxford. He holds an MA in Political Science from Queen's University, Belfast, and a PhD in Politics from the University of York. He is currently involved in an ESRC-funded project that considers the question of women's security and participation in post-conflict societies.

Nadim Shehadi is Director of the Centre for Lebanese Studies, an independent academic research institution affiliated to the Middle East Centre at St Antony's College, Oxford University. He is also an Associate Research Fellow at the Royal Institute of International Affairs, Chatham House, London.

Robin Wilson is Director of the Belfast-based think-tank Democratic Dialogue. He is an Honorary Senior Research Fellow at the Constitution Unit, University College, London, as well as a member of the board of the Institute of Governance at Queen's University, Belfast.

Stefan Wolff is Professor of Political Science at the University of Bath in England, United Kingdom, and Senior Non-resident Research Associate at the European Centre for Minority Issues in Flensburg, Germany. He holds an MPhil in Political Theory from Magdalene College, Cambridge, and a PhD in Political Science from the London School of Economics.

Marie-Joëlle Zahar is Assistant Professor of Political Science at the Université de Montréal. Her research interests and her most recent publications are centred in conflict-resolution, peace-building and post-conflict reconstruction with a focus on Lebanon and Bosnia and Herzegovina. She has held a number of research fellowships including positions at the Center for International Security and Cooperation (Stanford University) and the Munk Centre for International Studies (University of Toronto).

Index

Compiled by Sue Carlton

Karadžić, Radovan 133
Kashmir 5–6
King, Martin Luther 56
Knin 48
Kosovo 5–6, 48, 50
Kosovo Liberation Army (KLA) 49
Kosovo Polje, battle re-enactment
  48
Kumanovo 118
Kwok-Bun, Chan 216

Lal, Brij 208
Law on Local Self-Government
  (1994) (Macedonia) 118
leadership *see* political leadership
Lebanon 7, 18, 54, 138–52
  citizenship 148
  and consociationalism 24, 60,
    140
  educational reform 146
  electoral system 60, 141
  and inclusion 24, 36
  and national reconciliation 9,
    139, 143, 145, 146, 147–8
  power-sharing arrangements
    139–42
  programme for civic unity 142–6,
    147
  and religious pluralism 143–4
  return of displaced persons 146,
    148
  and women in politics 149–50
  see also Ta'if Accord (1989)
Lederach, John Paul 191
Liberal parties (Belgium) 95, 96
Lijphart, Arend 4, 24, 51, 59–60,
  126, 205–6, 208
  and electoral systems 25, 61–2,
    63–4
local government, and minorities
  38
lock-ins 66, 70–1, 213
Lund Recommendations on the
  Effective Participation of
  National Minorities in Public
  Life 36

Maalouf, Amin 211–12
MacCormick, Neil 18

Macedonia 7, 8, 15, 48, 49, 50,
  107–22
  and Albanian grievances 107–8
  army recruitment 117
  and coalition government 114–15
  electoral system 63, 65, 110–12
  and legislative veto 112–14
  police force 116–17
  public administration 115–17
  and small minority groups 107,
    109, 110–11, 112–13
  territorial self-government
    118–19
  see also Ohrid Agreement (2001)
McGarry, John 4
Malaysia 60
Mandela, Nelson 55
marginalisation 177, 178, 180, 205
Milošević, Slobodan 48–9, 123
minority issues 30–44
  assimilation 33–4
  autonomy 33–4, 37–9, 41, 42
  and changing majority-minority
    balance 32–3
  different approaches to 30–1, 41
  education 39–40
  flexible guidelines 35
  and human rights principles
    31–2, 35, 213
  integration 33–4, 35–7, 39–41
  languages 38, 40
  limitations of rights-based
    approach 42
  and local government 38
  and membership of public bodies
    36–7
  and policy choice 39–41
  political participation 36
  private-sector employment 40,
    214
  public-sector employment 37,
    115–17, 214
  residential segregation 40–1, 53
  and separate courts 38
  and strategy choice 33–41
  terminology 33–5
  territorial autonomy 38, 41
Montenegro 49
Montreal Declaration 36

mutual veto 20, 25, 80, 97–8, 126,
127–8, 164, 213

National Party, South Africa 55
Netherlands 4–5, 15, 52, 60
New Repertory Theatre,
    Birmingham 210
New Statesman 207
New Zealand 36
Nimni, Ephraim 209
North Atlantic Treaty Organisation
    (NATO) 123, 133
  Stabilisation Force (SFOR) 133,
    134, 135
Northern Ireland 7, 8, 71, 77–91
  and cabinet government 82
  changing attitudes 78, 86–7, 198
  community relations 85–8
  and criminal justice 80
  and demilitarisation 84
  District Policing Partnerships 85
  and education 87
  and equality 17, 80, 211
  and human rights 80
  Human Rights and Equality
    Commissions 37, 82–3, 195
  and inclusion 24, 25, 36
  institutionalising division 207–8,
    213
  and minority issues 40
  and national identity 77–9
  North–South Ministerial Council
    84
  parades 80, 88
  police force 37, 78, 80, 85
  political leadership 52–3, 54, 57
  and public-sector employment 37
  and reconciliation 54, 193–4,
    195, 198, 199–200
  and relational structures 172, 183
  and sectarianism 87–8, 89–90
  weapons decommissioning 78,
    79, 80, 83–4
  see also Belfast Agreement (1998)
Northern Ireland Life and Times
    Survey (NILT) 86–7, 198

Office for Democratic Institutions
    and Human Rights (OHIHR)
    110–11

Office of the High Representative
    (OHR) 131–2, 135
Ohrid Agreement (2001) 1, 8,
    107–10
  and electoral system 110–12
  and governmental practice 114,
    115
  and increasing segregation
    119–20
  and legislative veto 112–14
  and local-government reform 118
  and public administration reform
    115–17
Okin, Susan Moller 164, 210
O'Leary, Brendan 4
O'Neill, Shane 23
Orange Order 78, 88
Organisation for Security and Co-
    Organisation for Security and
    Co-operation in Europe (OSCE)
    110–11, 116, 213

Paisley, Ian 54
Pakistan 36
panachage 65
Papua-New Guinea 67
Parades Commission 88
partition 15
  see also separation
Party of Democratic Action (SDA)
    130
Party for Democratic Prosperity
    (PDP) 111, 114
Pateman, Carole 165
peace agreements
  implementation 2–3
  negotiation 1–2, 3
  see also Belfast Agreement (1998);
    Dayton Peace Agreement (DPA)
    (1994); Ohrid Agreement
    (2001); Ta'if Accord (1989)
Peace Implementation Council 132
personal autonomy 2, 4, 16, 19–22,
    26
  and inclusion 22, 25
  within groups 21
Petritsch, Wolfgang 132
Phillips, Anne 162, 166
pillarisation 178, 183, 184